Dispensationalism and the History of Redemption

A DEVELOPING AND DIVERSE TRADITION

D. Jeffrey Bingham and Glenn R. Kreider
General Editors

MOODY PUBLISHERS
CHICAGO

Edited by Jim Vincent
Interior and cover design: Erik M. Peterson

Library of Congress Cataloging-in-Publication Data

Dispensationalism and the history of redemption : a developing and diverse tradition /
D. Jeffrey Bingham and Glenn R. Kreider General Editors.
pages cm
Includes bibliographical references.
ISBN 978-0-8024-0961-4
1. Dispensationalism. 2. Redemption—Christianity. I. Bingham, D. Jeffrey (Dwight Jeffrey), editor.
BT157.D56 2015
230'.0463—dc23
2015016749

Moody Publishers
820 N. LaSalle Boulevard
Chicago, IL 60610

5 7 9 10 8 6 4

Printed in the United States of America

Contents

Foreword

This valuable work on dispensationalism, written by a unique set of qualified authors, represents an important contribution to the understanding and support of a dispensational interpretation of the Scriptures.

As you will see from the following chapters, a basic and broad unity of thought on the major tenets of dispensationalism coexists, with a diversity of opinions on some details. Depending on one's perspective, those details may be viewed as more or less important to the dispensational approach to the Scriptures. My prayer is that these presentations generate both gracious and profitable discussions among dispensationalists and a better perception of dispensationalism by others.

The continuity and discontinuity of the Bible has been and continues to be the subject of great debate and discussion. Dallas Theological Seminary historically has been known as an institution that advocates a dispensational system of theology. As a faculty, we believe that dispensationalism best accounts for both the unity as well as the diversity represented in the Bible. *Continuity* can be maintained by observing the primary purpose of God in history—to accomplish His kingdom and redemptive purposes on earth under a divinely appointed human representative who will both redeem and reign on His behalf. The *discontinuity* of the Bible rises from God's progressive revelation, by which He has revealed different responsibilities delegated to different people for varying durations of time.

As the book of Romans reveals, while salvation is always by grace through faith in any age of God's economy, people have been given responsibilities that have differed according to God's revelation and dealings with humanity up to that particular point in time. While discontinuity sometimes has been identified with the term *dispensations*, the successive stages in the progress of that revelation also reveal the continuity of God's purposes as He works to reclaim a kingdom usurped by an enemy and those who follow him, and to redeem, out of fallen humanity, those who will respond to His grace by faith in His Son who alone can save them.

A change in dispensation takes place when God reveals a change in the way He has chosen to orchestrate and administrate His plans for human history. With a dispensational change, some principles in the way God regulates His relationship with humanity are introduced that are new, some things continue from the previous period of God's government, some things may cease, and some things may simply change.

An illustration of the latter could be the concept of worship as practiced in four great periods of biblical history. With the patriarchs anyone could worship anywhere, at any time. Under Law nowhere could sacrifices be made except at the central sanctuary, by no one except an appointed Levitical priest, at times and in ways specifically designated by God. When Jesus talked to the Samaritan woman at Sychar He announced a radical shift for the immediate future that would take worship away from Jerusalem as the site of the central sanctuary. Looking forward, and assuming for the moment an earthly millennial reign of Messiah as the King-Priest, one can again see dispensational change as the Messiah superintends the worship of that period, very probably from a temple whose construction He will oversee (Zech. 6:12–13).

As various contributors will note, as a biblical hermeneutic dispensationalism is a system of analyzing and synthesizing the Scriptures that seeks to understand both the unity and the diversity of the historical workings of God on earth. Dispensationalists affirm the benefits of both textual analysis and theological synthesis. Dispensationalists also affirm those themes that unite the means as well as the ends of God's self-authenticating purposes:

- the vindication of His glory
- a redemption by grace through faith
- the mediation through a divine representative
- the restoration of a peaceful environment
- the experience and expression of unhindered worship

As you read this book, please do so carefully. Many of the straw men that have been erected and burned by opponents of dispensationalism are just that. In the following chapters you will read what is and what isn't dispensationalism. You will see that each contributor takes the text of Scripture seriously. Each is a friend, and all are current or former colleagues. All hold the historical, orthodox doctrines of the faith. None is pessimistic nor prone to an escapist mentality toward the present world.

Most of all, each holds the Savior in highest regard, and all anticipate the ultimate *shalom* that only God can bring as the ultimate end—that wondrous conclusion when He shall dwell with His people for all eternity.

Mark Bailey
President, Dallas Theological Seminary

List of Contributors

D. Jeffrey Bingham, Associate Dean of Biblical and Theological Studies, Wheaton College. BA, New Mexico State University; ThM and PhD, Dallas Theological Seminary

Craig A. Blaising, Executive Vice President and Provost, Professor of Theology, Southwestern Baptist Theological Seminary. BS, University of Texas; ThM and PhD, Dallas Theological Seminary; PhD, Systematic Theology, University of Aberdeen

Darrell L. Bock, Senior Research Professor of New Testament Studies, Dallas Theological Seminary. BA, University of Texas; ThM, New Testament, Dallas Theological Seminary; PhD, University of Aberdeen

Oscar A. Campos, Theology and Missiology Professor, Central American Theological Seminary. BTh and MA, Central American Theological Seminary; STM and PhD, Dallas Theological Seminary

Nathan D. Holsteen, Professor of Theological Studies, Dallas Theological Seminary. BS, Louisiana State University; ThM, Dallas Theological Seminary; PhD, University of Aberdeen

Glenn R. Kreider, Professor of Theological Studies, Dallas Theological Seminary. BS, Lancaster Bible College; ThM and PhD, Dallas Theological Seminary

Eugene H. Merrill, Distinguished Professor (Emeritus) of Old Testament Studies, Dallas Theological Seminary. BA and MA, Bob Jones University; MA, New York University; MPhil, Columbia University; PhD, Old Testament Interpretation, Bob Jones University; PhD, Ancient Near Eastern Studies, Columbia University

T. Maurice Pugh, Senior Pastor, New Life Fellowship, Arlington, TX. BA, University of Michigan; ThM and PhD, Dallas Theological Seminary.

Michael J. Svigel, Department Chair and Professor of Theological Studies, Dallas Theological Seminary. BS, Cairn University; ThM and PhD, Dallas Theological Seminary

Stanley D. Toussaint, Senior Professor Emeritus of Bible, Dallas Theological Seminary. BA, Augsburg College; ThM and ThD, Dallas Theological Seminary

Preface

Dispensationalism is an essential and enduring facet of the evangelical landscape. Its fivefold commitment to (1) the inspiration and inerrancy of the Bible, (2) the authority and relevance of the Word of God for Christian living, (3) the unity of the history of redemption, (4) the gospel and the need for conversion, and (5) global missions all bear this out. It is an evangelical tradition in service to the global church.

Like all enduring traditions, dispensationalism bears the scars of its battles. It has had to defend itself against its detractors, restore itself after its excesses, face the music of a history of cultural influences, weather the arduous process of both conscious and unconscious development, mourn the passing of some of its most ardent protectors, observe the decline of popular interest in major Bible prophecies and of things to come, and witness opposition to holistic narratives as well as the continued movement of biblical studies (in some quarters) away from canonical, theological interpretation.

Like all mature traditions, however, it rejoices in its sons and daughters, its granddaughters and grandsons who have dedicated themselves to the flourishing of the family heritage. They are always mindful of what and who has come before and ever thankful to God for their mentors, their companions, and new opportunities to serve the church as dispensationalists.

In this spirit these ten essays are offered. They focus on areas believed to be reflective of the past and present status of dispensationalism, strategic to the future of the tradition, and helpful to the gospel ministry. They are concerned with foundational matters of dispensationalism's evangelical identity, definition, history, and hermeneutics. In continued affirmation that one of its greatest blessings is providing insight into the one divine plan revealed progressively in the Bible, other essays trace this concern. Finally, attempting to situate dispensationalism more broadly, the volume concludes with chapters on the relationship of the tradition to other traditions and to the global context. In each essay, the writer attempts to represent both the unity and the diversity in the tradition with one's eyes focused on the faithful ministry of the gospel.

The writers of these essays are our teachers, colleagues, students, and friends. There are differences in opinions among us, but what we share in common is much more important. In these essays, our common heritage is what unites us.

We dedicate this book in gratitude to Charles C. Ryrie. His *Dispensationalism Today,* now simply *Dispensationalism,* has been the starting point for many conversations.[1] We remember and honor the legacy of Lewis Sperry Chafer and John F. Walvoord as dispensational theologians with a heart for the gospel. We also grieve the recent loss of Howard Hendricks, from whom we learned the skills of pedagogy, and J. Dwight Pentecost, from whom we learned to long for the things to come.[2] "The grace of the Lord Jesus be with all" (Rev. 22:21).

D. Jeffrey Bingham and Glenn R. Kreider
April 3, 2015 (115th anniversary of the ordination of Lewis S. Chafer.)

Notes

1. Charles Caldwell Ryrie, *Dispensationalism Today* (Chicago: Moody, 1965); and Charles C. Ryrie, *Dispensationalism*, rev. ed. (Chicago: Moody, 2007).
2. *Things to Come* (Zondervan) is the title of Pentecost's classic work, first published in 1958.

1

What Is Dispensationalism?

A PROPOSAL

GLENN R. KREIDER

I have fond and vivid memories of my childhood church experiences. In a small, rural Mennonite church I learned the Bible stories through my teacher's use of flannel graph characters. As a young child, I came to understand that I was a sinner and only through faith in the atoning sacrifice of Jesus Christ and His resurrection from the dead could I have the hope of eternal life. I believed that message, I trusted in Christ alone, and I looked forward to spending eternity with Him.

In this church, the Sunday school hour was followed by a corporate worship experience. Most of the women sat on the left side, the men on the right, and the teenagers sat in the back couple of pews. My mother and father sat together, usually on the right side with the men, and my sisters and I sat with them.[1] It was a rite of passage when I was allowed to leave my father's side and sit with my peers and the older teenagers in the back pew.

The music in this church was not contemporary nor seeker-sensitive; it was led by a man with a pitch pipe and the congregation sang four-part a cappella harmony. Then the pastor would come to the pulpit, open his large King James

Version *Scofield Reference Bible*, and begin to preach. His sermons were heavily expositional and applicational, and a reading from the Scripture almost always included the explanation, "And the Scofield note says . . ."

I was trained in dispensationalism from the beginning of my life. Although I eventually came to understand that not everyone was a Christian, I still thought all Christians were dispensationalists. During elementary school I never understood why my public school friends did not attend the prophecy conferences or Southern gospel hymn sings my family regularly attended.

When I was old enough to make my own decision about attending church, because I had a driver's license and a car, I began to attend an independent Bible church. The pastor of this church had been trained in the Scofield Correspondence Course.[2] He too preached expositionally and applicationally, and explained from the pulpit how to read the Bible as a dispensationalist. I learned to keep Israel and the church separate, that the hope of the church is the rapture, that the tribulation would be a terrible time on the earth, and that it would be followed by a millennium. During this thousand-year period, the promises made to Israel would be fulfilled literally and the church would be in heaven. Then, the end would come. The earth would be annihilated by fire and we would all go to heaven to be with Jesus.[3]

Yes, I am a dispensationalist, born into a dispensational home and brought to faith and nurtured in dispensational churches. I attended a dispensational Bible college where I was taught by several graduates of Grace Theological Seminary and Dallas Theological Seminary. I earned two degrees, a ThM and a PhD, from Dallas Theological Seminary and have been a full-time member of the teaching faculty since 2001.

I remain a dispensationalist, however, not merely because I have a heritage in the tradition. I have considered other theological positions. I have examined the history and the hermeneutics of dispensationalism. I have responded to questions and challenges from students over the years. I am not unaware of some of the problems and unresolved issues that still exist in my own theology. I believe, however, that a case can be made for dispensationalism from the text of Scripture.[4]

Dispensationalism is a popular, and populist, movement. It has had a huge influence in the evangelical Christian culture due to pastors and churches, pamphlets and books, seminars and conferences, radio and television programming, and mission agencies and parachurch ministries. Dispensational teaching is so widespread that a lot of people read the Bible this way, even if they are unaware that their position is dispensational. For many of them, it is all they know.

The purpose of this chapter is to describe what dispensationalism is and to defend this hermeneutical approach to the Scriptures from the Scriptures. But since dispensationalism is widely misconstrued and sometimes caricatured, we will first address several misunderstandings.[5]

WHAT DISPENSATIONALISM IS NOT

Dispensationalism is not a theological system—not in the same way that Calvinism, Lutheranism, Arminianism, and other theological traditions are systematic. Dispensationalists are Christians, Protestants and in the Reformed tradition. Dispensationalists confess the historic faith of the church, the Trinity, Chalcedonian Christology, the lostness of all humanity, salvation by grace alone through faith alone in Christ alone, the resurrection of the dead, the bodily return of Christ, etc. Dispensationalists do not have distinctive views of the Godhead, salvation, Christology, or the gospel. Rather, they affirm the doctrines of evangelical Christian orthodoxy.[6] The unique or distinctive beliefs of dispensationalism do not impact basic Christian doctrines. In short, dispensationalists confess orthodox Christianity.

Dispensationalism is not heterodox or heretical.[7] This charge persists in spite of numerous rebuttals.[8] No church council ever condemned the views found within mainstream dispensationalism, and no orthodox doctrines of the faith are compromised or denied in the tradition.[9] Specifically, dispensationalism does not teach multiple ways of salvation.[10] That God deals with His creation, especially people, differently from one era to the next does not imply that the means of salvation changes as the administrations change. Rather, like all Christians, dispensationalists believe that salvation is by grace alone, through faith alone, in Christ alone. Of course, it is not the case that people in every age were aware that salvation was provided through Christ, but their ignorance of the name of Jesus did not excuse them nor were they responsible for a content of beliefs that had not yet been revealed.[11] Dispensationalism affirms that the subject of the Scripture is the person and work of Christ in His first and second comings, that the Father sent the Son to accomplish His work in this world and then sent the Spirit to continue the work the Son began. The work of redemption will culminate in a new creation, where the Triune God will dwell with His people forever (Rev. 21:1–5).

Dispensationalism is not monolithic but it is a diverse and developing tradition.[12] There has never been a standard set of dispensational interpretations of biblical texts. A cluster of beliefs tends to characterize these Bible readers, rather than a standard set of dispensational interpretations of biblical texts. Blaising emphasizes this unity in the midst of diversity:

> There are a variety of dispensationalisms which one might encounter today. All of them emphasize the authority of Scripture, the importance of recognizing different dispensations for understanding Scripture, the distinctiveness of the church in the history of revelation, the importance of biblical prophecy and apocalyptic discourse, the imminent and premillennial coming of Christ, and a future for national Israel.[13]

Dispensationalism is not a hermeneutical approach that is imposed upon the Scriptures. It is, rather, a way of reading the Bible that can be supported by the Bible itself. Of course, not all Christians read the Bible this way. All do, however, read and interpret it with a set of preunderstandings and through an interpretive lens.[14] Dispensationalism is an interpretive lens.

Dispensationalism is not anti-tradition or sectarian nor "a cult or a sect since its basic ideas cross major denominational boundaries; it is not a new modern religion since it adheres to all basic elements of historic Christianity."[15] Although it is true that early dispensationalists viewed the institutional church negatively, dispensationalism does not reject denominations and church traditions.[16] Dispensationalists are found in a variety of Christian denominations, as well as in nondenominational churches and parachurch organizations.

Dispensationalism is not individualistic, at least not any more so than other American evangelical traditions.[17] Dispensationalism recognizes that the church is the body of Christ, that world evangelization is a corporate responsibility, that spiritual giftedness is described through analogy to the human body (1 Cor. 12), and that sanctification or growth in godliness occurs in the context of the church. The important distinction between Israel and the church is rooted in the reality that both are corporate. Israel is not merely a group of individuals who relate to God; she is a nation composed of families, clans, tribes, villages, and communities. Similarly, the church is one body made up of many parts. That dispensationalism recognizes a distinction between Israel and the church does not deny the unity of one people of God, saved by grace alone through faith alone in Christ alone.[18]

Dispensationalism is not primarily an eschatological position. Most dispensationalists believe in the pretribulation rapture of the church, at which time Christ will come to the earth, the dead in Christ will be raised, and those who are alive will be caught up and glorified (cf. 1 Thess. 4–5) seven years before Christ returns to the earth to establish a thousand-year reign over the earth from the throne in Jerusalem. Dispensationalism is rooted in premillennial eschatology, but since not all premillennialists are dispensational, it would not be accurate to equate dispensationalism and premillennialism. Further, there is much more to dispensationalism than a view on the end times.[19]

Dispensationalism does not necessarily pit the soteriological purpose of God against the doxological purpose.[20] Rather, dispensationalists agree with the Westminster Shorter Catechism in affirming "man's chief end is to glorify God and enjoy him forever."[21] Further, dispensationalists understand the biblical story as the story of redemption. From creation through the fall and God's work of redemption in a fallen world to the new creation when all the effects of sin have been removed, the Bible is the story of a Creator and Redeemer who is at work in His world. And His work of redemption glorifies Him.

Dispensationalism is not an academic tradition, although there have been dispensationalists who have served Christ in the academy.[22] It is, rather, a grassroots and populist movement. Dispensationalists are usually found in churches, colleges, mission agencies, television and radio ministries, and other practical ministries.[23]

Dispensationalism is not necessarily a pessimistic philosophy of history. Some dispensationalists emphasize that each dispensation includes a test and ends with human failure. Scofield, for example, wrote, "Each of these Dispensations may be regarded as a new test of the natural man, and each ends in judgment—marking his utter failure."[24] But as Charles Ryrie points out, not every dispensation ends with failure. In fact, according to Ryrie, "The presence of a test, failure, and judgment is not the *sine qua non* of a dispensational government of the world."[25] Perhaps more importantly, Ryrie argues that dispensationalism's view of God's redemptive work in history is "optimistic . . . [since] the dispensational pattern does not form a repetitive cyclical pattern, but rather an ascending spiral."[26] He even contrasts the optimism of dispensationalism with the pessimism of other views of history when he writes, "If there were not 'cyclical' interventions, then the course of human history would only be downward and entirely pessimistic."[27] In short, dispensationalism's view of history is optimistic; the trajectory of human history is improving, not because of evolutionary development, but because of God's grace progressively revealed and experienced in history.[28]

Dispensationalism is a biblical theology. It is rooted in the teaching of the Scriptures and claims to be a way of reading the Scripture that is taught therein. Demonstrating that claim from the Scripture follows in this chapter. But first, I propose a working descriptive definition of dispensationalism.

WHAT DISPENSATIONALISM IS

The covenant theologian Michael Horton argues that "covenant" is the "architectronic structure, a matrix of beams and pillars that hold together the structure of biblical faith and practice. . . . It is not simply the concept of the covenant, but the concrete existence of God's covenantal dealings in our history that provides the context within which we recognize the unity of Scripture amid its remarkable variety."[29]

Dispensationalists read the same Scriptures as covenant theologians and all other Christians. Dispensationalists recognize that God makes covenants with His people and that His faithfulness to those covenants is a major biblical theme. But dispensationalists, unlike covenantalists, do not believe that the "covenant" establishes the framework of the biblical story. This does not mean that dispensationalists deny the importance of covenants in the biblical story but that they believe that covenants are subsidiary to another structural construction.

The Scriptures reveal a God who is the sovereign Creator of everything that is. He not only brought the world into existence, He sustains it and cares for it. He is actively involved in the world that He has made. Like all good stories, the biblical story has a plot line that unfolds over time. The Bible tells the story of God's work of redemption, from the fall (Gen. 3) to the new heaven and new earth (Rev. 21–22). As God interacts with His world, and particularly with the humans He created in His image and likeness, His relationship with His creation is mediated differently at different times. Although God is unchanging, His plan for His creation unfolds progressively over time.

Dispensationalism is rooted in a biblical word and a biblical concept. The word "dispensation" (*oikonomia*), which is sometimes translated as "administration," or "stewardship," gives the hermeneutical approach its name. But more important than the label is that there are distinguishable eras or periods of time revealed in the biblical story.

A Definition

In his classic work *Dispensationalism Today*—now simply *Dispensationalism*—Charles Ryrie defined a dispensation as a "distinguishable economy in the outworking of God's purpose."[30] Later he summarized:

> Dispensationalism views the world as a household run by God. In this household world God is dispensing or administering its affairs according to His own will and in various stages of revelation in the process of time. These various stages mark off the distinguishably different economies in the outworking of His total purpose, and these economies are the dispensations. The understanding of God's differing economies is essential to a proper interpretation of His revelation within those various economies.[31]

Thus, a dispensation is not merely a period of time, an age, but a distinguishable period of time during which God administers His plan of redemption differently from other eras or periods. This change happens in history; God brings one economy or administration to an end, and then inaugurates a new one. There is continuity between dispensations; there is only one God and He has one unified plan of redemption. There is discontinuity between dispensations; the way God administers the plan of redemption changes. Sometimes the changes are cataclysmic and other times they are more incremental, but there are clear institutional and administrative changes from one dispensation to the next.

Dispensationalism is characterized by a hermeneutical approach that interprets the biblical story as the progressive revelation of God's unified work of redemption. Although dispensationalists recognize continuity in the plan of God, they believe that the Scriptures reveal distinguishable periods of time in the administration of God's relationship with His creation. The elements of discontinuity in these eras do not indicate different means or ways of salvation, since salvation is always by grace through faith and based in the person and work of Christ. Some dispensationalists emphasize that each period of time includes a divine test and each dispensation ends with the failure of humanity. Some dispensationalists recognize seven periods while others see as few as three. Dispensationalists believe that the Scriptures teach a distinction between Israel and the church within the unified people of God. Although in this dispensation believing Israelites become part of the church through faith in the Messiah, there is still the hope of future eternal blessings for believing ethnic Israel within dispensational theology.[32]

The label "dispensationalism" is rooted in the New Testament usage of the Greek word *oikonomia*. It is to an examination of the usage of that term we now turn. Then, a brief overview of the biblical story will illustrate the revelation of dispensations in the unfolding story of God's work of redemption.

Dispensationalism in Luke 16

In Luke 16, Jesus told a parable about a rich man and the steward or manager of his household. The rich man suspected his manager had misused his assets. So he summoned him and asked for an accounting of his stewardship. The unjust manager demonstrated shrewdness; he called his master's debtors and decreased the amount each of them owed. The master commended this dishonest manager for his shrewdness in this matter yet, presumably, brought his administration to an end. The dishonest steward was replaced by a new steward, which meant there would be a new stewardship. A change in steward brings a corresponding change in administration.

Jesus' application follows: "And I tell you, make friends for yourselves by how you use worldly wealth, so that when it runs out you will be welcomed into the eternal homes" (Luke 16:9 NET).[1] In this application, Jesus implies a dispensational change, from life in this world to the age of eternal dwellings.

This wealthy man has hired a manager of his household possessions. The manager does not own the assets; they belong to the rich man. The manager is accountable to his employer for his management. In this case, the manager has been unfaithful or unethical in his employment so he is dismissed from his position. His administration comes to an end and is replaced by another manager and another administration.

This is a parable rooted in the culture of the time, but could also be situated in a variety of cultural contexts. Wealthy people often hire others to manage their possessions. Those managers are not self-employed; they work for their employer. They are accountable to the owner for the way they handle the rich person's possessions.

Dispensationalism views the world as a divine household, in which God is the owner and humans are stewards of God's possessions. In a way similar to a wealthy landowner who hires a manager to care for his possessions, God has entrusted the care of creation to humans. Everything we have has come from Him. Everyone is a steward of what God has created. Our "possessions" do not belong to us; we are merely stewards. This is explicitly taught in the creation mandate:

> Then God said, "Let us make humankind in our image, after our likeness, so they may rule over the fish of the sea and the birds of the air, over the cattle, and over all the earth, and over all the creatures that move on the earth."
>
> God created humankind in his own image, in the image of God he created them, male and female he created them.
>
> God blessed them and said to them, "Be fruitful and multiply! Fill the earth and subdue it! Rule over the fish of the sea and the birds of the air and every creature that moves on the ground." (Gen. 1:26–28 NET)

Having been created to rule over God's creation, divine imagers will be accountable to God for their stewardship of His possessions. And, as Jesus taught in Luke 16, all Christians look forward to the eschatological hope of "eternal homes" (Luke 16:10).

Dispensationalism in Paul's Epistles: Ephesians 3

In Luke 16, the word "dispensation" is used in a technical, or concrete, sense for an administration of a household. In the book of Ephesians, the apostle Paul uses the word *oikonomia* or "dispensation"[33] in a broader, theological sense. He uses it to describe eras in redemption history.

In Ephesians 3, Paul introduces his ministry for the sake of the Gentiles with a reminder of the "stewardship of God's grace" given to him for their sake (Eph. 3:2). This stewardship of the gospel (Eph. 3:7) was given to him by God's grace, "to preach to the Gentiles the unfathomable riches of Christ" (Eph. 3:8). This dispensation of God's grace "had for ages been hidden in God who has created all things" (Eph. 3:9) but now has been disclosed "to the rulers and the authorities in the heavenly places" (Eph. 3:10). This dispensation of the gospel is not disconnected from the eternal redemptive plan of God; rather, it is "in accordance with the eternal purpose which He carried out in Christ Jesus our Lord, in whom we have boldness and confident access through faith in Him" (Eph. 3:11–12).

If a dispensation was given to Paul, and this new dispensation is the gospel, the good news that Jesus has united Jews and Gentiles in one new man, then there must have been a dispensation prior to this one.[34] If this dispensation was accomplished in the work of Christ, it could not have existed in this form prior to the coming of Christ. Further, "new" implies there was an "old."

The content of this dispensational change is explained in Ephesians 2 as the work of Christ in His incarnation, life, death, and resurrection. In that text, Paul expresses the contrast between Israel and Gentiles this way: "Therefore remember that formerly you, the Gentiles in the flesh, who are called 'uncircumcision' by the so-called 'circumcision' that is performed on the body by human hands—that you were at that time without the Messiah, alienated from citizenship of Israel and strangers to the covenants of promise, having no hope and without God in the world" (Eph. 2:11–12 NET). This state of hopelessness and godlessness does not mean that Gentiles were unable to experience the covenantal blessings promised to Israel. Many Gentiles did. It meant that, normatively, Gentiles would receive the blessings of God along with Israel by becoming part of the nation. And many did.

Things are different for both Jews and Gentiles after the coming of Christ. Paul continues, "But now in Christ Jesus you who were formerly far away have been brought near by the blood of Christ. For He Himself is our peace, who made both groups into one and broke down the barrier of the dividing wall, by abolishing in His flesh the enmity, which is the Law of commandments" (Eph. 2:13–15a). In the incarnation, but particularly in the work of atonement on the cross, Jesus took on Himself the hostility and opposition between Jews and Gentiles and He brought peace to the two through His own body. He created "in himself one new man out of two, thus making peace, and to reconcile them both in one body to God through the cross, by which the hostility has been killed. And he came and preached peace to you who were far off and peace to those who were near, so that through him we both have access in one Spirit to the Father" (Eph. 2:15b–18 NET).

One new man has been created out of two ethnic groups. The people of God has always been constituted by those who were joined to Him and to one another by grace through faith. Israel was God's people by grace through faith. Gentiles, the nations, could come to God by means of the covenant YHWH had made with the nation of Israel, by grace through faith in this God. The law of Moses would have regulated their worship of and relationship with God. Now, in Christ

Jesus, God has created one new man, one people made up of Jews and Gentiles. Gentiles will no longer be required to undergo circumcision and become part of Israel. Rather, now, in the Israel whose name is Jesus, ethnic Jews and ethnic Gentiles are united together in Him. No longer separated by circumcision, they are together, at peace with God and one another in Christ. "So then you are no longer strangers and aliens, but you are fellow citizens with the saints and are of God's household, having been built on the foundation of the apostles and prophets, Christ Jesus Himself being the cornerstone, in whom the whole building, being fitted together, is growing into a holy temple in the Lord, in whom you also are being built together into a dwelling place of God in the Spirit" (Eph. 2:19–22).

From one people of God, known as Israel, to one people of God made up of people of all ethnicities, tongues, and nations, the Christ event results in a change of administration. No longer are practices like sacrifices, festivals, circumcision, dietary restrictions, and Sabbath regulations the means of identifying this people, the means by which their ongoing relationship with God is mediated. No longer does the Mosaic law regulate the ceremonial practice of the people. Now, through Christ, a new age has come. But the means by which people join the community of God's people is by grace through faith, as has always been the case.

Dispensationalism in Galatians 3–4

In the book of Galatians Paul also describes this dispensational change. He reminds the Christians in Galatia of the promise that God had made to Abraham. "Now the promises were spoken to Abraham and to his descendant. Scripture does not say, 'and to the descendants,' meaning many, but 'and to your descendant,' referring to one, who is Christ" (Gal. 3:16 NET). God's promises to Abraham were made, then, not to Israel but to Christ. Long before there was an Israel, even before Jacob was born, God promised to bless all nations through the seed of Abraham: "And the scripture, foreseeing that God would justify the Gentiles by faith, proclaimed the gospel to Abraham ahead of time, saying, 'All the nations will be blessed in you' " (3:8 NET).

God's plan, culminating in the gospel of the resurrected Christ, has always been to bless the nations. In the old dispensation this occurred through Israel. In the new dispensation, blessing comes through and in Christ, the descendent of Abraham. "For you are all sons of God through faith in Christ Jesus. For all of you who were baptized into Christ have clothed yourselves with Christ. There is neither Jew nor Greek, there is neither slave nor free man, there is neither male nor female; for you are all one in Christ Jesus. And if you belong to Christ, then you are Abraham's descendants, heirs according to the promise" (vv. 27–29). Of course, Paul is not denying that there are differences between Jew and Gentile, slave and free, male and female; that would be silly. Rather, in Christ those differences do not matter like they did in the dispensation that immediately preceded the Christ event. In Christ, in this new dispensation, Jews and Gentiles, slaves and free, men and women, are equal members of the people of God.

Then, Paul compares the dispensation of law to a minor who "is under guardians and managers [*oikonomous*] until the date set by the father" (Gal. 4:2). Although this child is an heir and "is owner of everything" (Gal. 4:1), he does not have access to his inheritance until the father gives management to him. In the same way, "we, when we were minors, were enslaved under the basic forces of the world. But when the appropriate time had come, God sent his Son, born of a woman, born under the law, to redeem those who were under the law, so that we may be adopted as sons with full rights" (Gal. 4:3–5 NET).

Paul describes a change in dispensations, from stewardship by the law to the stewardship of the gospel of Christ, from the focus on Israel to the inclusion of all nations, from the old to the new. What does not change is the means of salvation; it is always by grace alone through faith alone in Christ alone. What does not change is that God has made promises to Abraham; these include the blessing of all nations. Both dispensations are rooted in the gospel, the promise that all peoples would be blessed through Abraham.

What does not change is that God remains gracious to His people—although the administration of His grace has changed, and things are better under the new dispensation than under the old. It is better to live after the resurrection of Christ than before Christ came, after His atoning sacrifice than when animals died to atone for sin, under His priesthood than under the Aaronic priesthood (cf. Heb. 7). Christ brings not only a new age but also a better age, because Christ is better than Moses, the angels, and the prophets.

Dispensationalism in Ephesians 1

This redemptive trajectory, that each dispensation is better than the previous one, is also seen in one other text where Paul uses "dispensation." In Ephesians 1:10, he looks forward to the "administration suitable to the fullness of the times" in which God will sum "up all things in Christ, things in heaven and the things on earth." All things in heaven and earth will one day be redeemed, all creation will be redeemed, sin and all its effects will be removed; Christ will be the head. In this, still future, dispensation, the prayer Jesus taught His followers will be realized, "your kingdom come, your will be done on earth as it is heaven" (Matt. 6:10). Only in the eternal state will all God's enemies be defeated and all things in heaven and earth be summed up or brought to submission under Christ (cf. 1 Cor. 15:25–28).

CONCLUSION

Dispensationalism is defined as the view that the Bible teaches that there are distinguishable periods of time in which God administers His plan for creation differently. The coming of Christ inaugurates a new way of relating to God. If the gospel brings a new dispensation, then there was a dispensation that preceded it (Eph. 2–3; Gal. 3–4). Paul also looks forward to a dispensation of the fullness of times, when the work of redemption will be completed. Thus, there is biblical support for three dispensations. As Ryrie puts it, "There can be no question that the Bible uses the word dispensation is exactly the same way the dispensationalist does."[35]

The doctrinal statement of Dallas Theological Seminary defines these three dispensations this way: "We believe that different administrative responsibilities of this character are manifest in the biblical record, that they span the entire history of mankind. . . . We believe that three of these dispensations or rules of life are the subject of extended revelation in the Scriptures, viz., the dispensation of the Mosaic Law, the present dispensation of grace, and the future dispensation of the millennial kingdom. We believe that these are distinct and are not to be intermingled or confused, as they are chronologically successive."[36] There are biblical grounds for these three dispensations. That does not mean that others are not taught in Scripture, just that the Bible does use the term "dispensation" to describe these three in Ephesians and Galatians.

It is not the number of distinguishable administrations that defines dispensationalism.[37] Most dispensationalists defend more than these three. In what follows, I will defend seven.

DISPENSATIONALISM IN BIBLICAL THEOLOGY

For many Christians, the dispensational hermeneutic appears to be self-evident. When they read the Bible, they observe that God's relationship with His people and with creation changes over time.[38] In fact, many have adopted a dispensational reading of the Scriptures without being aware of it.[39] Toussaint explains that dispensationalism "simply results from an investigation into the progress of God's plan as revealed in the Scriptures. It recognizes various administrations or economies in the outworking of God's plan in history."[40]

The earlier section argues for dispensationalism based upon the way the term *oikonomia* is used in the New Testament, particularly in Galatians and Ephesians. Dispensationalism can also be defended by observing the changes in the way God administers His sovereignty over creation. Several changes are seen in the biblical story of creation, fall, and redemption. Roy Aldrich observes, "The dispensational position is not entirely dependent on the meaning of the word [dispensation] or its various uses in the New Testament. Even if no such word were found in the Bible, some term would have to be chosen to describe the concept of dispensational truth. Correct theological terms are not always Biblical words."[41]

Creation: At Home in the Garden

The Bible begins with the account of the creation of heaven and earth. The eternal God, for reasons known only to Him, chose to create an earth; He separated land from water, created vegetation on the earth, and created living things to fill the land, seas, and skies. God is the source of everything that is.

God created a man and a woman in His image and likeness and gave them the responsibility to populate the earth and care for the creatures and the earth that He had made (Gen. 1:26–28). Their responsibility would be to represent God and reveal Him in and to creation. They will be the visible representation of the invisible God. God, who is perfectly capable of caring for the earth all by Himself and who would have done a more efficient and effective job than will billions of human caretakers, turns over the care of His precious possession to them. Since no one human could do this alone, they are commanded to reproduce and fill the earth (Gen. 1:26). They are placed in a garden, given access to anything they wanted to eat, except the fruit from one tree (Gen. 2:17), and given the task of caring for God's world. God's plan for his Creation will be administered through them.

Fall: Exiled from the Garden

Disastrously, the story quickly takes a tragic twist. An enemy of God, the serpent, comes into the garden. He entices the couple to follow his plan, to eat from the Tree of Knowledge of Good and Evil. God's word was clear and direct: "You must not eat from the tree of the knowledge of good and evil, for when you eat from it you will surely die" (Gen. 2:17 NET). Instead, according to the serpent, "Surely you will not die, for God knows that when you eat from it your eyes will open and you will be like divine beings who know good and evil" (Gen. 3:4–5 NET). God threatened death for eating; the serpent promises knowledge and life. The two humans listen to the serpent, eat the fruit, and experience the consequences of fear, shame, guilt, and ultimately, death.

After their act of rebellion, God comes to visit them (Gen. 3:8). He meets them in the world that He created for them. When they hide from Him, God finds them and confronts them with their rebellion. Then He pronounces judgment on them and exiles them from the garden, blocking the way back to ensure that they will never return to the place. The ground is cursed because of their sin and an animal dies to cover their nakedness (Gen. 3:21). Because they rebelled against God, they will return to the dust from which they were taken. They will die after a lifetime spent in painful toil (Gen. 3:19).

But this is not the end of the story. The man and woman, although exiled from the garden and the presence of God, remain alive on the earth.[42] That human life continues reveals that God's plan has not come to an end. Rather, God now administers His plan differently than He had prior to the fall. He does not destroy these rebellious creatures, He does not replace them with another species of caretakers, and He does not change their responsibility to fill the earth and care for it. Instead, it is the context of their task that changes; they will carry out their responsibility to care for the world in a world marked by sin and all of its effects. And in the end, they will die.

The author of Genesis does not use the term "dispensation" to describe the change that occurs in Genesis 3, but the alteration in the administration of God's plan is obvious. Human rebellion brings divine judgment and a corresponding modification in the relationship between the Creator and His world.

No longer are they living in the garden in a world of life and peace; they are kicked out of the garden to live in a world of painful toil that eventually ends in their death as well as the death of every other living thing.

After the Flood: The Rise of Nations

With the worldwide flood comes another change in the administration of God's plan for His creation. God's heart was grieved and filled with pain (Gen. 6:6) because the earth was filled with violence (Gen. 6:11, 13). So, God promises to destroy all living creatures and the earth itself (Gen. 6:13, 17), except for Noah, his family, and the animals that Noah would take into the ark (Gen. 6:18–20).[43] He also preserved food for all the inhabitants of the ark (Gen. 6:21). As in Genesis 3, the failure of the caretakers of the earth leads to the destruction of all living things on the earth. The destiny of the earth is tied inextricably to the behavior of the human caretakers. These caretakers had failed in their stewardship of the earth, filling the earth with violence instead of blessing (cf. Gen. 1:26–28). As a result, they are judged, the earth is purged, and a new dispensation begins, as Noah and his family come out of the ark to repopulate the earth.

The preservation of Noah and his family, as well as every kind of living creature that lives on the earth, is a gracious act of God. Even in the midst of severe judgment, God preserves life and provides for the ongoing care of His creation. God's plan for the earth does not change, even though the means by which He administers it does change.

When Noah and the rest of his family begin a new dispensation, the patriarch builds an altar and sacrifices animals to the God who had delivered him from judgment.[44] He and his family hear the words, familiar to the reader of Genesis 1:

> God blessed Noah and his sons and said to them, "Be fruitful and multiply, and fill the earth. The fear of you and the terror of you will be on every beast of the earth and on every bird of the sky; with everything that creeps on the ground, and all the fish of the sea into your hands are given. Every moving thing that is alive, shall be food to you; I give all to you, as I gave the green plants." (Gen. 9:1–3)

Later, God says, "As for you, be fruitful and multiply; Populate the earth abundantly and multiply in it" (v. 7).

To the first humans, God had spoken blessing, commanded reproduction, and given responsibility to rule over the creatures on the earth, in the air, and in the water (Gen. 1:28). Their diet was to come from "every plant yielding seed that is on the surface of all the earth and every tree which has fruit yielding seed" (Gen. 1:29). The animals had the same diet (Gen. 1:30). Now, things are different. The imagers still have the responsibility to rule over the world that God had made. But now, the creatures will live in terror of them. The reason for this terror might be very simple: because the animals have something to fear. Prior to the flood, humans and animals were vegetarian; after the flood, humans and animals will eat living things. This dietary change demonstrates a change in the way God administers His plan for creation. There is continuity; the divine imagers are still the means by which the plan is administered. But there is a change in the way it occurs. The dietary changes as well as the shortened life span of the caretakers are evidence of this (Gen. 6:3).

The writer of Genesis does not emphasize the change in administration. In fact, there is little attention devoted to this episode beyond the reason for the judgment and the devastating destruction the flood brought. But there clearly is a new day dawning. The flood does not destroy all life, it does not destroy the earth, and it does not bring an end to God's plan. It does, however, radically change the way God's rule over His earth is managed.

Call of Abraham: Blessing of All Nations

Many dispensationalists see another administrative change in the call of Abraham. The descendants of Noah have settled in Shinar (Gen. 11:1–2). They have, apparently, been fruitful. They are not, however, filling the earth and ruling over it. Instead, they plan to build a tower in order to "make a name for ourselves. Otherwise we will be scattered across the face of the entire earth" (Gen. 11:4 NET). God confounds their language and scatters them (Gen. 11:9), resulting in a variety of people groups (Gen. 10).

Once again, there is failure that culminates in judgment. The rebellion at Babel deserves death, but God does not destroy these rebels. Instead, He confuses their speech. God is gracious and redemptive even in judgment. The multiplicity of languages and the corresponding cultural diversity will make communication difficult. Yet in the midst of this judgment, God gives humans the gift of multiculturalism (cf. Rev. 7:9).

A significant change in the administration of God's plan occurs when He chooses Abram, from Ur of the Chaldeans (Gen. 11:31), and promises to bless him and through him to bless all peoples on earth (Gen. 12:1–3). Rather than dealing with individuals and families, God's plan of blessing will be administered through one man and his descendants. God's plan from the beginning has been to bless all creatures. He blessed living creatures created on the fifth day (Gen. 1:22) and then human beings created on the sixth day (Gen. 1:28). Now, this blessing of all peoples will be mediated through one man and his descendants. According to Paul (Gal. 3:8), this promise to Abram is the gospel.

The Exodus: The Giving of the Law

The transition from the dispensation of Abraham and his family to the law of Moses is less climactic than the change that happens in the fall or the flood. This change is not based on failure and judgment of God's people.[45] There is judgment on the Egyptians in the exodus. But the deliverance of God's people, the promise of their return to the land promised to Abraham, Isaac, and Jacob, the giving of the law at Mt. Sinai, and the leadership under Moses seems designed more as a demonstration of God's faithfulness than judgment on human failure. Yahweh declares, "They shall know that I am the Lord their God who brought them out of the land of Egypt, that I may dwell among them. I am the Lord their God" (Exod. 29:46).

During this administration of God's plan, the law of Moses is the constitution of God's people. Among a myriad of examples that could be cited of a dispensational change[46] is the story of a man gathering wood on the Sabbath (Num. 15:32). Several witnesses bring him to Moses, who inquires of the Lord. The response is clear: "The man shall surely be put to death; all the congregation shall stone him with stones outside the camp" (Num. 15:35). This is the penalty for working on the Sabbath (Exod. 31:14–16; 35:1–2). Prior to the giving of the law, working on the Sabbath was acceptable. Now, working on the Sabbath made one a lawbreaker and subject to the death penalty.[47]

Another clear example of an administrative change is the dietary regulations of the Law. Of course, dietary regulations existed in previous dispensations. The instructions to Adam are clear: "You may freely eat fruit from every tree of the orchard, but you must not eat from the tree of the knowledge of good and evil, for when you eat from it you will surely die" (Gen. 2:16–17). Eating the fruit from one tree was thus a capital crime. All the rest of the vegetation was acceptable for food. Eating animal flesh was forbidden (Gen. 1:29–30).

After the fall, the diet remains the same, except that now "you will eat the grain of the field. By the sweat of your brow you will eat food until you return to the ground, for out of it you were taken; for you are dust, and to dust you will return" (Gen. 3:18–19). The food provisions remain the same, except there will be no access to the trees in the garden, especially not the tree of life (Gen. 3:22–23). What changes is that the work of providing food will be through painful toil.

After the flood, the regulations change again: "You may eat any moving thing that lives. As I gave you the green plants, I now give you everything. But you must not eat meat with its life (that is, its blood) in it" (Gen. 9:3–4 NET). In addition to eating plants and vegetation, humans are now allowed to eat meat, but not blood.

Now, in the Mosaic law, the regulations are much more extensive (Lev. 11; Deut. 14). Living creatures are divided into two categories: "This is the law of the land animals, the birds, all the living creatures that swarm on the land, to distinguish between the unclean and the clean, between the living creatures that may be eaten and the living creatures that must not be eaten" (Lev. 11:46–47 NET). In short, before the Law was given at Sinai, a member of the community of Israel could enjoy a delicious rabbit stifado. When the Law was given, eating that same dish is forbidden under penalty of defilement: "By these . . . you will be made unclean; whoever touches their carcass becomes unclean until evening, and whoever picks up any of their carcasses shall wash his clothes and be unclean until the evening" (Lev. 11:24–25).

This change in dietary regulations indicates a change in the administration of God's plan for His world. It is one of many changes. The law of Moses adds a number of other requirements, including the construction of a place and objects to be used in worship, festivals and feasts, sacrifices and offerings, laws and ordinances for government, and legal and judicial requirements.

The Spirit: Blessing of All Nations

All Christians acknowledge a transition from the old covenant to the new covenant. The coming of Jesus, the Messiah, in fulfillment of biblical prophecy introduces a new age. Jesus lived a perfect life, died as a substitute for sinners, and was resurrected to provide hope of life everlasting. His first advent ends with His ascension to the Father. The Spirit, promised to the disciples in the Upper Room Discourse (John 13–17), is poured out on the day of Pentecost (Acts 2).

In Christ, Jews and Gentiles are united in one new man, the body of Christ (Eph. 2). Salvation comes by grace through faith to those whose trust is placed in Christ. And then, having believed, they receive the gift of the Spirit (Eph. 1). Believers in Jesus are indwelt by the Spirit and baptized into the body of Christ (1 Cor. 12:13). In Ephesians 3, as argued above, Paul calls this a "stewardship [dispensation] of God's grace" (Eph. 3:2).

With the transition from the dispensation of Mosaic law to the new covenant, the Sabbath and dietary regulations change again. No longer are people of faith required to keep the Sabbath or face execution, or keep strict dietary laws or risk excommunication. Rather, because of Christ's atoning sacrifice, Paul instructs Christians: "Therefore no one is to act as your judge in regard to food or drink or in respect to a festival, or new moon, or a Sabbath day—things that are a mere shadow of what is to come, but the substance belongs to Christ" (Col. 2:16–17).[48] The Sabbath and dietary regulations of the law of Moses are no longer in effect. Jesus makes that point explicitly when He explains to His disciples, "Are you so foolish? Don't you understand that whatever goes into a person from outside cannot defile him? For it does not enter his heart but his stomach, and then goes out into the sewer" (Mark 7:18–19a NET). Mark explains, "This means all foods are clean" (v. 19b).

After the day of Pentecost, Peter is reminded of this change in dietary regulations when he sees a vision of a sheet carrying a variety of clean and unclean animals (Acts 10:9–16). A voice from heaven instructs him to eat. Three times the voice commands and three times Peter refuses. The command to eat comes with a rebuke: "What God has made clean, you must not consider ritually unclean" (v. 15 NET). When he arrives at Cornelius's house, Peter explains what he had learned from the vision: "God has shown me that I should call no person defiled or ritually unclean" (v. 28 NET). Thus, the vision had broader application than to dietary laws, but it was based upon removal of those regulations. In other words, Peter now understands that the removal of the dietary restrictions is connected to the way he should view people. In light of the redemptive work of Christ, he can no longer view Gentiles as unclean.

That the rest of the apostles did not readily and easily accept this change is clear by their response. They summon Peter to Jerusalem to explain himself. They ask him why he shared a meal with a Gentile (Acts 11:2–3).[49] When they hear that the Spirit had come to these Gentiles, they "ceased their objections and praised God, saying, 'So then, God has granted the repentance that leads to life even to the Gentiles' " (Acts 11:18 NET).

Apparently these followers of Jesus did not yet understand that the Great Commission was a command to make disciples of all nations (Matt. 28:19). Nor did they really understand the promise that they would be witnesses to the ends of the earth (Acts 1:8). It took Peter's multiple visions and the repeated command from heaven to eat unclean animals and his trip back to Jerusalem to explain his visit to the house of a Gentile for the disciples to understand that a change had occurred in God's administration of the work of redemption. It is now through the church that God will bless all nations, by means of the indwelling Holy Spirit.

This does not mean, as replacement theology, or supersessionism, teaches, that the church has replaced Israel, that God is through with Israel, and that God has no intention of keeping the promises He has made to Abraham, Isaac, and Jacob.[50] Rather, God's plan for ethnic Israel will be fulfilled in the future (Rom. 11:1).[51] The plan for Israel will be fulfilled in Jesus and, through Him, to those who are united to Him by grace through faith.

The New Heavens and Earth: Redemption Completed

The final dispensation, from the millennium into eternity, begins with the return of Christ to the earth (Rev. 19). This event includes a great feast: "Let us rejoice and be glad and give the glory to Him because the marriage of the Lamb has come, and his bride has made herself ready. . . . Blessed are those who are invited to the marriage supper of the Lamb!" (Rev. 19:7, 9).[52]

The writer of Hebrews predicts that "a Sabbath rest [remains] for the people of God. For the one who has entered His rest has himself also rested from his works, as God did from His. Therefore let us be diligent to enter that rest, so that no one will fall, through following the same example of disobedience" (Heb. 4:9–11). The fulfillment of the Sabbath awaits the consummation of all things, when Christ will be all in all. Jesus is the fulfillment of the Sabbath and He provides rest for those who are in Him (cf. Matt. 11:28–30).[53] Those who came before Him, those who lived by faith in earlier dispensations, "did not receive what was promised. For God had provided something better for us, so that they would be made perfect together with us" (Heb. 11:39–40 NET). Together with that great cloud of witnesses (Heb. 12:1), we look forward to receiving "a kingdom that cannot be shaken" (Heb. 12:28), "the city that is to come" (Heb. 13:14).

Our hope, and the hope of all the redeemed, is found in "Mount Zion . . . the city of the living God, the heavenly Jerusalem, and to myriads of angels, to the general assembly and church of the firstborn, who are enrolled in heaven, and to God, the Judge of all, and to the spirits of the righteous made perfect, and to Jesus, the mediator of a new covenant, and to the sprinkled blood, which speaks better than the blood of Abel" (Heb. 12:22–24).

In the Apocalypse, John sees the fulfillment of this promise.

> Then I saw a new heaven and a new earth, for the first heaven and the first earth had passed away, and the sea was no more. And I saw the holy city, new Jerusalem, coming down out of heaven from God, prepared as a bride adorned for her husband. And I heard a loud voice from the throne saying, "Behold, the dwelling place of God is with man. He will dwell with them, and they will be his people, and God himself will be with them as their God. He will wipe away every tear from their eyes, and death shall be no more, neither shall there be mourning, nor crying, nor pain anymore, for the former things have passed away."
>
> And he who was seated on the throne said, "Behold, I am making all things new." Also he said, "Write this down, for these words are trustworthy and true." And he said to me, "It is done! I am the Alpha and the Omega, the beginning and the end. To the thirsty I will give from the spring of the water of life without payment. The one who conquers will have this heritage, and I will be his God and he will be my son." (Rev. 21:1–7 ESV)

Thus, the prediction of the prophet Ezekiel will be experienced on the earth. This is a promise of an eternal covenant: "I will make a covenant of peace with them; it will be an eternal covenant with them. I will establish them, increase their numbers, and place my sanctuary among them forever. My dwelling place will be with them; I will be their God, and they will be my people. Then, when my sanctuary is among them forever, the nations will know that I, the LORD sanctify Israel" (Ezek. 37:26–28 NET).

God's Plan for His Creation

From the beginning of the biblical story, God has been carrying out His plan for His creation. He created the heavens and the earth and created divine imagers to represent Him in the world. Their rebellion against Him did not catch

God by surprise. He had planned their redemption even before they fell. His plan is carried out in time and space. It is progressively revealed and progressively accomplished. There are distinguishable periods of time during which God administers His plan differently. Each dispensation, or administration, is better than the previous one, culminating in a new creation, a new heaven and earth in which God makes the earth His home forever.

The redeemed of all ages spend eternity with Him. Nothing could be better than that.

THEOLOGICAL DISTINCTIVES OF DISPENSATIONALISM

In 1965, Ryrie asserted that "dispensationalists are conservative and affirm complete allegiance to the doctrines of verbal, plenary inspiration, the virgin birth and deity of Christ, the substitutionary atonement, eternal salvation by grace through faith, the importance of godly living and ministry of the Holy Spirit, and hope for the future in the coming of Christ."[54] Later he makes this point: "Whether nondispensationalists want to acknowledge it or not, dispensationalists do believe in the unity of the plan of salvation, the spiritual seed of Abraham, and even the possible validity of the covenant of grace!"[55]

In 1992, Blaising and Bock described dispensationalism very similarly:

> We speak of dispensationalism as a tradition within American evangelicalism, sharing common features of evangelical orthodoxy. It is a tradition that has emphasized the universal church as the framework for Christian unity and spirituality, seeking its practical manifestation in ways that do not conflict with the concept of the local church. It has advocated the authority of Scripture and has emphasized the theological relevance of biblical apocalyptic and prophecy. It is a futurist premillennialism that has strongly maintained the imminent return of Christ and a national and political future for Israel. It is characterized by a canonical approach to Scripture that interprets discontinuities of the Old and New Testaments as historical changes in divine-human dispensations reflecting different purposes in the divine plan. As an element of dispensational change, it has emphasized unique features in grace of the present dispensation of the church.[56]

Dispensationalism is not a theological position that is rooted in denominationalism. It grew out of denominations, but it is not a denomination. It was rooted in the conviction that denominations had lost their theological moorings. But dispensationalists hoped to purify and revive Christianity within those denominations. Dispensationalists played a major role in the rise of independent Bible churches. In planting such churches, the focus shifted from revitalizing existing churches and denominations to planting new, independent churches. Yet, dispensationalism is not antidenominations. It has an independent and entrepreneurial spirit which is nondenominational not antidenominational. In fact, many dispensationalists today serve in mainline denominational churches and organizations.

Dispensationalism, like the American evangelicalism where it has found a home, is a gospel-centered theological position. Dispensationalists are convinced that humanity is lost, "essentially and unchangeably bad apart from divine grace."[57] The only solution to the condition of lost humanity is found in the good news that Jesus Christ took upon Himself the sin of the whole world, died as a substitute for sinners, was raised from the dead to give hope of eternal life, ascended to the Father who sent the indwelling Holy Spirit, and is coming back to the earth to complete the work of redemption. Christ gave to the church the Great Commission, the privilege and responsibility to communicate this gospel message to the whole world and to make disciples of Jesus. Dispensationalism emphasizes individual or personal evangelism and the worldwide missionary mandate given to the church. It is, thus, not surprising that many faith-based mission agencies were founded by dispensationalists.[58]

Related to dispensationalism's emphasis on the Great Commission is its church and parachurch focus. The task of making disciples has been given to the church, but much of the work in making disciples is carried out through parachurch organizations. These are ministries, founded by Christians, which are designed to come alongside the church to perform ministerial tasks. Parachurch ministries do not replace the church; they serve alongside, as an arm of the church. Yet the relationship between the two has not always been harmonious. At times and in certain places, parachurch ministries sometimes seem as if they are more important than the church, as if they don't need the church.[59] Dispensationalism's strong entrepreneurial ethos and pragmatic bent have contributed to this. But in the best-case scenario, churches and parachurch organizations work together to accomplish the tasks of evangelism, training, teaching, discipleship, missions, and otherwise producing followers of Jesus who obey everything He commanded.[60]

Dispensationalists have a premillennial eschatology. Premillennialism is the view that Christ will return to the earth bodily (Acts 1:11) to inaugurate a one-thousand-year period of time during which He reigns over the earth from Jerusalem (Rev. 19–20). It is called premillennial because the return of Christ is prior to the millennium. All dispensationalists are premillennial but not all premillennialists are dispensational.[61] Most dispensationalists believe that seven years prior to the return of Christ to the earth, He will descend in the clouds and resurrect those who have died in faith and glorify believers who are still alive, and take both groups back to heaven with Him. This event is called the rapture of the church and because it precedes a seven-year tribulation period, it is called a pretribulation rapture position. This position is not limited to a dispensational reading of the Scriptures nor is it an essential view of dispensationalism.

UNRESOLVED TENSIONS

The focus in this chapter has been on the views that dispensationalists hold in common, on what unites those who adopt the position, who willingly associate with the hermeneutical approach, who are comfortable within the fold. There is much that unites dispensationalists today, but there remain unresolved issues, and some views divide dispensationalists from one another.[62]

This chapter has not made much of the recent development described as progressive dispensationalism. The focus has been on what unites rather than what divides. To say it another way, what all dispensationalists hold in common is much more important than the nuances of distinction between dispensational views. Further, since dispensationalism has never been monolithic, there have always been areas of disagreement among dispensationalists.

Understandings of the Covenants

A number of issues of disagreement or diversity remain within dispensationalism. Among them are the understandings of the covenants. Dispensationalists are united in seeing the Abrahamic covenant as foundational to the redemptive plan of God. Some see a covenant in Genesis 12 while others believe that the promises God made in Genesis 12 are put into a covenant in Genesis 15. Some believe that the promises are specifically limited to Israel while others emphasize that God promises to bless Israel and the nations. Others emphasize that the promises are fulfilled in the Seed of Abraham, Jesus Christ.

How does the Mosaic covenant relate to the new covenant? Did the new covenant replace the Abrahamic covenant?[63] Are some aspects of the old covenant in force today? Will the old covenant sacrificial system be reestablished as a means of worship in the millennium?

Dispensationalists disagree in the way they understand the new covenant. Some insist that since the covenant was promised to Israel and Judah it can only be fulfilled to Jews. Others understand the New Testament to teach that the new covenant was inaugurated with the coming of the Spirit and that Jews and Gentiles receive new covenant blessings together, which still look forward to a future for ethnic Israel in God's plan in the future.

The Davidic covenant is acknowledged to promise an eternal kingdom under the reign of the Son of David, Jesus the Christ. But what about Christ's current reign? Is His reign from heaven an inaugurated fulfillment of that covenant promise or is the Davidic covenant reign only future?

The Nature of the Kingdom

Dispensationalists also differ on the nature and definition of the kingdom, whether it is present or solely future, whether it is earthly or heavenly, whether it is material or immaterial, or both. Many dispensationalists understand the Gospels to teach that Jesus offered a kingdom to Israel and, because the people rejected their king, the offer was then withdrawn and the kingdom postponed. Others believe the New Testament to teach that Jesus did not merely offer a kingdom but He came bringing the kingdom or bringing a new stage of the kingdom.[64]

Dispensationalists universally believe that there is a future for ethnic Israel in the redemptive plan of God and that the church and Israel must be distinguished. What is not quite as clear is the variety of ways "Israel" is used in the Bible and within theological and biblical literature. Similarly, "church" is defined differently within dispensationalism. Like evangelicalism as a whole, dispensationalists need to devote attention to the definition and mission of the church. This is particularly seen when dispensationalists correctly affirm that the church is made up of both Jews and Gentiles.[65]

A variety of views of the eternal state are found within dispensationalism. Some believe that the Bible teaches that in the final judgment, the earth will be annihilated and pass out of existence. This earth will be replaced with a new earth; there will be no essential connection between the old and the new.[66] Others believe that there will be some degree of continuity between this world and the new creation, that re-creation will not destroy and begin anew but the earth that was corrupted by sin will be redeemed and last forever. Dispensationalism has always had a strong earthly focus, at least for Israel, but it, like much of American evangelicalism, has sometimes viewed heaven as the final home of the redeemed.

The Hermeneutical Approach

Finally, dispensationalism is a hermeneutical approach to the Scriptures. Ryrie has described the hermeneutics of dispensationalism as "consistently literal, or plain . . . historical-grammatical hermeneutics."[67] This is the second of his *sine qua nons*. He explains, "The word *literal* is perhaps not as good as either the word *normal* or *plain*, but in any case it is interpretation that does not spiritualize or allegorize as nondispensational interpretation often does."[68] Blaising and Bock describe their hermeneutical approach as "historical-grammatical-literary-theological."[69] They also emphasize that Bible reading is not an individual task:

> Scripture's role is to transform us daily as we address it and look for it to challenge us. But our dialogue does not occur in a vacuum, nor should our deliberations be private. Others read the text with us. Though we do not always agree with others on what the Bible says, these differences reflect our limitations in understanding. Sometimes our dialogue with others helps us see our own blind spots.[70]

As Ryrie notes, the term "literal" might not be the best descriptor of the hermeneutical approach. But dispensationalists continue to use it to describe their hermeneutics. For example, Elliott Johnson defends its use and defines it this way: "*Literal* interpretation entails those meanings which the author intended to communicate in the expressions of the text (grammar) in the original setting (historical). *Literal* thus works with a text within the frame of an author and his communication."[71]

The strength of dispensationalism is that it is a biblically based system. Like evangelicalism, "as a community, we share a heritage that takes the divine message of the Bible seriously."[72] At its best, dispensationalism has been a community of biblical scholars, theologians, historians, pastors, evangelists, missionaries, and other Christian ministers wrestling with the issues facing them in this world under the authority of the Word of God. Since there are real enemies of the gospel we all face together, our goal should be to join with like-minded Christians with dispensational convictions, as well as with the bigger community of orthodox Christianity, in order to love and serve God and call others to follow Him in discipleship. Dispensationalism has been a place where such discussions take place "among biblical students and scholars who seek to handle the Word of God carefully and continue to evaluate their findings under its authority."[73] And these discussions continue as we together seek to submit to the authority of the Scriptures and reach the world with the good news of a resurrected Savior.

Notes

1. My parents were part of a transitional generation that changed this practice of separating men and women in the worship service. It might be too strong to call their decision to sit together an act of rebellion, but it certainly was a violation of the social mores in the church.
2. This pastor was an excellent biblical expositor, even though the Scofield course was the only formal theological training he had. On the history of Scofield's course see Glenn R. Goss, "Cyrus Ingerson Scofield and the Scofield Reference Bible, 1843–1921," http://www.ebccnet.com/scofield.php.
3. Of course, this is not a summary of dispensational teaching, merely the summary of what I learned growing up dispensationalist.
4. None of the contributors to this book would argue that dispensationalism is the only legitimate hermeneutic, but all believe that it is a legitimate way to read the Bible and, not surprisingly, that it is preferred to other options.
5. Darrell L. Bock argues, "Dispensationalism has been the object of caricature for at least four decades." Bock, "Current Messianic Activity and OT Davidic Promise: Dispensationalism, Hermeneutics, and NT Fulfillment," *Trinity Journal* 15 (1994): 55.
6. Blaising and Bock write, "We speak of Dispensationalism as a tradition within American Evangelicalism, sharing common features of evangelical orthodoxy," in Craig A. Blaising and Darrell L. Bock, "Dispensationalism, Israel, and the Church," in *Dispensationalism, Israel and the Church*, ed. Craig A. Blaising and Darrell L. Bock (Grand Rapids: Zondervan, 1992), 379. Mark S. Sweetnam, "Defining Dispensationalism: A Cultural Studies Perspective," *Journal of Religious History* 34 (2010): 198, lists "a commitment to evangelical doctrine" as one of the "markers" of dispensationalism.
7. One of the most strident of those charges is by John Wick Bowman, "The Bible and Modern Religions: II. Dispensationalism," *Interpretation* 10 (1956): 172–73. Bowman wrote: "Here is a teaching which, regardless of the amount of incidental true doctrine which it may contain, is—by virtue of certain dominant concepts which ramify the teaching at every point . . . something other than the historic faith of the Christian church." He argues the dispensationalism of the *Scofield Reference Bible* "is to be classed with the type of Pharisaism that opposed our Lord and the Judaizing branch of the early church that hounded Paul across the Roman Empire."
8. See Charles C. Ryrie, *Dispensationalism Today* (Chicago: Moody, 1965), 111–31; cf. Charles C. Ryrie, *Dispensationalism,* rev. ed. (Chicago: Moody, 2007), 122–40. Although he does not use the term "heresy," Sam Storms charges that premillennial dispensationalism is a view that "*the New Testament explicitly denies*" (italics in the original). Sam Storms, *Kingdom Come: The Amillennial Alternative* (Ross-Shire, Scotland: Mentor, 2013), 137.
9. On the charges of heresy brought against Lewis S. Chafer, see R. Todd Mangum, *The Dispensational-Covenantal Rift: The Fissuring of American Evangelical Theology from 1936 to 1944*, Studies in Evan-

gelical History and Thought (Waynesboro, GA: Paternoster, 2007).

10. For one example of this charge, see John H. Gerstner, *Wrongly Dividing the Word of Truth: A Critique of Dispensationalism* (Brentwood, TN: Wolgemuth and Hyatt, 1991), 262. Gerstner concludes, "If we have shown anything in this present volume, it is that Dispensationalism does teach more than one way of salvation—and that in doing so it teaches no salvation at all." In spite of consistent and repeated denials by dispensationalists, the charge continues to be leveled. More recently, Michael Horton, *Introducing Covenant Theology* (Grand Rapids: Baker, 2009), 149, characterizes dispensationalism as holding to the view that "commits old covenant Israelites to salvation by works in contrast to salvation by grace in the new covenant."

11. Thus the doctrinal statement of Dallas Theological Seminary reads, "We believe that it was historically impossible that they should have had as the conscious object of their faith the incarnate, crucified Son, the Lamb of God, and that it is evident that they did not comprehend as we do that the sacrifices depicted the person and work of Christ." http://www.dts.edu/about/doctrinalstatement/. Yet Walter C. Kaiser Jr. claims that this dispensational view means that one can be saved today "by simply saying, 'I believe there is a God!' 'I am a theist' "; in "Is It the Case that Christ Is the Same Object of Faith in the Old Testament? (Genesis 15:1–6)," *Journal of the Evangelical Theological Society* 55/2 (2012): 292. This is a caricature of the dispensational view.

12. Sweetnam, "Defining Dispensationalism," 193, asserts: "Dispensationalism is very far from being a monolithic system of belief." Darrell L. Bock, "Current Messianic Activity and OT Davidic Promise," 55, writes, "Dispensationalism has never been as monolithic as its opponents have portrayed it."

13. Craig A. Blaising, "Contemporary Dispensationalism," *Southwestern Journal of Theology* 36 (Spring 1994): 13.

14. Harold W. Stone and James O. Duke observe: "The biblical text does not speak for itself; every reading is someone's interpretation of it," in *How to Think Theologically* (Minneapolis: Fortress, 1996), 46. Also see Grant R. Osborne, *The Hermeneutical Spiral* (Downers Grove, IL: InterVarsity Press, 1991), 6.

15. Dale S. DeWitt, *Dispensational Theology in America* (Grand Rapids: Grace Bible College, 2002), 2.

16. Charles C. Ryrie, "Update on Dispensationalism," in *Issues in Dispensationalism*, ed. Wesley R. Willis and John R. Master (Chicago: Moody, 1994), 17, summarizes Darby's view that "the established church was in ruins and apostasy." On Darby and dispensationalism, see Larry V. Crutchfield, *The Origins of Dispensationalism: The Darby Factor* (Lanham, MD: University Press of America, 1992). See also Mark Sweetnam and Crawford Gribben, "J. N. Darby and the Irish Origins of Dispensationalism," *Journal of the Evangelical Theological Society* 52 (2009): 569–77.

17. See Nathan O. Hatch, *The Democratization of American Christianity* (New Haven, CT: Yale University Press, 1989). See also Stephen J. Nichols, *Jesus Made in America: A Cultural History from the Puritans to* "The Passion of the Christ" (Downers Grove, IL: InterVarsity, 2008).

18. Early dispensationalists sometimes made too sharp a distinction between the church and Israel, between the heavenly people and the earthly people. According to Ryrie, *Dispensationalism Today*, (Chicago: Moody, 1965), 146, "Any apparent dichotomy between heavenly and earthly purposes is not actual."

19. Craig A. Blaising, "Premillennialism," in *Three Views on the Millennium and Beyond*, ed. Darrell L. Bock (Grand Rapids: Zondervan, 1999), 155–227; and Blaising, "A Case for the Pretribulation Rapture," in *Three Views on the Rapture*, ed. Alan Hultberg, 2nd ed. (Grand Rapids: Zondervan, 2010), 25–73.

20. Ryrie, *Dispensationalism Today*, 46–47, has argued that dispensationalism holds to a doxological purpose while covenant theology holds to a "man-centered" soteriological purpose. This is inaccurate and unhelpful. See John S. Feinberg, "Systems of Discontinuity," in *Continuity and Discontinuity: Perspectives on the Relationship between the Old and New Testaments* (Westchester, IL: Crossway, 1988), 84–85.

21. "Westminster Shorter Catechism," http://www.reformed.org/documents /WSC.html.

22. Sweetnam, "Defining Dispensationalism," 192, notes, "Dispensationalism has, for most of its existence, remained below the academic radar; with the exception of a handful of historical and sociological works its cultural power has remain unacknowledged and unexamined."

23. John D. Hannah, *An Uncommon Union: Dallas Theological Seminary and American Evangelicalism* (Grand Rapids: Zondervan, 2009), 292–93, describes the connection between Dallas Theological Seminary and the Bible conference movement. Much of what he says about the seminary could also be said about dispensationalism. See also Glenn R. Kreider, "Dispensationalism," in *The Routledge Encyclopedia of Protestantism*, 4 vols., ed. Hans Hillerbrand (New York: Routledge, 2004), 2:599–600.

24. C. I. Scofield, *Rightly Dividing the Word of Truth* (Findlay, OH: Fundamental Truth, 1947), 13.

25. Ryrie, *Dispensationalism Today*, 39; cf. Charles C. Ryrie, *Dispensationalism* (Chicago: Moody, 2007), 42.

26. Ibid., 44. Surely he overstates the case when he claims, "Only Dispensationalism presents a properly optimistic philosophy of history."

27. Ibid, 43. Ryrie is responding to the claim of C. Norman Kraus, *Dispensationalism in America: Its Rise and Development* (Richmond, VA: John Knox Press, 1958), 126. Kraus wrote: "The final answer of the dispensationalist to the problem of development in history seems to be an implicit denial of the possibility of progress, claims to the contrary notwithstanding. Reacting against a false optimism and the assumption of inevitable evolutionary progress, Dispensationalism reverted to an equally pagan concept of history which denies the possibility of progress and asserts the inevitability of futility on the historical level."

28. Paul David Nevin, "Some Major Problems in Dispensational Interpretation," PhD dissertation, Dallas Theological Seminary, 1965, 196, wrote, "If Dispensationalism is to have an adequate philosophy of history, it must not only have unity and diversity, it must also have progress. God must not only have a goal in history, He must be getting there." He then demonstrates five ways that the dispensations show historical progress (197–204).

29. Michael Horton, *Introducing Covenant Theology*, 13. Later he explains, "The covenant is the framework" of Reformed theology (14).

30. First published in 1965, the book is still in print fifty years later; it was retitled *Dispensationalism* in 1995 and further revised in 2007. Ryrie's definition appears on page 33 of *Dispensationalism* (Chicago: Moody, 2007).

31. Ryrie, *Dispensationalism*, 34–35. In the foreword Frank E. Gaebelein calls dispensationalism a "system of Bible interpretation" (7).

32. This paragraph is adapted from my article "Dispensationalism," in *Encyclopedia of the Bible and Its Reception*, ed. Hans-Josef Klauck et al. (Berlin: De Gruyter, 2012), 6:923–24.

33. *Oikonomia* can be also translated as "stewardship," "management," and "administration."

34. The gospel had been announced in advance to Abraham (Gal. 3:8) but was accomplished in the work of Christ (Eph. 2:11–22).

35. Ryrie, *Dispensationalism*, 32. Italics removed. Ryrie reiterates this point one paragraph later: "The Scripture on at least two occasions does use the word in the same way the dispensationalist does."

36. At http://www.dts.edu/about/doctrinalstatement/.

37. See the chart in Ryrie, *Dispensationalism*, 81. See also Blaising and Bock, *Progressive Dispensationalism* (Wheaton: Victor, 1993; repr., Grand Rapids: Baker, 2000), 118–19.

38. Lewis Sperry Chafer, "Dispensationalism," *Bibliotheca Sacra* 93 (Oct–Dec 1936): 391, surely overstates the case when he claims, "Any person is a dispensationalist who trusts the blood of Christ rather than bringing an animal sacrifice . . . and any person is a dispensationalist who observes the first day of the week rather than the seventh." Yet, his basic point is accurate; for a period of time, God required sacrifices and the keeping of the Sabbath. He no longer does.

39. Craig A. Blaising, "Dispensationalism: The Search for Definition," in *Dispensationalism, Israel and the Church*, ed. Craig A. Blaising and Darrell L. Bock (Grand Rapids: Zondervan, 1992), 15, observes

that "many ideas and concerns associated with dispensationalism have become part and parcel of mainstream evangelicalism."

40. Stanley D. Toussaint, "A Biblical Defense of Dispensationalism," in *Walvoord: A Tribute*, ed. Donald K. Campbell (Chicago: Moody, 1982), 109.
41. Roy L. Aldrich, "A New Look at Dispensationalism," *Bibliotheca Sacra* 120 (1964): 42.
42. The man, Adam, will live for 930 years (Gen. 5:5).
43. Clearly, this language is hyperbolic: "I have decided that all living creatures must die, for the earth is filled with violence because of them. Now I am about to destroy them and the earth" (Gen. 6:17). The earth was not destroyed. When the floodwaters subsided, the ark settled, and Noah and the rest of the inhabitants came out of the ark and settled on the earth. In 1 Peter 3, Peter compares the destruction by water in the flood to the destruction by fire in the day of the Lord. See Gale Z. Heide, "What Is New about the New Heaven and the New Earth? A Theology of Creation from Revelation 21 and 2 Peter 3," *Journal of the Evangelical Theological Society* 40 (1997): 3–56.
44. One of the reasons for the command to Noah to take seven (or seven pairs of) clean animals onto the ark (Gen. 7:2–3) is to provide animals for these sacrifices. God provided what Noah would need after the flood, both for food and sacrifice.
45. Ryrie, *Dispensationalism*, 42, explains, "The presence of a test, failure, and judgment is not the *sine qua non* (absolute essential) of a dispensational government of the world."
46. As explained earlier, in Ephesians 3, Paul uses the term "dispensation" of this period of time.
47. This puts Sabbath breaking in the same category as murder (Exod. 21:12–15), kidnapping (Exod. 21:16), cursing parents (Exod. 21:17), sorcery (Exod. 22:18), adultery (Lev. 20:10), incest (Lev. 18:22), and blasphemy (Lev. 24:14–16). Only murder (Gen. 9:5–6) is specifically condemned as a capital crime prior to the giving of the Law.
48. Norman Geisler, "Colossians," *The Bible Knowledge Commentary: New Testament*, ed. John F. Walvoord and Roy B. Zuck (Wheaton: Victor Books, 1983): 678, argues that the Sabbath regulations have passed away.
49. Their reaction here is eerily similar to their response when they saw Jesus talking to a Samaritan woman (John 4:27).
50. See Michael J. Vlach, *Has the Church Replaced Israel?* (Nashville: B&H, 2010). For a Reformed view of the future for Israel and a nuancing of "replacement theology," see Brian Warner, "Replacement Theology," http://replacementtheology.org.
51. See J. Lanier Burns, "The Future of Ethnic Israel in Romans 11," in *Dispensationalism, Israel and the Church*, ed. Craig A. Blaising and Darrell L. Bock (Grand Rapids: Zondervan, 1992), 188–229.
52. There is no menu given for this banquet, but perhaps it will include rabbit stifado.
53. Ray C. Stedman, "Jesus Is Our Sabbath Rest," http://www.ldolphin.org/sabbathrest.html.
54. Ryrie, *Dispensationalism Today* (1965), 210–11. In the revised edition, the list is different: "hope for the future in the coming of Christ" is replaced with "the future coming of Christ, and the eternal damnation of the lost." Charles C. Ryrie, *Dispensationalism*, rev. and exp. ed. (Chicago: Moody, 1995), 212. The list remains the same in the 2007 edition (p. 247).
55. Ryrie, *Dispensationalism Today*, 211. This list is also revised in the new edition: "Dispensationalists do believe in the unity of the plan of salvation, the unity of God's people of all ages, the present aspect of the kingdom of God, the single basis of salvation, and the spiritual seed of Abraham." Ryrie, *Dispensationalism* (1995), 212. This list, too, remains unchanged in 2007 (p. 247).
56. Craig A. Blaising and Darrell L. Bock, "Dispensationalism, Israel, and the Church: Assessment and Dialogue," in *Dispensationalism, Israel and the Church*, ed. Blaising and Bock, 379.
57. The doctrine of total depravity is expressed this way in "DTS Doctrinal Statement," http://www.dts.edu/about/doctrinalstatement/.

58. For a list of ministries rooted in dispensationalism, see Craig A. Blaising and Darrell L. Bock, *Progressive Dispensationalism: An Up-to-Date Handbook of Contemporary Dispensational Thought* (Wheaton: Victor, 1993), 10–14.

59. See B. L. Shelley, "Parachurch Groups (Voluntary Societies)," in *Dictionary of Christianity in America*, ed. Daniel G. Reid, Robert D. Linder, Bruce L. Shelley, and Harry S. Stout (Downers Grove, IL: InterVarsity Press, 1990), 863–65.

60. Sometimes parachurch organizations function to unite the church, as members of a variety of denominations join together to achieve a common ministry goal.

61. See, for example, the defense of historic premillennialism in *A Case for Historic Premillennialism*, ed. Craig L. Blomberg and Sung Wook Chung (Grand Rapids: Baker, 2009).

62. For one attempt to address several areas of disagreement see Herbert W. Bateman IV, ed., *Three Central Issues in Contemporary Dispensationalism: A Comparison of Traditional and Progressive Views* (Grand Rapids: Kregel, 1999). In a concluding essay, "Dispensationalism Tomorrow," Bateman writes: "This tradition is not monolithic, as some have believed. . . . Dispensationalists are, however, agreed and like-minded in their stress on the uniqueness of the church and their confidence that a future exists for national Israel" (309).

63. This is not "replacement theology," the view that the church replaces Israel as the recipient divine blessing. Rather, it is the view that the old covenant was fulfilled in Christ and the new covenant is the means by which God blesses Israel and the church together in this dispensation.

64. My view is that the kingdom has always been, that from the creation of the world God mediated His rule over the world through humans. He has never stopped being the king and He has mediated His reign in a variety of increasingly better ways. In the incarnation, God Himself came to the earth. When He left, He sent the Spirit, which is better than when the King was present. One day He will return to the earth and reign for a thousand years. But that is not the end, for the millennium will be followed by an eternal reign over the earth on the earth by the eternal King.

65. For example, the doctrinal statement of Dallas Theological Seminary: "We believe that by the same Spirit all believers in this age are baptized into, and thus become, one body that is Christ's, whether Jews or Gentiles, and having become members one of another, are under solemn duty to keep the unity of the Spirit in the bond of peace, rising above all sectarian differences, and loving one another with a pure heart fervently." http://www.dts.edu/about/doctrinalstatement/.

66. Earlier dispensational views of two peoples and two destinies has largely disappeared from the tradition. On this development see Stanley D. Toussaint, "Israel and the Church of a Traditional Dispensationalist," in *Three Central Issues*, ed. Bateman IV, 228–30.

67. Ryrie, *Dispensationalism* (2007), 47. This language is unchanged from the 1965 edition.

68. Ibid. The language is unchanged from the 1965 edition, although Ryrie adds a qualification not found in the first edition: "To be sure, literal/historical/grammatical interpretation is not the sole possession or practice of dispensationalists, but the consistent use of it in all areas of biblical interpretation is."

69. Blaising and Bock, *Progressive Dispensationalism*, 77.

70. Ibid., 104–5.

71. Elliott E. Johnson, "A Traditional Dispensational Hermeneutic," in *Three Central Issues*, 65. Robert L. Thomas, "The Hermeneutics of Progressive Dispensationalism," in *Progressive Dispensationalism*, ed. Ron J. Bigalke, Jr. (Lanham, MD: University Press of America, 2005), 2, describes the hermeneutics of progressive dispensationalism as "a hermeneutical shift away from literal interpretation."

72. Blaising and Bock, *Progressive Dispensationalism*, 76.

73. Charles R. Swindoll, "Foreword," in *Three Central Issues*, 11.

2

Evangelicalism, Dispensationalism, and the Bible

D. JEFFREY BINGHAM

Something is tragically lost when the Bible is read merely as a set of ancient, distant documents, a relic from antiquity. The refusal of evangelicals, throughout their history, to principally conceive of Scripture in these terms is one of their most winsome qualities. They have always, to their credit, even during and after the age of criticism, revered the Bible as a contemporary agent. To them, it is the living word of God.

Some know the Bible only as individual verses, a chapter here and there, a story or psalm with which they identify deeply. Others have parsed it in Hebrew or Greek, performed word studies, and compared its contents to accounts from the Ancient Near East. Some have studied it in groups; others have meditated on it only in private. Some take notes when it's preached; others only sing its words in a refrain. Some have a perspective on its overall theme; others have a life verse.

All have sought life from its pages: redemption from guilt, truth rather than lie, wisdom over foolishness, comfort within death's terror, love in the face of hatred, joy under a cloud of sorrow, companionship after abandonment. At times, tears, laughter, sighs, confession, curses, and thanksgiving accompany evangelical readings of the Bible.

My interest here is to describe, in part, the ways in which everyday reading of the Bible takes place within evangelicalism and the factors that may influence those readings. I also will explore the relationship between evangelical biblicism and dispensationalism.

My claims are simple. Modern and contemporary evangelicals in their various approaches to the Scriptures, both in Britain and America, demonstrate a unique devotion to the Bible. This devotion is based largely on their view of the Bible: the Scriptures have (1) authority, (2) perspicuity, and (3) immediate relevance to one's relationship with God and the affairs of daily life. However, despite this common set of assumptions, there are divergences in actual interpretive practice.

For example, some evangelical approaches to the Bible, influenced by this threefold view and various cultural factors, disregard the notion of a unified biblical narrative in favor of more idiomatic, fragmentary readings. In contrast, other evangelicals, faithful to the same view and influenced by similar cultural forces, have emphasized the importance of a unified biblical theology for Bible reading. Dispensationalism is a biblical theology that in its various models offers accounts of the unified biblical narrative. As such, dispensationalism exemplifies the latter approach. Thus *dispensationalism represents, in its various forms, an essential facet of evangelicalism.*

BIBLICISM AND THE IDENTITY OF EVANGELICALISM

The Centrality of the Bible in Evangelicalism

Scholars readily acknowledge the centrality of the Bible within the spirituality, history, and culture of evangelicalism, beginning with Ryle's declaration in the nineteenth century that "Evangelical Religion [assigns] absolute supremacy to Holy Scripture as the only rule of faith and practice, the only test of truth, the only judge of controversy."[1] David Bebbington, speaking of the "four qualities" that have marked the "Evangelical religion," lists as the third, "*Biblicism*, a particular regard for the Bible."[2] Evangelical "devotion to the Bible," he goes on to say, resulted from the "belief that all spiritual truth is to be found in its pages."[3] Evangelicals throughout the generations agreed on the divine inspiration of the Bible, although the meaning of the doctrine was variously understood, and in Bebbington's view, led eventually to schism among evangelicals. Likewise, George Marsden writes that one "essential evangelical belief" is "the Reformation doctrine of the final authority of the Bible."[4] Alister McGrath describes the "six central beliefs" upon which evangelicalism is grounded and notes that each is "thoroughly rooted in Scripture," with the first belief being "the supreme authority of Scripture."[5] And within Timothy Larsen's five-point definition of evangelicalism we find that an evangelical is one "who has a preeminent place for the Bible in her or his Christian life as the divinely inspired, final authority in matters of faith and practice."[6]

Evangelicals display the preeminent position they give to the Bible in their theological method, their private daily devotional reading, their commitment to expositional preaching as the pinnacle of worship, their memorization of the Bible, the effort they have given to translating the Bible as a component of their ministry of evangelization, and group Bible studies.[7] Such high placement carries forth the Reformation principle of *sola Scriptura* and maintains, in contrast to the modern spirit, faith in Scripture's identity as the unique, reliable Word of God.[8]

Even those who take issue with evangelicalism's "biblicism" help to demonstrate the Bible's prominence within the tradition. Christian Smith argues that American evangelicalism's view of the Bible is "misguided and impossible," fails "to live up to its own claims," and "needs to be abandoned for a better approach to Christian truth and authority."[9] Introducing his thesis, he provides one analysis of evangelicalism's view of the Bible:

> I am suggesting, therefore, that biblicism of the kind I describe below represents the epistemological center of gravity of much of American evangelicalism (and conservative Protestantism more generally) and so warrants the kinds of questions raised in this book.
>
> By "biblicism" I mean a theory about the Bible that emphasizes together its exclusive authority, infallibility, perspicuity, self-sufficiency, internal consistency, self-evident meaning, and universal applicability.[10]

Those within the broader culture recognize evangelicalism's passionate allegiance to the Scriptures. In a recent *Newsweek* essay, Kurt Eichenwald criticized an alleged "biblical illiteracy" among American evangelicals.[11] Now, no doubt, biblical illiteracy, in some fashion, exists among America's evangelicals. The illiteracy that concerns Eichenwald, however, is one founded upon what he believes to be a naiveté regarding the sad, unreliable history of the origin, authorship, transmission, translation, interpretation, and use of the Bible's texts, its inner contradictions, as well as the crooked history of doctrinal and creedal formulation. Eichenwald's scholarship is shoddy, indiscriminate, prejudicial, and selective.[12]

Nevertheless, his article proves a point: American society, sometimes with disdain, notices evangelicals' allegiance to the Bible.

Evangelical Biblicism in Anthropological Perspective

Malley has studied the Bible within evangelicalism from an anthropological perspective.[13] His model begins with the observation that regardless of variance in how actual Bibles appear, American evangelicals share beliefs about the distinctiveness of the forms of "the Bible" along with beliefs about the distinctiveness of its message.[14] Furthermore, they ascribe authority to the Bible, both in principle and practice, and such attribution serves as a matter of evangelical self-identity. When they ascribe authority to the Bible in principle, they do so on the basis of the doctrine of biblical inspiration and they view this quality as one that makes them different from others, particularly within an environment that is characterized by religious pluralism.

When evangelicals attribute authority to the Bible, in practice they assume a relation of transitivity between text and ideas, Malley writes. That is, evangelicals regard their interpretations of biblical texts to be identical with a biblical text; semantic equivalence exists between what is written and what is read. This hermeneutical assumption undergirds their reading of the Bible.[15] The tradition presents the text as an object for hermeneutic activity, but the goal of that hermeneutic activity is not so much to establish the meaning of the text as to establish transitivity between the text and beliefs. The tradition emphasizes the fact of connection more than of particular connections. And thus a great deal of "what the Bible says" may be transmitted quite apart from actual exegesis.[16]

Evangelical interpretive practice, he notes, must navigate between two extremes: hermeneutic freedom and irrelevance.[17] At times, the freedom exercised in interpretation "mines the riches of individuals' hermeneutic imaginations." If there exists "too much hermeneutic freedom," "the tradition disintegrates" and it loses "its epistemological appeal." If the hermeneutic is too restrictive the Bible is reduced to an "irrelevant historical artifact." As merely an artifact, for the evangelical, it ceases to be the living word of God. The evangelical tradition requires, then, "both hermeneutic freedom and determinacy." While there may be rigorous exegetical standards within the training centers of evangelicalism, its seminaries and colleges, by and large, on a popular ecclesiological level, such standards are ignored. Malley understands this distinction as the practical response of the tradition to the two boundaries: "biblical relevance in the pews and hermeneutic determinacy in the classroom."

He believes his analysis offers a more precise notion of Scripture for this particular tradition than the more general one presented in the comparative study of Ninian Smart and Richard Hecht, which is loosely summarized by Miriam Levering.[18] From the Smart and Hecht study she lists six common parameters for a "category of 'sacred text.' "[19]

Malley's painstaking analysis of the authority of the Bible in principle and practice within evangelicalism is a helpful move forward. The particular cognitive factors he identifies as undergirding American evangelicalism's biblicism are helpful as well.[20] First, he sets forth the epistemological factor. Evangelicals believe the inspired Bible provides spiritual truth, thus satisfying the human need for a way of knowing. Second, biblicism meets the human compulsion for relevance. Through the various means of exposition, meditative reading, and its faith tradition focused on soteriology, the attributes of God, and morality, evangelicalism offers a structure that resonates with this drive. Third, evangelical biblicism allows for and promotes the construction of analogies between scriptural material and the life experience of the reader and thereby is in tune with our ability and need to match patterns. Dissimilarities in context and history are overlooked in preference for perceived similarity in faith, struggle, or triumph. Readers are permitted to discover their own connections of relevance and this also contributes a certain pleasing plasticity to the tradition. Finally, this biblicism agrees with our attraction to the story and meaning we find within a text, sometimes in substitution for the text. This returns to what he has termed the transitivity between text and belief, a relationship that informs the factor of the drive for relevance. This factor is worthy of deeper analysis.

THE RELEVANCE OF THE BIBLE IN EVANGELICALISM

The relevance of the Bible, its immediate relation to the matters at hand, is paramount in evangelicalism's biblicism. Stanley Grenz put it this way, "We believe that the scriptural texts are intended for living in the present."[21] Beyond higher critical issues and sometimes even beyond issues of how to address Scripture's truthfulness, "evangelical people seek in the Scriptures answers for daily living."[22] Performed in this manner, Bible reading is frequently joined with prayer into a daily devotional or "quiet time" during which the person speaks to God and God replies. But this kind of faith in the Bible's relevancy is not limited to how evangelicals read the Bible in their prayer closets. It is a belief that permeates how pastors exposit and how the audience listens to the Bible in communal services. For example, Tanya Luhrmann's study of evangelicals in Chicago points out that "the pastor's sermon teaches the congregation to use the Bible to relate to God, both as a God of power and as a best friend. Church is a class in which you learn how to hear what God has to say."[23]

Todd M. Brenneman more fully develops the third anthropological cognitive factor that is set forth by Brian Malley in *How the Bible Works: An Anthropological Study of Evangelical Biblicism*: the construction of analogies between scriptural material and the life experience of the reader. (Recall that Malley's first two factors are [1] epistemological and based on [2] the human need for relevance.) Brenneman's concern is the role of sentimentality within evangelicalism. Developing his thesis that popular evangelicalism is deeply emotional and nonintellectual, he speaks of evangelical readings that modernize the biblical narrative by "assimilating the reader and biblical character."[24] The narrative is understood in such a way that the reader shares the emotions and experience of the person within the text. The reader can have an "experience of the text that is therapeutic and emotional."[25] The reader's problems may differ in specifics from those of the biblical character, but the healing can be shared. "The trope of ordinariness," the democratic principle that the Bible's message is meant for everyone, not merely a certain group, is fundamental to this type of reading.[26]

As Luhrmann notes in relationship to the Jesus People of the 1960s, this perspective also involved a confidence that the Bible was a contemporary document written for the time of the reader.[27] Her study shows that this holds true for churches in the twenty-first century as well. She writes as embedded researcher:

> There is no sense that texts from the past hide from us behind authorial intentions we can no longer understand, or that they were written for a social and economic community we do not live in now. On Sunday mornings and in house group, we would read the most obscure and historical texts—Judges, for example—as if they were written for us, to help us understand how God wanted us to be with him.[28]

Such confidence among evangelicals is usually joined to the traditional Christian belief in the perspicuity of Scripture, a belief largely founded in the nineteenth century that continues to inform contemporary thought and practice. An anonymous author for *The Revival* reminds us that for some evangelicals, faith in the authority of the Bible is joined with faith in the perspicuous or self-interpreting nature of the text: "The truth that the Bible is self-interpreting is as precious and all-important as the corresponding truth that it is the inspired Word of God. The message from heaven would, indeed, be of no use to men if it required any interpreter besides itself."[29] In many contexts this concern with the text is highly emotional. Nevertheless, certainty about the Bible's clear and contemporary nature is at least partly rooted in the perceived trustworthiness of the scientific method and Protestant loyalty to Scottish common sense realism, touted as plain, popular, and actual, rather than theoretical and philosophical.[30] Here was planted the flag that "Nature and Scripture were equally perspicuous."[31] In the same way that the laws of nature were believed to be fixed, universal, and immutable, obvious biblical truths were not bound by time or culture.

Even though the secular basis for perspicuity might be philosophical and scientific, evangelical pneumatology with its quest for holiness through personal experience of the divine was able to apply the hermeneutic to matters of the heart: emotional comfort and morality.[32] In this vein, Yale President Timothy Dwight preached:

> The Scriptures themselves are . . . everywhere filled with instruction; but they are also filled everywhere with persuasion. Instead of being a cold compilation of philosophical dogmas, they are filled with real life, with facts, with persons, with forcible appeals to the imagination, and with powerful applications to the heart. With these the instruction is everywhere interwoven. By these it is continually embodied. In the Bible no affection of the human heart is unaddressed. Our hope and fear, our love and hatred, our sorrow and joy, our desire and aversion, nay, our taste for beauty, novelty, and sublimity, for moral glory and greatness, are all alternately and most forcibly applied to, in order that the whole man, as a being possessed of imagination and affections, as well as of understanding, may be alarmed, allured, and compelled, to return from sin, embrace holiness, and live for ever.[33]

The evangelical confidence in the Bible's clear, immediate, personal relevancy is perhaps nowhere more pronounced than in the practice of *Sortes biblicae*, the opening of the Bible at random in search of guidance.[34] Critics have pointed to its parallels with divination, its sentimentalism and departure from reason, as well as its disharmony with a true perspective of God and Bible study.[35] Nevertheless, it is still practiced today, with a history in early and medieval Christianity, and a revival within evangelicalism between 1730 and 1900. There are several reasons evangelicals employ the device of *Sortes biblicae*. They use it to discover answers to theological questions. They use it to find personal assurance that they are redeemed. Preachers practice it in order to receive direction as to which passages they should proclaim. Anxious, downhearted believers open the Bible to random passages out of need for encouragement from God's uplifting voice. Others embrace the practice in search of answers to specific questions, not necessarily theological in nature. Finally, it serves to provide guidance in the many personal choices life presents.[36]

The roots of *Sortes biblicae* are not unique to this practice, but seem to inform much of popular evangelicalism's relationship to the Bible.[37] Of course, the populism within the movement, its identity with the common people, fed the notion that anyone could hear from God in this fashion. Romanticism with its individualism, emotionalism, and sensitivity to the supernatural provided a bridge to the notion that God speaks immediately to a reader through a randomly discovered text. *Sola Scriptura*—consult only the Scriptures—also stands behind its popularity. In this approach, the all-encompassing authority and scope of the Bible reaches down to inform every aspect of a believer's life and choices.

Evangelicals embrace the Bible's relevance in a variety of ways, and different influences may account for their practices. Whatever other theological or cultural forces explain its popularity, one, it seems, stands paramount: The belief among the people that the Bible is not just any other book and therefore should not be read like one. Higher criticism opposed this pious belief, yet time and again in the face of modernity evangelicals returned to what some thought were naive practices of faith. John Nelson Darby wrote these representative words:

> I think that the mass of the poor have more reality of thought than reasoners, —see more justly the true character of things. Their occupation with labour gives this; they toil to exist. That is now God's ordinance. What they get outside this, must be real. Speculation has no place here. They may know nothing of a revelation, but if they have the thought that there is one, they want one that is a revelation from God—something He has told them, not an improved Shakespeare.[38]

EVANGELICALISM AND A UNIFIED BIBLICAL NARRATIVE

We have reviewed a variety of popular ways that evangelicals in different ages have lived out their devotion to the Bible. However, one aspect to this devotion, according to Collin Hansen, may be minimized: "Even weekly churchgoers who know the names and places [of the Bible] struggle to put it all together and understand the Bible as a single story of redemption."[39] In the twenty-first century the evangelical interest in the contemporary relevance of the Bible can lead to a piecemeal reading strategy that demotes the value of a unified narrative of the history of redemption and of a unified testimony to Christian doctrine. Some precedent can be found in the period that W. R. Ward has called "Early Evangelicalism" (1670–1789). In his treatment of Zinzendorf's tendency toward mysticism, Ward discusses the pietist's default to "the usual evangelical rant against 'system,' [which] assured that the dear God had planted no theoretical system in the Bible, and that to look for one was really rather provincial."[40] Ward's treatment of Zinzendorf is closely connected to his larger thesis that involves his "evangelical hexagon," a cluster of six themes that are helpful in describing the background and cohesive nature of evangelicalism.

Opposition to Connection and a Unifying Narrative (Metanarrative)

In departure from others, Ward does not list a theme that specifically includes evangelicalism's relationship to the Bible. Two of his themes, however, have important ramifications for evangelical perspectives on the Bible: Evangelicalism's "close association with mysticism" and its "anti-Aristotelianism and hostility to theological system."[41] Such hostility to systems would include even distaste for a synthesis of the Bible's message and of the Bible with other disciplines.[42]

Also involved in some evangelical opposition to synthesis, connection, and structure was the Arminian-Calvinist debate. According to Charles Simeon, "Calvinism is a system. God has not revealed his truth in a system; the Bible has no system as such. Lay aside system and fly to the Bible; receive its words with simple submission, and without an eye to any system. Be Bible Christians and not system Christians."[43] He then warned against forced linkage of passages and assuming contradictions between passages. Such opposition to systems, especially when joined to mysticism and the drive for relevance, would not only steer evangelicals away from theological systems and traditions, but would also leave them suspect of models offering narratives on the whole of the history of redemption. They were much more comfortable "flying to the Bible" without charts of the areas they were attempting to navigate. Their reading was frequently private and prayerful as they hunted for immediate relevance to their life circumstances.

Some versions of a theological system or metanarrative of the history of salvation seem to attract stronger responses than others. Beyond Simeon's reaction to Calvinism, William Miller would label New England Calvinism "a system of craft rather than the truth."[44] He put aside traditional sources and sought to understand the Bible for himself. Popular evangelical confidence in the contemporary nature of the Bible may mean that a dispensational account will find less and less adherents. In the mainstream, it is known for its delineation of distinctive characteristics and features among history's dispensations or ages, one or more of which are in the past. Given such a reputation, its popularity with those who want to minimize or dismiss historical distance may very well shrink.[45]

The Role of Democratic Cultural Values and Individualism

From the beginning of the nineteenth century in America, it has been difficult to separate this practice from the close connection between democratic cultural values, individualism, and popular approaches to Bible reading. Americans have sewn together the fabrics of the common person and common sense while they rent themselves apart from interpretive authorities, arrangements, and systems.[46] Pluralism has made its own contribution to the weakening of evangelical faithfulness to confessions.[47] One can hear the result in the evangelical slogan, "no creed but the Bible," and can witness it in the popularity of individual Bible study done in isolation from gifted teachers, tradition, and a holistic perspective on the Bible's message. Such isolation frequently leads to conclusions that are solipsistic and not textually grounded.[48]

This approach to the Bible permeated American life. Even President Grover Cleveland, an old-fashioned Presbyterian disinterested in higher criticism, was heard frequently to say, "The Bible is good enough for me, just the old book under which I was brought up. I do not want notes or criticisms, or explanations about authorship or origins, or even cross-references. I do not need, or understand them, and they confuse me."[49]

Influence of the Novel

An unexpected force also influenced the mid-nineteenth-century departure from confidence in a biblical theology or system that unified the diverse components of the Bible: the growth of Christian literary fiction, in particular, the novel. The impact is still felt. Although evangelicals would formally confess Scripture's unity, the expansion of the novel's popularity challenged the traditional hermeneutic predisposed to a unified message.[50] Knight and Mason would call the novel "a textual form marked by interpretive indeterminacy."[51] Interpretive indeterminacy was, in some manner, in keeping with the evangelical desire to find personal relevance in the text and to be free from ecclesiological dogma. Now, however, a contemporary, popular cultural form added fuel to the fire. It threatened the formal "Evangelical reliance on the alleged univocality, transparency, and simplicity of the Gospel message."[52]

The Influence of Sentimentality and Historical Criticism

The tendency to move away from systems, doctrines, and unified narratives can also be understood from another perspective. Again, Brenneman analyzes it as a function of sentimentality. "When explored through a sentimental worldview," he writes, "the doctrinal is diluted in favor of the experiential and emotional."[53] With this orientation a reader's interest is not in a metanarrative, a system, a doctrine, or necessarily in what is reasonable. "Instead someone reads the Bible, as Warren says, to 'become best friends with God.' "[54]

In *The Eclipse of Biblical Narrative,* Hans W. Frei gave the classic account of the decline of biblical metanarratives in the eighteenth and nineteenth centuries. He argued that the pre-critical view of biblical narratives as testimonies to real events and truths together formed a "single storied or historical sequence," "one cumulative story," "one narrative," "a common narrative," "a single history."[55] Then modernity, through historical criticism, introduced increasing distance between narrative and reality. Neither historical-critical reconstruction of events nor the biblical theology movement was able to reclaim the ancient high ground of the unity between reality and narrative.[56] Postmodernity, according to Jean-François

Lyotard, was the final move: "Simplifying to the extreme, I define postmodern as incredulity toward metanarratives."[57]

In a volume entitled, *The Futures of Evangelicalism*, Graeme Goldsworthy contributes the essay, "Evangelicalism and Biblical Theology." In it he offers testimony to the benefit that a unified narrative of the history of redemption can bring to popular evangelical reading of the Bible.

> My own experience of thirty years of teaching biblical theology in theological colleges and in local church ministry has convinced me of a couple of things. First, that there is a great need when teaching the Bible to help people see something of the one grand plan of God's revelation. Second, that ordinary Christians of all ages become more enthusiastic for study of the Bible once they begin to glimpse its overall unity and coherence.[58]

A Return to a Panoramic View of the Bible's Message

Goldsworthy's experience resonates with a method of biblical interpretation popular with evangelical scholars early in the twentieth century. Higher criticism had reduced the Bible to its parts. A multidimensional evangelical response included a popular emphasis on biblical unity.[59] "The synthetic study of the Bible," as James M. Gray called it, studied the whole Bible, whole books, and related them to each other.[60] He sought to put the parts together rather than to separate them. Weary of the fragmentary method that focused on individual verses disconnected from the whole, he proposed that study begin with the big picture. "Give people to see for themselves what the Bible is in the large, and then they will have a desire to see it in detail. Put a telescope in their hands first, and a microscope afterwards."[61] Gray advocated reading each book of the Bible in sequence. One should read each book through at one sitting, repeatedly, independently, and prayerfully.

Although Gray advocated a method that included reading the Bible independently, he did not mean complete independence from study aids or from a biblical theology that provided structure and coherence. His reasons for an independent first reading are largely to train the reader as a thinker and teacher who has struggled with the challenges of interpretation. But, even though the student should temporarily set tools aside, Gray had in mind a particular overarching biblical theology that provided an account of the way the parts related to the whole. His panorama was dispensationalism:

> Get the whole Bible in your mind first in one grand broad view, see it in its dispensational relations, and then you can study it by chapters, or by topics or in any other way to your heart's content, and with increasing profit to yourself and others. Begin any other way, and you will live and die wishing you had begun the right way.[62]

In his *Synthetic Bible Studies*, Gray writes that the "dispensational teaching of the Bible" is the plan of the Bible that he was trying to "emphasize somewhat."[63] But even this plan needed to be applied to the Bible only with the aid of the Holy Spirit.

In some quarters of evangelicalism, then, reaction against systems led back to panoramic views of the biblical message. Many proponents of this approach believed these panoramic views, however, were to be built from the bottom up, by following the biblical facts and evidence wherever they led, not by faithfulness to a set of preconceived, philosophical assumptions. Basically, these evangelicals replaced "Aristotelian" structures with Baconianism, substituting one philosophy for another.[64] But Francis Bacon's outlook was perceived as objective, rational, inductive, based on common sense, and therefore as a tradition-free, certain path to truth. According to Lamar, "Bacon destroyed the influence of dogmatism in scientific research."[65] What Bacon had worked out for the physical sciences, evangelicals applied to the Bible. Whether in science or biblical studies, one simply gathered and classified the facts with confidence.

With the inductive method of Bible study, J. S. Lamar and others sought to remove the same types of idols, prejudices, and theories from Bible reading. "The Scriptures," wrote Lamar, "admit of being studied and expounded upon the principles of the inductive method; and that, when thus interpreted, they speak to us in a voice as certain and unmistakable as the language of nature heard in the experiments and observations of science."[66] A. T. Pierson put it like this: "One likes a *Biblical* theology . . . framed on the Baconian system, first gathering the teachings of the Word of God, and then seeking to induce some general law under which those facts can be classified and arranged."[67]

Explicit in Pierson's words is a self-conscious debt to Baconianism and its emphasis on arranging and classifying biblical facts. He has no matching consciousness of Baconianism's own assumptions, prejudices, and dogmas.[68] Evangelicalism's use of Bacon demonstrates the tradition's link to modern culture. Significantly, its ability to move from fragmentation to a biblical plan of the ages that was not perceived to be dogmatic was the result of their philosophical context, a context for which, in other dimensions, they had much disdain. Nevertheless, we must not miss three key points: (1) driven by a search for relevance in the text and other cultural influences, some evangelicals tended toward a fragmentary approach to the Bible, (2) influenced by their faith in the text's relevance and other cultural factors, other evangelicals, even within modernity, returned to the ancient view of a united biblical narrative, and (3) even though evangelicals continued to be influenced by their surroundings in a variety of ways in their different hermeneutical approaches, the Bible was the authoritative and perspicuous object of their attention.

DISPENSATIONALISM AND THE BIBLE

As Lori Anne Ferrell points out, the paradox created by Protestantism is that while there is increased "textual availability" there is also "textual inaccessibility."[69] "The Bible is hard," she writes, and modernity introduced in a new way "biblical *unknowing*" through increased availability.[70] In a fever to gain access to God's Word some evangelicals abandon guidance and wander into the wilderness of fragmentary, solipsistic, wilding, imaginative, and unorthodox readings. Dispensationalism, in its various models, with all its other features and interests, is an evangelical biblical theology that affirms the Bible's relevance and offers Bible readers unified accounts of the history of redemption for the purpose of providing guided access to the available text.

Darby and the Twin Emphases

We can see these twin emphases, relevance and unified biblical narrative, as early as John Nelson Darby. Responding to Benjamin W. Newton's commentary on Revelation, Darby argued that Newton lacked a perception of the whole plan of God manifested in the Bible.[71] He is frustrated with works, like Moses Stuart's study of the Old Testament canon, that focus, in his mind, on "present personal edification," but do not treat the Bible holistically.[72] Understanding the relevance of the Bible is linked to understanding its dispensational history: "No man can get fully the real evidence for the Bible, unless he views it as a whole given of God. That is its value; and if God gives me His whole view of man from the creation to the eternal state—is that not instructive, the most instructive possible of all knowledge?"[73]

In the conclusion to a collection of articles written by Darby and William Kelly, F. G. Patterson summarizes the connection between relevance and biblical holism, that is, the relationship between the godly Christian life and a dispensational understanding.

> The soul that has been established in dispensational truth, and that has ascertained the ways of God during the various dispensations (and even when the testimony entrusted to men in each dispensation has been corrupted and destroyed), learns how to respond to God's *way;* how to walk before Him in accordance with His mind and will; even when the dispensation has fallen into ruins. Surely one judges that the path marked out in one dispensation, would be unsuited for another; and judges, too, with spiritual discernment, that a path right in the *beginning* of a dispensation, necessarily changes its character when the dispensation has fallen into ruins through the unfaithfulness of those to whom the testimony is entrusted; yet all the while recognizing that divine principles *never* have changed, even while the vessel proved that it could not hold the treasure committed to it.[74]

For Darby, God's displays of His glory and power may differ from dispensation to dispensation, so the believer's affections, life, and responsibilities may differ as well. These differences are pivotal to how the text is applied by a reader.[75] This, of course, extends to principles of Christian ministry. They, too, are consequences of the nature of the present dispensation.[76]

Scofield, Chafer, Walvoord, and Ryrie

With appeal to Augustine's words, "Distinguish the ages and the Scriptures will harmonize," C. I. Scofield contended that his account of the dispensations and covenants maintained orthodox commitment to the harmonious unity of the Bible and provided a schematic for Bible reading that could be used by all.[77] Like those before him, a proper understanding of the ages would help the reader grasp relevant "ethical truth."[78] The orientation of all his editing labor was to help readers study the Bible by locating the books historically, placing them within the Bible's holistic narrative, and providing interpretive notes.[79] In the mind of Scofield, the main cause of any believer's failure to understand the Bible is "the fact that no particular portion of Scripture is to be intelligently comprehended apart from some conception of its place in the whole."[80]

The linkage between understanding the Bible, comprehending its dispensational structure, and accurate application of its teaching to daily life became a standard feature of the tradition. It modeled the evangelical concern for the Bible's relevance. Its texts were not old and cold; they were fresh and alive, but one needed to appreciate how to live in light of them. Irenaeus in the second century and Augustine in the fifth needed to point out Scripture's harmony by rightly accounting for differences within its contents in order to maintain the church's and its members' purity. In the same way, dispensationalists have taken that responsibility in more recent times. Lewis Sperry Chafer and John F. Walvoord are quite explicit. First, they generally state the importance of dispensationalism for biblical interpretation.

> In the study of Scripture, it is important to understand that scriptural revelation falls into well-defined periods. These are clearly separated, and the recognition of these divisions and their divine purposes constitute one of the important factors in true interpretation of the Scriptures. These divisions are termed "dispensations," and in successive periods of time different dispensations may be observed.[81]

Next, these words are soon followed by a comment regarding the importance of dispensationalism for application of the Bible to everyday life.

> Since the child of God depends wholly on the instructions contained in the Bible for his direction in daily life, and since the principles obtaining in the various dispensations are so diverse and even at times contradictory, it is important that he recognize those portions of the Scriptures which directly apply to him if he is to realize the will of God and the glory of God.[82]

Charles Ryrie affirms the same connection. Noting that all interpreters recognize some distinctions in the unfolding of redemption, he underscores that such distinctions are basic to correct interpretation of the Bible. For him, of course, dispensationalism offers the right perspective on these distinctions. As he provides warrant for this hermeneutical principle, he turns to issues of Christian practice. Distinctions or dispensations are basic to the Christian relation to animal sacrifices and to worship on the Lord's Day.[83]

Despite the expressed importance of the dispensations and a view of the whole for a correct reading of Scriptures, dispensationalists were still hesitant to see themselves as acting in faithfulness to a hermeneutical assumption or system. Although Darby, for instance, frequently pointed out Newton's loyalty to a "system," he preferred not to label his own hermeneutical disposition as one.[84] "System" for him was frequently conceived as an evil framework of worldliness.[85]

Ryrie, too, preferred to emphasize that his distinction between Israel and the church arose from a literal hermeneutic. It was the result of inductive Bible study, "not a scheme superimposed upon the Bible" or the consequence of preconceived notions.[86]

Dispensationalism and the Relevance of the Bible

The growing popularity of premillennialism and prophecy with dispensationalism had a connection to the common person's drive for relevance as well.[87] Various historical contexts of angst—local and global, nineteenth, twentieth, and twenty-first century—brought forth several attempts to correlate biblical prophecies with current events. As prophecies were linked to specific current events throughout the years, many evangelicals of all classes became more interested in signs of the end times and developed a keen sense of eschatological expectation. In addition to providing a context for understanding and enduring their own tumultuous times in history, these readings motivated moral reform and evangelism.[88] Whether William E. Blackstone's *Jesus Is Coming* (1878), Hal Lindsey's *The Late Great Planet Earth* (1970), or Charles H. Dyer's *The Rise of Babylon* (2003), dispensationalists attempted to demonstrate the Bible's relevance to current issues in light of unified biblical narrative. Over the years, also, dispensationalism developed and the tradition became more and more self-conscious of its own relation to culture and change.[89]

But the association among a dispensational framework, an accurate understanding of the Bible, and the relevance of the Bible for Christian life remained a basic principle for the tradition. The language and commitments in 1993 were very similar to those that had come before. For Blaising, comprehending the dispensations in relation to the biblical covenants "is crucial to understanding the history and theology of the Bible. Understanding the Bible dispensationally is especially important for understanding God's relationship with human beings today. It helps us focus on those distinctive relationships He institutes today and the explicit responsibilities He gives us."[90]

Blaising's comments on particular responsibilities include reflections on social and political righteousness, multiculturalism, an appeal to avoid speculation, sensationalism, and intimations of prophetic authority in treatment of prophecy and current events—and a reminder of the yet future consummation of promises to Israel, and a Chalcedonian, dispensational, and Christological doxology.[91]

CONCLUSION

Devotion to the Bible is a hallmark of evangelicalism. It is a book of profound relevance for evangelical readers. However, there is a tendency for these readers to see the Bible as a pastiche of divinely inspired, but disconnected, stories and principles. Readers, it seems, in the name of relevancy can sometimes dismember the object of their devotion.

James Kugel explains that one of the four assumptions of ancient interpreters was that the Bible was "relevant," it "was a book of lessons directed to readers in their own day."[92] He goes on to explain that as modern interpreters began to put forward new assumptions, the ancient ones were denied. Within modernity, the eternal validity of the text, on the basis of its restrictive, historical settings, was denied.[93] It applied only to some people within the contexts of its original composition. This taxonomy allows for little nuance, but it does help illumine a crucial aspect of dispensationalism.

Between the extremes of the ancient and modern assumptions, as set forth by Kugel, dispensationalism provides a helpful *via media.* It epitomizes throughout its history and forms a devotion to the Bible's relevance for persons of all eras. Yet it accounts for the unity of the history of revelation and redemption, with attention to elements of diversity and historical circumstance. In this way it helps to carry the Christian from textual availability to prudent textual accessibility. Dispensationalism has always had a commitment to the edification of all Bible hearers and readers through explication of the Bible's relevance, meaning, and application in light of its unity and historical, dispensational, economical differences. Dispensationalism is a thoroughly evangelical way of reading the Bible that maintains its ageless relevance, its elements of dissimilarity, and its unity as a connected account. This makes the tradition worthy of continued reflection.

NOTES

1. J. C. Ryle, "Evangelical Religion," in *Knots Untied, Being Plain Statements on Disputed Points in Religion From the Standpoint of an Evangelical Churchman*, rev. ed. (London: National Protestant Church Union and Charles Murray, 1898), 4.
2. David Bebbington, *Evangelicalism in Modern Britain: A History from the 1730s to the 1980s* (London/New York: Routledge, 1989), 2, 12–13.
3. Ibid., 12.

4. Ibid., 13–14; and George Marsden, *Understanding Fundamentalism and Evangelicalism* (Grand Rapids: Eerdmans, 1991), 4.
5. Alister McGrath, *Evangelicalism and the Future of Christianity* (Downers Grove, IL: InterVarsity, 1995), 59–64.
6. “Defining and Locating Evangelicalism,” in *The Cambridge Companion to Evangelical Theology*, ed. Timothy Larsen and Daniel J. Treier (Cambridge: Cambridge University, 2007), 1.
7. Larsen, “Defining and Locating Evangelicalism,” 7–8. For a study of evangelical group Bible study see James S. Bielo, *Words Upon the Word: An Ethnography of Evangelical Group Bible Study* (New York/London: New York University, 2009).
8. Ibid., 8.
9. Christian Smith, *The Bible Made Impossible: Why Biblicism Is Not a Truly Evangelical Reading of Scripture* (Grand Rapids: Brazos, 2012), ix, 3.
10. Ibid., viii.
11. Kurt Eichenwald, “The Bible: So Misunderstood It's a Sin,” *Newsweek*, 23 December 2014, http://www.newsweek.com/2015/01/02/thats-not-what-bible-says-294018.html.
12. E.g., Michael Brown's “A Response to *Newsweek* on the Bible,” *Newsweek*, 15 January 2015. There have been several responses to the article on evangelical websites.
13. Brian Malley, *How the Bible Works: An Anthropological Study of Evangelical Biblicism* (Walnut Creek, CA: Altamira, 2004).
14. Ibid., 71.
15. Ibid., 83–84.
16. Ibid., 87.
17. Ibid., 123, 146.
18. Ibid., 12–13; *Sacred Texts of the World: a Universal Anthology*, ed. Ninian Smart and Richard Hecht (New York: Crossroad, 1982), xiv–xvi.
19. Miriam Levering, “Rethinking Scripture,” in *Rethinking Scripture: Essays from a Comparative Perspective*, ed. M. Levering (Albany: State University of New York, 1989), 8–9. The first two parameters Levering summarizes for a “category of sacred text” are (1) There are often beliefs that the text is of divine origin, or the product of special insight and (2) Whatever their origin, they are regarded and treated as sacred, that is, powerful and inviolable, to be treated with respect.
20. Malley, *How the Bible Works*, 152–55.
21. Stanley Grenz, *Revisioning Evangelical Theology* (Downers Grove, IL: InterVarsity, 1993), 31.
22. Ibid., 32.
23. T. Luhrmann, *When God Talks Back: Understanding the American Evangelical Relationship with God* (New York: Knopf, 2012), 6.
24. Todd M. Brenneman, *Homespun Gospel: The Triumph of Sentimentality in Contemporary American Evangelicalism* (Oxford: Oxford University, 2013), 44.
25. Ibid., 44.
26. Ibid., 45.
27. Luhrmann, *When God Talks Back*, 23.
28. Ibid., 12.
29. “Unity of Creed: The Union of the Christian Church,” *The Revival: An Advocate of Evangelical Truth* 15 (1866): 71–73.
30. Cf. Andrew R. Holmes, “The Common Sense Bible: Irish Presbyterians, Samuel Davidson, and Biblical Criticism, *c.* 1800–65,” in *Dissent and the Bible in Britain,* c. *1650-1950*, ed. Scott Mandelbrote and

Michael Ledger-Lomas (Oxford: Oxford University, 2013), 176–204.

31. George M. Marsden, "Everyone One's Own Interpreter? The Bible Science and Authority in Mid-Nineteenth-Century America," in *The Bible in America*, ed. Nathan O. Hatch and Mark Noll (New York/Oxford: Oxford University, 1982), 80.
32. See Marsden, "Everyone One's Own Interpreter?," 84–85.
33. "Sermon 136," in Timothy Dwight, *Theology Explained and Defended in A Series of Sermons*, 5 vols. (London: J. Haddon, 1824), 4: 492.
34. For the description that follows, see Laura Bartlett, "Consulting the Oracle: *Sortes Biblicae* in Evangelicalism to 1900," *Scottish Bulletin of Evangelical Theology* 29 (2011): 205–18. I am grateful to Tim Larsen for this reference.
35. Bartlett, "Consulting the Oracle," 216–18.
36. Ibid., 207–11.
37. Ibid., 215–16.
38. John Nelson Darby, *Dialogues on the Essays and Reviews by One Who Values Christianity for Its Own Sake, and Believes in It as a Revelation from God*, 2nd rev. ed. (London: W. H. Broom, 1863), 5–6. Cf. *Dissent and the Bible in Britain*, Mandelbrote and Ledger-Lomas, 29. Their comment as they conclude this introductory essay is important: "Where can the biblical culture and learning of British Dissenters be found today? One answer is within the conservative evangelicalism of the modern United States" (35).
39. Collin Hansen, "Why Johnny Can't Read the Bible," *Christianity Today*, May 2010, 38. In the same article Timothy George, the founding dean of Beeson Divinity School, notes how the school is taking steps to ensure that "students don't just have a superficial knowledge of Scripture but can explain the Bible as a connected story."
40. W. R. Ward, *Early Evangelicalism: A Global Intellectual History, 1670–1789* (Cambridge: Cambridge University, 2006), 111.
41. Ibid., 4.
42. Ibid., 156.
43. Charles Simeon, "Notes on Calvinism and Arminianism," in *The Evangelical and Oxford Movements*, ed. Elisabeth Jay (Cambridge: Cambridge University, 1983), 22; cf. Ward, *Early Evangelicalism*, 188.
44. Quoted in Joshua V. Himes, *A View of the Prophecies and Prophetic Oracles* (Boston: Moses A. Dow, 1841), 9, 11; cf. Nathan O. Hatch, "*Sola Scriptura* and *Novus Ordo Seclorum*," in *The Bible in America*, ed. Nathan O. Hatch and Mark Noll (New York/Oxford: Oxford University, 1982), 75.
45. Luhrmann, *When God Talks Back*, 23.
46. Nathan O. Hatch, "*Sola Scriptura* and *Novus Ordo Seclorum*," in *The Bible in America*, 74.
47. Cf. Richard Lints, *The Fabric of Theology: A Prolegomenon to Evangelical Theology* (Grand Rapids: Eerdmans, 1993), 91–92.
48. One YMCA handbook on Bible study encouraged private over communal study: "Magnify private, daily devotional Bible study. . . . The more secret Bible study there is by the members of the class with reference to their own inner lives, the more interest, freshness, zest, and life will there be." John R. Mott, *The Bible Study Department of the Student Young Men's Christian Association* (New York: The International Committee of Young Men's Christian Associations, 1899), 32.
49. George F. Parker, *Recollections of Grover Cleveland* (New York: The Century Co., 1909), 382.
50. Mark Knight and Emma Mason, *Nineteenth-Century Religion and Literature* (Oxford: Oxford University, 2006), 132–35.
51. Ibid., 134.
52. Ibid., 135.
53. Brenneman, *Homespun Gospel*, 73.

54. Rick Warren, *The Purpose-Driven Life* (Grand Rapids: Zondervan, 2002), 87.
55. Hans W. Frei, *The Eclipse of Biblical Narrative: A Study in Eighteenth and Nineteenth Century Hermeneutics* (New Haven, CT: Yale University, 1974), 1–2.
56. Ibid., 4–8.
57. Jean-François Lyotard, *The Postmodern Condition: A Report on Knowledge*, trans. Geoff Bennington and Brian Massumi (Minneapolis: University of Minnesota, 1984), 24.
58. Graeme Goldsworthy, "Evangelicalism and Biblical Theology," *The Futures of Evangelicalism*, ed. Andrew West, Craig Bartholomew, and Robin Parry (Grand Rapids: Kregel, 2004), 125.
59. See Timothy P. Weber, "The Two-Edged Sword: The Fundamentalist Use of the Bible," in *The Bible in America*, 112-13.
60. James M. Gray, *How to Master the English Bible* (Chicago: Winona, 1904), 34.
61. Ibid., 36.
62. James M. Gray, *Bible Problems Explained* (Chicago: Moody, 1913), 18–19. See his comments on the benefit to understanding the features of different dispensations (49, 60, 69, 80, 82).
63. James M. Gray, *Synthetic Bible Studies*, rev. ed. (New York: Fleming H. Revell, 1923), 288.
64. See on Baconianism and the Bible: Theodore Dwight Bozeman, *Protestants in an Age of Science: The Baconian Ideal and Antebellum American Religious Thought* (Chapel Hill: The University of North Carolina, 1977), 132–59; Marsden, "Everyone One's Own Interpreter?," 81–84.
65. J. S. Lamar, *The Organon Of Scripture or The Inductive Method Of Biblical Interpretation* (Philadelphia: J. B. Lippincott & Co., 1860), 159. For Bacon in Lamar's thinking see pp. 174–211.
66. Ibid., 176.
67. Arthur T. Pierson, *The Coming of the Lord* (New York/Chicago: Fleming H. Revell, 1896), 7; cf. Matthew Avery Sutton, *American Apocalypse: A History of Modern Evangelicalism* (Cambridge, MA: Harvard University, 2014), 15–16.
68. Bozeman presents the following summary: "These, then, are the principal elements of 'Baconianism' as elaborated by the Scottish School: 1. A spirited enthusiasm for natural science. 2. A scrupulous empiricism, grounded upon the confident 'trust in the senses' and in the reality of the outer world supplied by the Realist doctrine of 'judgment.' 3. A sharp accent upon the limits of scientific method and knowledge, directed to the inductive control of generalizations by continuous reference to 'facts.' Abstract concepts not immediately forged from observed data have no place in scientific explanation. 4. A celebratory focus upon 'Lord Bacon' as the progenitor of inductive science; a flat identification of Newtonian methods with Bacon's 'induction' "(*Protestants in an Age of Science*, 21).
69. Lori Anne Ferrell, *The Bible and the People* (New Haven/London: Yale University, 2008), 156.
70. Ibid., 127–28.
71. John Nelson Darby, *Thoughts on the Apocalypse*, 2nd. rev. ed. (London: Houlston and Sons, 1853); J. N. Darby, *The Irrationalism of Infidelity, Being a Reply to "Phases of Faith"* [by Francis W. Newman] (London: Groombridge and Sons, 1853), 229. Repeatedly, Darby points out what he thinks are failures of Newton to think rightly about the different dispensations and provides his own thoughts (J. N. Darby, *An Examination of the Statements Made in the "Thoughts on the Apocalypse" by B. W. Newton and an Enquiry How Far They Accord with Scripture* [London/Plymouth: J. B. Rowe, 1848], 6–31, 78–96, 131–46, 170–88, 239–59).
72. Moses Stuart, *Critical History and Defence of the Old Testament Canon* (New York: Mark H. Newman, 1845); Darby, *The Irrationalism of Infidelity*, 229, n. *.
73. Darby, *The Irrationalism of Infidelity*, 229, n. *.
74. "Conclusion," *The Bible Treasury* 5 (1864–65): 157–58.
75. Darby, *An Examination of the Statements Made in the "Thoughts on the Apocalypse,"* 32.
76. J. N. Darby, *On Ministry: Its Nature, Source, Power, and Responsibility* (London: D. Walther, 1844), 3.

77. *Sermon* 32.10 (Ben. 82.7); PL 38.511: *Distribute tempora, et concordat Scriptum. Scofield Reference Bible*, ed. C. I. Scofield (New York/Oxford: Oxford University, 1909), iii. Cf. "The Scofield Reference Bible, compiled by Cyrus Ingerson Scofield, provided a dispensational template through which evangelicals read the Scriptures" (Randall Balmer, *Blessed Assurance: A History of Evangelicalism in America* [Boston: Beacon, 1999], 52).

78. *Scofield Reference Bible*, iii.

79. Cf. R. Todd Mangum and Mark S. Sweetnam, *The Scofield Bible: Its History and Impact on the Evangelical Church* (Colorado Springs: Paternoster, 2009), 93–134.

80. *The Scofield Reference Bible*, v.

81. Lewis Sperry Chafer and John F. Walvoord, *Major Bible Themes: 52 Vital Doctrines of the Scriptures Simplified and Explained*, rev. ed. (Grand Rapids: Zondervan, 1974), 126.

82. Ibid., 127.

83. Ryrie, *Dispensationalism*, rev. ed., 16–17. Ryrie cites L. S. Chafer, *Dispensationalism* (Dallas: Dallas Seminary Press, 1936), 9.

84. E.g., Darby, *An Examination of the Statements Made in the "Thoughts on the Apocalypse,"* 1, 17, 19, 25, 29, 44-45, 59, 67, 86, 96, 114, 138.

85. E.g., Darby, *An Examination of the Statements Made in the "Thoughts on the Apocalypse,"* 286–89.

86. Ryrie, *Dispensationalism*, 85.

87. Cf. Sutton, *American Apocalypse*, 8–15.

88. Note the testimony of George E. Ladd concerning these authors: "It is doubtful if there has been any other circle of men who have done more by their influence in preaching, teaching and writing to promote a love for Bible study, a hunger for the deeper Christian life, a passion for evangelism and zeal for missions in the history of American Christianity"; in *Crucial Questions About the Kingdom of God* (Grand Rapids: Eerdmans, 1952), 49.

89. Craig A. Blaising, "Developing Dispensationalism: Part 1: Doctrinal Development in Orthodoxy," *Bibliotheca Sacra* 145 (1988): 133–40; "Developing Dispensationalism: Part 2: Development of Dispensationalism by Contemporary Dispensationalists," *Bibliotheca Sacra* 145 (1988): 254–80; Craig A. Blaising, "History," in Craig A. Blaising and Darrell L. Bock, *Progressive Dispensationalism* (Grand Rapids: Baker, 1993), 9–56.

90. Craig A. Blaising, "Exposition," in *Progressive Dispensationalism*, 127. Blaising concludes: "In other words, interpreting the Bible dispensationally focuses especially on this dispensation, clarifying what the church is and what are the principles of Christian living and the nature of Christian responsibility."

91. Craig A. Blaising, "Theology and Ministry," in *Progressive Dispensationalism*, 284–300. The final section reveals Blaising's expertise in both patristic and biblical Christology.

92. James L. Kugel, *How to Read the Bible* (New York: The Free Press, 2007), 15, 21.

93. Ibid., 32.

3

The History of Dispensationalism in Seven Eras

MICHAEL J. SVIGEL

Like Bob Dylan's iconic, often repeated "Blowin' in the Wind," numerous disparate renditions of the history of dispensationalism have been performed throughout its relatively brief history. Some have attempted to emphasize dispensationalism's allegedly radical departure from other doctrinal patterns.[1] Others tell a story of dispensationalism's gradual positive development as legitimate growth in doctrinal understanding from its original simple explication.[2] Others have shown a gradual "maturing" of dispensationalism from its controversial birth through an awkward adolescence and into a more respectable adulthood.[3]

Still others suggest a tale of an eventual distortion and even apostasy away from its original doctrinal simplicity and purity.[4] Some have attempted to demonstrate dispensationalism's lack of historical precedence in some of its more unique doctrines or its lack of precedence as a definable system.[5] Others have attempted to defend its rightful place within the diversity of conservative Protestantism, often drawing attention to some elements of historical continuity with orthodox teachers of the past,[6] or appealing to a theory of doctrinal development that legitimizes newly discovered dispensational perspectives.[7]

But to chase down the origins and history of dispensationalism, one must first be able to identify what it is one is chasing. This leads to the question, "What is dispensationalism?" The answer to this is, in many people's minds, blowing in the wind. Part of the problem is that dispensationalism is not a "doctrine."[8] It has quite frequently been referred to as a "system,"[9] though much of what is unique about dispensationalism does not affect most areas of systematic theology.[10] Dispensationalism is not a denomination but an interdenominational movement, its proponents hailing from a host of both denominational and independent churches.

How should we then define dispensationalism for the purpose of discussing its origins and trajectories? Taking into account its entire past and considering its current manifold expressions, dispensationalism can at least be regarded as a *stable pattern of distinct biblical interpretations and doctrines.*[11] It is, therefore, best referred to as a "tradition" that both transcends and inhabits various Protestant evangelical denominations and confessions.[12]

SEVEN ERAS IN THE HISTORY OF DISPENSATIONALISM

In the interest of an orderly chronological survey of dispensationalism, I present the following narrative of the history of dispensationalism in seven successive "eras": (1) innocent beginnings; (2) conscious self-identity; (3) governing principals; (4) promising propagation; (5) legalizing precepts; (6) gracious considerations; and (7) new millennial anticipations.[13]

1. Innocent Beginnings (1800–1845)

Dispensationalism developed innocently enough, growing steadily from a fertile ground of eschatological exploration, innovation, and rediscovery that had been under way for several centuries since the Reformation. It reached a fever pitch in the nineteenth century. During this time there appeared the conceptual antecedents of the pattern of doctrines and interpretations that would become dispensationalism in the nineteenth century.

From Barrington and Watts to Chandler

In 1725, John Shute Barrington, in the preface to his two-volume *Miscellanea Sacra,* noted:

> I could wish with all my heart, that some able pen would state the several periods previous to that of Jesus. . . . I am satisfied the true way to get a thorough understanding of the scriptures would be, to make one's self master of each of these periods, as they are described and distinguished in the Bible, and as they stand in order of time; the former of these preparing always for the latter, and the latter still referring to the former; so that we must critically understand each of these, before we can have the whole compass of that knowledge, and the proof of the truth of it, which the Bible is designed to give us.[14]

A few years later Barrington fulfilled this desire himself in a treatise in which he defined "dispensations" as "the various Methods, in which God has extraordinarily discovered himself to Mankind" and "those Methods, by which he has conveyed [further] Knowledge to them, than they could arrive at by the bare Use of the natural Powers he has given them."[15] Though not the kind of definition that would tend to dominate nineteenth- and twentieth-century dispensational writers, Barrington's writing serves as an example of a variation on a common eighteenth-century theme: God's ordered dispensations of redemptive history.

Hymn writer and theologian Isaac Watts (1674–1748) also propounded some of the doctrines and interpretations that would later constitute the pattern of dispensationalism. It would be grossly anachronistic to call Watts a dispensationalist in the modern sense.[16] However, his work is still important in the history of dispensational development because of his definition of dispensations as distinct stages in the history of the covenants of works and redemption[17] and the special attention he gave to the hermeneutical value of such a system.[18] Also significant was his claim to have arrived at his unique dispensational scheme through an unprejudiced reading of Scripture alone, "rather than by any human creeds, confessions or systems, either ancient or modern."[19]

Yet even more importantly, at the close of his treatise Watts invited others to improve upon his scheme, following his same method. Inevitably his invitation influenced others to reconstruct his dispensational scheme in a variety of directions. One writer in 1827 expressly cited Watts as a motivation for his own attempt at creating a dispensational scheme.[20]

In his Bampton Lectures of 1825, George Chandler (1779–1859), an Anglican priest and postmillennialist, specifically mentioned previous works by men like John Taylor[21] and Jonathan Edwards[22] as being "so often coincident with the subject-matter" of his own lectures that he might appear to have borrowed his own material from them, which he flatly denied.[23] This demonstrates the broad tendency among writers and thinkers of the eighteenth and early nineteenth centuries to be thinking and writing about "the scheme of divine revelation," a pursuit that ultimately led to the development of a stable dispensationalism. In fact, Chandler described this pursuit for a better dispensational scheme in the following terms: "To trace through a long course of ages the plan of divine wisdom, is one of the noblest efforts of which the human mind is capable."[24]

The Search for a Scheme of God's Redemptive Plan

From these examples, one observes that during the eighteenth and nineteenth centuries, Christian thinkers from a variety of perspectives were engaged in what might be likened to a "quest for the holy grail" of systematic biblical theology: a comprehensive, consistent, and compelling scheme of God's redemptive plan. To further underscore this milieu, I refer to the appeals of a reviewer of Townsend's 1822 *New Testament, Arranged in Chronological and Historical Order*, which cheerfully recommended Townsend's work but also reflected on similar works that had attempted to present biblical truth according to a dispensational structure up to his day, beginning with Barrington's *Essay on the Several Dispensations of God* published a century earlier. Yet the reviewer lamented, "This work [of Barrington] is, however, to be considered only as an outline, according to his own suggestion; and a complete treatise on, if we may be allowed the expression, dispensational theology is still wanting."[25] The reviewer then mentioned "some few efforts" that had been made by others, but these, he said, "have not succeeded to the full extent of our wishes."[26]

The nineteenth-century dispensational system, then, developed in the midst of eschatological, dispensational, and prophetic investigations that were wildly popular at the time, especially in England and North America. John Nelson Darby, himself an erstwhile Anglican before furiously aligning with the Brethren movement, is often regarded as the father of dispensationalism.[27] However, in light of the "gold rush" atmosphere in which Darby and his associates mined the Scriptures for the ultimate dispensational scheme, he is probably better regarded as one who expedited the search for the mother lode than the one who found it. Though his own dispensational system may be without historical precedence, none of the pattern's individual doctrines or interpretations is entirely without historical predecessors or contemporary parallels.

In the early period of formulation, Darby himself exhibited a degree of hesitancy and flexibility in some areas that would later become fixed in dispensationalism, even in his own thinking. For example, in a letter dated 1843, Darby seemed to wrestle with the question of a complete rapture of all believers or a partial rapture of only the faithful: "It may be some will pass through [the tribulation], but I am more than ever confirmed that it is not presented to our faith, but the contrary, and that the faithful will be kept from it."[28] In fact, during his period of formulating his understanding of prophetic matters, he appeared to be quite open and gracious in his dealings. "Mistakes in the interpretation of Revelation, one may exercise much patience with. . . . I hold to love much more than to my views, or to those of others, or sustaining or destroying the views of others."[29]

However, within ten years this toleration of diversity and patience with others' interpretations and doctrines seems to have vanished in Darby's immediate circles as the stable pattern of dispensational theology began to take form.[30]

2. Conscious Self-Identity (1845–1875)

Over the course of several decades of study, teaching, discussion, and debate, the proto-dispensationalists settled more and more on what would become the unique pattern of doctrines and interpretations that is dispensationalism.

Darby and Newton

A falling out between Benjamin Wills Newton (1807–1899) and John Nelson Darby in the 1840s provides a relevant marker in the development of dispensationalism's self-identity. Though not strictly speaking a Darbyite, Newton shared many of the doctrines and interpretations of Scripture characteristic of dispensationalism. For example, his dispensational scheme included a pattern of successive failures, including the deterioration of the church dispensation.[31] Newton also expected that after the tribulation Israel would be reestablished and "the preserved Israel shall enter on their sphere of earthly service in the kingdom below, when the Church of the first-born shall be called into their mansions of glory in the kingdom above."[32]

Despite these similarities, during the 1830s Darby and Newton began to experience tensions over eschatology, especially with regard to Darby's recently solidified doctrine of the pretribulation rapture and some of its implications on biblical interpretation, namely, whether the saints suffering through the tribulation in Matthew 24 referred to Jewish believers or to the church.[33] The breaking point between Newton and Darby can be fixed more firmly after 1845, after Newton published his *Thoughts on the Apocalypse* (1846), which defined his futurist, premillennial, dispensational, but non-pretribulational and non-Darbyite doctrines and interpretations. In response to this, Darby wrote a sharp rebuttal in 1848, in which he remarked, "The whole system maintained in the 'Thoughts' is untenable and worthless as a system."[34] For Darby, Newton's rejection of the pretribulation rapture marked a failure of Newton's eschatological system as a whole.[35]

Here we see that Darby regarded his unique interpretations and doctrines—even the details of the order of the rapture and the tribulation—as identity-forging markers of dispensationalism *as a system*. From about 1845 to 1875, then, the pattern of doctrines and interpretations that would become known as dispensationalism took a more fixed form. The child that had been forming in the womb of early modern millennialism was born.

Darby and Trotter

Another attendant at the birth of dispensationalism was Plymouth Brethren leader William Trotter (1818–1865), whose writings had a direct influence on the thinking of American dispensationalists.[36] In the period of "innocent beginnings," Trotter had read widely in prophetic studies, claiming no originality "in the strict sense of the word," but also acknowledging that some of his views he had never seen treated elsewhere. Yet, typical of many in his day, he suggested that all things must be judged by the standard of Scripture alone.[37]

Like Darby,[38] Trotter taught that "heaven, not earth" is to be the church's dwelling place,[39] and in 1853, he noted, "When its formation and discipline are completed, it will be removed to its own heavenly sphere. . . . The church was formed by the descent of the Holy Ghost on the day of Pentecost. . . . All true believers in Christ are its members."[40] In keeping with this distinction, Trotter also held to a difference between the coming of Christ *for* His saints and a later coming *with* His saints, which "implies that they have been previously caught up to him, and glorified."[41] After the catching up of the church in the rapture, Israel would be restored and judgments of Christ would be poured out during the tribulation, during which many Jews and Gentiles would be saved.[42] Though emphasizing the covenantal and prophetic distinctions between Israel and the church, Trotter believed the only saints who had an earthly calling were the survivors of the tribulation—Jews and Gentiles who would enter the millennium in mortal bodies, repopulate the earth, and constitute the blessed kingdom of Israel and nations during the thousand-year reign.[43]

In keeping with other mainstream dispensationalists of his day, Trotter insisted on soteriological continuity in every dispensation.[44] His primary emphasis with regard to dispensations was not different ways of relating to God, different tests of man's obedience, or different means of salvation or sanctification. Rather, for Trotter dispensations were primarily distinct means of "divine government of the earth."[45]

Swiss Pastor Guers and Dispensationalism's Methodological Foundations

Though generally limited to the Brethren movement of which Darby and Trotter were influential figures, dispensationalism at this time began to spread into other parts of Europe among other Brethren assemblies. The Genevan Brethren pastor Émile Guers must be regarded as evidence of the emergence of a distinct dispensational identity between 1845 and 1875. His "methodology and the resulting doctrinal conclusions were essentially the same as that of John Nelson Darby."[46] Yet in 1856, sometime after the falling out between Darby and Newton, Guers pointed back to Newton's insistence on a literal approach to prophecy as a major influence on his own methodology.[47] This not only demonstrates an international dispensational self-identity beyond England and Ireland, but it also reveals Guers's independence from what might be called "Darbyism"—a form of dispensational dogmatizing connected to the man himself.

Guers is probably best regarded, though, as an early example of an articulation of dispensationalism's methodological foundations, an emphasis that would be highlighted in various streams of dispensationalism later in its history. In two letters published in 1862, Guers defended the literal interpretation of prophetic Scripture as a view that "existed long before J. N. Darby or B. W.

Newton, and before me; it is as old as Christianity."[48] For Guers, the dispensational doctrine of an earthly millennium during which the prophecies of Israel were to be fulfilled was the result of a literal approach to biblical prophecy.[49]

German Pastor Brockhaus on Holiness and the Church's Mystical Union

Also during this time the Brethren movement in Germany found its distinct identity after a break by Carl Brockhaus (1822–1899) from the Elberfelder evangelischen Brüderverein (the Elberfeld Protestant Brethren Association) in 1852 primarily over a proper understanding of holiness.[50] As Brockhaus traveled throughout Germany, Holland, and Switzerland between 1852 and 1895, his influence over the various Brethren congregations, or Brüdergemeinde, spread.[51] During this time, however, the uniqueness of the Brethren's theology and practice contrasted sharply with other traditions: Lutheran, Methodist, Baptist, and others. In fact, by 1875 Brockhaus even distinguished himself from John Nelson Darby—with whom he continued to enjoy a very close personal friendship[52]—because they had not provided the best testimony for the German Brethren when they prayed the Lord's Prayer at every gathering, a practice that Brockhaus and his circle rejected as trappings of dead ritualism.[53]

Brockhaus adopted Darby's ecclesiological emphasis on the mystical union of the church as the body of Christ, completely distinct from local churches and denominations, especially "worldly" or "weak" churches. Yet Brockhaus pushed this teaching to its extreme, leading to a split even between the German and English Brethren.[54] Though the details of eschatology were not a particularly strong emphasis in Carl Brockhaus's theology, he was an ardent proponent of Darby's dispensational ecclesiology, and his son, Rudolf Brockhaus, would play a significant role in the popularizing of dispensational distinctives in the early twentieth century.

Though sharing the basic content and trajectory of Darby's dispensationalism, the French-speaking Émile Guers and the German-speaking Carl Brockhaus illustrate the diversity of emphases and priorities that existed within the movement beyond Darby and English-speaking dispensationalism. Between 1845 and 1875, within this international movement an increasing consciousness of a dispensational self-identity would pair with both unity and diversity.

3. Governing Principals (1875–1900) Who Shaped Dispensational Theology

After much travel, speaking, and writing throughout Europe and North America, John Nelson Darby died in 1882. By this time, and largely due to his influence, the stable doctrinal pattern known as dispensationalism had come into its own.[55] In the period from 1875 to 1900, as Darby's dispensational flame ignited numerous lights around the world, dispensational theology developed an even more distinct identity with the ascendancy of what might be called "governing principals," individual pastors, theologians, and authors who would later be regarded as "authorities" and "leaders" of dispensationalism. These principals became skilled in articulating, defending, and promoting dispensational theology in ways that emphasized points of unity with increasing clarity as well as continuing to permit areas of diversity. By the end of the nineteenth century these governing principals enjoyed the doctrinal consensus of a system, the cooperation of a movement, and the authority of an alliance of like-minded leaders.

The Role of the Niagara Conference and Other Bible Conferences

The Niagara Bible Conference was one major contributing factor in the establishment of these governing principals. Though launched in 1875 by conservative Protestants from a broad spectrum of confessional backgrounds, eventually premillennial dispensationalists (mostly Presbyterians) dominated the conference. Under the leadership of James H. Brookes, who had been influenced by Darby and other Brethren dispensationalists,[56] the Niagara conference in 1878 added the premillennial return of Christ to their doctrinal statement, among the fundamentals of the faith. By the end of the nineteenth century, dispensational premillennial leaders had reproduced the Bible conference movement far and wide, disseminating the seeds of dispensational theology.[57]

Dispensationalists in America had not only survived challenges and conflicts brought to light through the Niagara Bible Conference, but they also outpaced historicist premillennialists, who viewed the fulfillment of prophecies in Revelation as having been (and continuing to be) fulfilled throughout the history of the church. Dispensationalists' doctrine of a pretribulation rapture affirmed that the prophecies of Daniel and Revelation were to be fulfilled only after the removal of the church from the earth. As one historian notes, "By the end of the nineteenth century, futurist dispensational premillennialism prevailed."[58]

Also during this period the primary governing principals of dispensationalism transitioned from mainly Brethren teachers in Europe to a more interdenominational leadership, especially in the United States. With this change, Darby's emphasis on the collapse of the institutional church was not thoroughly received. His antidenominationalism became a softer interdenominationalism. Early American dispensationalists remained for some time in traditional denominations like Presbyterianism, Congregationalism, and Baptist churches. However, they transferred their pessimism to American and global culture in general, emphasizing the collapse of the political, social, and cultural institutions as well as the demise of mainline churches. One writer notes, "Dispensationalism was introduced into the United States by pastors of middle and upper middle class churches at just the moment when intellectual change on these social levels was creating near panic in the late 1870's and 1880's."[59]

Two Influential Spokesmen: Scofield and Parlane

Within this historical setting, the establishment of dispensationalism's governing principals can be illustrated well by comparing two examples of dispensational articulation at the close of the twentieth century: W. A. Parlane and C. I. Scofield, the latter a "world-famous prince" in the dispensational kingdom, the former a "working-class provincial."[60] The prince reveals how the leaders were governing the realm; the provincial demonstrates how this theology was being received and re-articulated by educated lay people.

Though published two years after Parlane's book, Scofield's wildly influential 1896 pamphlet, *Rightly Dividing the Word of Truth*, deserves first mention. The sixty-four-page pamphlet consisted of ten chapters touching primarily on eschatology and ecclesiology from a dispensational perspective.[61] In the first chapter, entitled "The Jew, the Gentile, and the Church of God," Scofield set forth the fruit of half a century of dispensational distinctions between Israel and the church: the two groups are "distinct," each having "a peculiar relation to God" and each having received "specific promises."[62] With his earthly/heavenly distinction between Israel and the church, Scofield stood in continuity with earlier dispensationalists and in unity with his contemporaries in the late nineteenth century.[63] Though non-dispensationalists had held the same thing,[64] Scofield emphasized the common dispensational view, that the church had its beginning at Pentecost —and that the church age would end at the pretribulational rapture.[65]

Chapter 2 set forth Scofield's now famous seven dispensations: (1) man innocent, (2) man under conscience, (3) man in authority over the earth, (4) man under promise, (5) man under law, (6) man under grace, and (7) man under the personal reign of Christ. Scofield regarded these dispensations as "periods of time," each of which demonstrated the utter inability of humans to be responsible before God.[66]

In the third chapter Scofield contrasted the two advents of Christ—the first as the humble sacrificial Lamb, the second as the heavenly Judge and King, which he described as premillennial and pretribulational.[67] The coming millennial kingdom was further developed in Scofield's fourth chapter on the distinction between the two resurrections, and in the fifth chapter he outlined five distinct judgments in Scripture.[68]

Scofield then asserted what he regarded as the "most obvious and striking division of the Word of truth" in chapter 6: the difference between law and grace, which "characterize the two most important dispensations: the Jewish and Christian." Though a sharp distinction between law and grace also marked many Protestant thinkers, Scofield gave the division a dispensational foundation. In Scofield's scheme, Scripture "never, in any dispensation, mingles these two principles" of law and grace.[69]

An important aspect of Scofield's dispensational ecclesiology emerged in chapter 10, which he opened with the following statement: "Ever since God has had a people separated to Himself they have been sorely troubled by the presence among them of those who professed to be, but were not, of them." This distinction between the true believers and the professors has led many dispensationalists to emphasize the invisible, spiritual church in radical distinction from the visible, worldly churches that could be overrun by the unregenerate. Such a state of the church was expected as a mark of the end of the church age. Though not itself unique to dispensationalism, the notion of the invisible, true church versus the visible, professing church was insisted upon by dispensationalists in a way that was consistent with their eschatological expectations and ecclesiological explications.

The importance of this survey of Scofield's late-nineteenth-century thought can be summed up in two points. First, Scofield presented basic dispensational teachings in a simple, straightforward, and authoritative style, quoting Scripture, mostly without commentary, in support of the doctrines. These teachings included (1) the pronounced dispensational distinctions between Israel and the church; (2) seven dispensations as periods of time during which God deals with humans differently; (3) the contrast between the dispensation of the law and the dispensation of grace, implying a sharp difference between the law and grace principles in the lives of believers; (4) the church age as a period beginning at Pentecost and ending at a pretribulational rapture; and (5) the future millennium as a time of blessing to Israel in literal fulfillment of Old Testament promises and prophecies, and therefore the distinction between Israel as an earthly people in the future restoration and the church having a heavenly calling.

Second, Scofield's dispensational teachings were delivered in the form of a *pamphlet*—a basic summary that could easily be read, studied, memorized, or used as outlines for lessons or sermons. Its succinct, to-the-point packaging and confident tone made *Rightly Dividing the Word of Truth* an authoritative writing by an emerging prince among the governing principals of dispensationalism.

W. A. Parlane's *Elements of Dispensational Truth* (1894), which preceded Scofield's *Rightly Dividing* (1896), was also fairly brief, just ten pages more than the Scofield pamphlet. In its preface, Parlane claimed that his "elementary treatise" or "short outline" on dispensationalism, "suitable for enquirers," represented a kind of synthesis of earlier dispensational thinkers. In fact, Parlane suggested that "the teachings of past years have been condensed in this book."[70]

With regard to his ecclesiology, Parlane, like Scofield, set as a defining issue the fact that the church of God began at Pentecost and concluded at the rapture. Also like Scofield, Parlane had a distinctly "mystical" ecclesiology, emphasizing the universal and spiritual company of all believers rather than a corporately ordered institution on earth.[71] For Parlane, the "church of God" always meant the genuine elect, while the visible, institutional organization often called the "church" was actually referred to in Scripture as the "Kingdom of Heaven" or "Kingdom of God."

Regarding his kingdom theology, then, Parlane identified the "Kingdom of Heaven" and "Kingdom of God" as "synonymous expressions," contrary to some dispensationalists who would distinguish the two, and he regarded this kingdom as having both present aspect ("the Kingdom in mystery") and a future aspect ("the age to come").[72] The present kingdom had been present for some time prior to the establishment of the church.[73] Thus, the church of God was not to be equated with either the kingdom of God present nor with the kingdom of God future.

The future kingdom of God (or heaven), according to Parlane, would be established on the earth when Christ reigns on the throne of David from Zion, fulfilling the expectations of the Old Testament prophets. Parlane left no room for an inaugurated form of the kingdom with Christ currently sitting on David's throne.[74] Rather, he saw the final gathering and restoration of Israel as something that would take place "at the commencement of the millennial age," when Christ would sit upon the millennial throne to reign as king.[75]

With regard to the hermeneutical method, Parlane explicitly rejected what he called the "pernicious art of spiritualizing" the prophecies of the Old Testament, clearly holding to a literal interpretation of the promises to restore national Israel.[76] He pointed out methodological inconsistencies of non-literalists, observing that "whenever the [prophetic] words . . . were found in connection with denunciations and woe, they were applied literally to the Jewish people, but if these words were connected with promises of future glory and triumph they were interpreted spiritually, and were said to mean the Church."[77]

In keeping with the main dispensational authorities prior to and contemporary with his writing, Parlane held to a two-stage coming of Christ—His coming *for* the church before the tribulation and His coming *with* the church after the tribulation.[78] Like Scofield, Parlane also held to a distinction between the separation of sheep and goats described in Matthew 24:31–46 and the great white throne judgment in Revelation 20:11–15.[79] However, the church would have no part in either of these judgments, having been caught up and rewarded prior to the tribulation.

Thus we see in Parlane's booklet lines of clear unity and continuity within dispensationalism as well as indications of "wiggle room" for diversity of understanding some of the details of interpretation and doctrine, especially with regard to the nature of the kingdom of God and the interpretation of particular passages of Scripture. With Scofield and Parlane—one a prince and the other a provincial of the dispensational realm—we find expressions of a stable, clear pattern of doctrines and interpretations, including methodological presuppositions, that could be easily propagated in the next generation.

4. Promising Propagation (1900–1950)

Dale DeWitt rightly observes that dispensationalism "gained many converts at first through its popular preaching, pamphleteering and reference edition of the Bible."[80] With a number of dispensational authorities established in the previous period of "governing principals," during the first half of the twentieth century the dispensational pattern would spread like wildfire, especially among those on the conservative side of the modernist-fundamentalist controversy. One scholar has described the period this way: "As the movement baked in the oven of opposition it gradually leavened existing ecclesiastical structures, eventually rising into a transdenominational empire of loosely affiliated churches, parachurch organizations, and educational institutions."[81]

Already in the closing years of the nineteenth century, much of the machinery and raw materials that would spread dispensationalism around the world had been firmly established. In 1886 Moody Bible Institute was founded by leaders associated with the Bible conference movement. William E. Blackstone's (1841–1935) *Jesus Is Coming*, published in 1878 and undergoing several editions since, had a profound influence on popular premillennial and dispensational thought in the late nineteenth and early twentieth centuries. Blackstone appears to have been directly influenced by Plymouth Brethren teacher William Trotter.[82] Dispensationalists continued to hold conferences, found Bible schools, plant churches, travel and preach widely, write books, and eventually establish colleges and seminaries. A few examples of this period of promising propagation will suffice to illustrate how the stable, easily packaged system that emerged from the late nineteenth century could be "sold" to an evangelical public already caught in the throes of the modernist-fundamentalist controversy.

The Influence of Scofield and His Reference Bible

First, in 1909, C. I. Scofield published the *Scofield Reference Bible*, which consisted of numerous study notes that propounded not only the classic conservative Protestant theology of fundamentalism, but also the eschatology and ecclesiology of dispensationalism. Crutchfield writes, "It was the *Scofield Reference Bible* that provided the most effective tool for the dissemination of dispensationalism in America." Likewise, Mangum and Sweetnam note, "Historically speaking, *The Scofield Reference Bible* was to dispensationalism what Luther's Ninety-Five Theses was to Lutheranism, or Calvin's Institutes to Calvinism."[83] Published by Oxford University Press, Scofield's Bible enjoyed an international and interdenominational success, giving dispensationalism as a system the reputation of not only a viable—but also an acceptable and respectable—alternative among Protestant orthodoxies.

Scofield was also instrumental in establishing the Philadelphia School of the Bible in 1914, which later merged with Bible Institute of Philadelphia to become Philadelphia Bible Institute in 1951. Throughout the twentieth century this school trained numerous preachers, teachers, and lay people from a dispensational perspective. On the other side of the country, the Bible Institute of Los Angeles (BIOLA), founded in 1908 by Lyman Stewart and led by dispensationalist R. A. Torrey (1856–1928), also contributed to the propagation of dispensationalism. Lewis Sperry Chafer (1871–1952), a direct disciple of Scofield and his successor at the First Congregational Church of Dallas, Texas (later renamed Scofield Memorial Church), founded Dallas Theological Seminary in 1924. Though Dallas Theological Seminary began with a faculty teaching from a variety of eschatological perspectives, Chafer was a convinced dispensationalist and by the 1952 revision of the institution's doctrinal statement, dispensationalism was permanently fixed.[84] With Dallas Seminary, too, dispensationalist teachers acquired a voice in evangelical scholarship when the faculty took over the publication of the journal *Bibliotheca Sacra* in 1934.[85]

Larkin's and Chader's Dispensational Charts

Another force in the popularization of dispensationalism especially among lay people was the publication of dispensational charts used as teaching tools by propagators of the theology. Especially important was Clarence Larkin's (1850–1924) *Dispensational Truth*, first published in 1918. A Baptist pastor with an ability to produce stunning charts, Larkin presented now classic visual teaching aids with explanations that promoted dispensational distinctives, including seven dispensations like Scofield's scheme. For many years to come dispensationalist pastors and teachers would use Larkin's charts or produce similar timelines to visually represent "God's Plan and Purpose in the Ages."

Sixteen years later C. A. Chader published a chart and explanatory book first in Swedish and later in English. This book represented "over forty years of Bible study" and the chart, measuring twenty-seven feet by nine feet, was intended to be used in preaching biblical messages on God's plan through the ages.[86] Unlike Scofield, Chader's chart actually had eight dispensations, "and not seven, as many writers hold," as he believed that the period of Tribulation should be understood as a distinct epoch.[87] This demonstrates not only the international and intercultural portability of this kind of promotion of dispensational theology but also the diversity of dispensational schemes during this period and the next.[88]

Sauer's Influence in Europe and Russia

Finally, through the teaching and writing of Erich Sauer, dispensationalism continued to influence conservative Protestants ("Kreisen der Gläubigen") in German-speaking countries in the early 1900s. From his teaching ministry at the Bibelschule Wiedenest, first established in 1905 by the German "Open Brethren," Sauer's distinct form of dispensational teaching, which developed parallel to North American dispensationalism, was promoted not only among the free churches in Germany, but also in Russia, Hungary, Romania, Bulgaria, Yugoslavia, and Czechoslovakia in the 1920s and 1930s. In the following decades it continued to have ever-widening influence in European and world missions, and through these efforts the distinctive dispensational form of Sauer continued to spread worldwide among free evangelical churches and ministries.[89]

5. Legalizing Precepts (1950–1980)

Here is our story thus far. After its gradual emergence (see "Innocent Beginnings"), the distinctive pattern of doctrines and interpretations formed a definable theological tradition with Darby and the Brethren known as "dispensationalism" ("Conscious Self-Identity"). This led to succinct, authoritative expressions of this pattern by key leaders of the movement from a variety of denominational backgrounds ("Governing Principals"). This in turn resulted in a promotion of dispensationalism far and wide ("Promising Propagation").

Battles Inside and Outside the Camp

During the next period dispensational theology would become increasingly solidified and institutionalized. The period between 1950 and 1980 might be regarded as an era of attempted "codification" of dispensational theology. In some circles, the diversity of details and different emphases that had once coexisted gave way to what might be called "dispensational orthodoxy." However, without any real authority structures to enforce such "correct opinion" on debated issues, the attempt would simply fail. Yet while the precepts of dispensationalism were being hammered out, dispensationalism became embroiled in both defensive and offensive battles with other perspectives both inside and outside its own camp.

Scofield's disciple and founder of Dallas Seminary, Lewis Sperry Chafer, died in 1952, but not before bequeathing to dispensationalism an eight-volume *Systematic Theology*, "the first distinctly premillennial, pretribulational, dispensational synopsis of theology from the perspective of Protestant orthodoxy."[90] Between 1950 and 1975, this multivolume work and other publications by a generation trained by dispensational institutions would help to promote a distinct brand of dispensationalism. John F. Walvoord became president of Dallas Theological Seminary in 1953, having been hand-picked by Chafer. During his tenure he both promoted and defended dispensational premillennialism in numerous volumes written at an accessible lay level.[91] Prominent Dallas Seminary faculty members as well as dispensational leaders from around the world continued to consolidate its base of supporters.[92] At the same time, a number of detractors and defectors criticized elements of dispensationalism with increased fervor.[93]

Already in 1938 dispensationalist H. A. Ironside wrote a critique of what had become known as "ultra-dispensationalism," a theological system that claimed, among other things, that the church began long after Pentecost, that some Christian rites such as baptism were not for the Gentile church, and that some books of the New Testament were written only to Jewish followers of Jesus and did not belong properly to the Gentile church dispensation.[94] Dispensationalists of the Scofield/Chafer tradition were quick to distinguish themselves from such perspectives. When ultra-dispensationalists tried to claim support for their views from Scofield and Chafer as well as an insistence on a more faithful application of the principle of literal interpretation, Dallas Theological Seminary, under Walvoord's leadership, emended the school's doctrinal statement in 1952 to exclude ultra-dispensationalism, thus further solidifying and codifying their form of dispensationalism.[95]

The Sixties: Dispensationalism Today and the New Scofield Reference Bible

Two events in the 1960s helped to promote a form of American dispensationalism that had emerged since the late nineteenth and early twentieth centuries. In 1965 Charles C. Ryrie published *Dispensationalism Today*, in which he famously defined dispensationalism with three *sine qua nons*, or essentials without which the system itself was not dispensationalism.[96] These were the distinction between Israel and the church,[97] a consistent use of literal hermeneutics,[98] and the glory of God as the unifying theme throughout the dispensations.[99]

The second event in the 1960s that served to promote a particular form of dispensationalism was the publication of the *New Scofield Reference Bible* in 1967 under the leadership of dispensationalists who did not share all of Scofield's earlier dispensational convictions. The fact that the old *Scofield Reference Bible* continued to be published indicates that not everybody was interested in the perceived modifications or changes to the system. Others believed the editorial committee did not change enough.[100]

Bateman explains that in the 1950s to 1970s, the older dispensational distinction between the "kingdom of God" and the "kingdom of heaven" and the emphasis on a single new covenant were modified.[101] Prior to this, many dispensationalists, including Scofield and Chafer, argued that *the kingdom of heaven* and *the kingdom of God* were two completely different phrases describing two completely different programs of God; this was the view presented in the old *Scofield Reference Bible,* Chafer's *Systematic Theology*, and Larkin's *Dispensational Truth*. Also, whereas Darby believed in one new covenant strictly for Israel, Chafer had made the suggestion that there were two new covenants, one for Israel, the other for the church, a view advanced by Ryrie as well, before eventually being abandoned as biblically indefensible.[102] Toussaint further confirms that early dispensationalists like Darby, Gaebelein, Larkin, Scofield, and Chafer held to a heavenly/earthly dualism between the church and Israel.[103] However, in the 1950s and 1960s, this radical distinction faded in major writers like Walvoord, Pentecost, and Ryrie.[104]

Though Ryrie's attempt at succinctly defining dispensationalism in his three *sine qua nons* has come under great scrutiny since its initial articulation, it does demonstrate that during this time in the 1950s through the 1970s, an attempt was being made by some dispensationalists to "standardize," "codify," or prescribe what might be called a dispensational "orthodoxy." Yet as we have already seen through this historical survey, dispensationalism has always been a movement marked by diversity in the midst of unity. Therefore, such an attempt to legislate its principles was bound to fail. Any *sine qua non* would end up being too broad (including many who would never characterize themselves as dispensationalists); or it would be too narrow (excluding many key figures and principal leaders in its history). The best we can make of Ryrie's *sine qua non* is that it was a snapshot of one significant segment of dispensationalism at one particular point in time.

Summing up the period that brought forth Ryrie's *Dispensationalism Today* and the *New Scofield Reference Bible*, Blaising writes:

> In the late '50s and '60s, some dispensationalists introduced important revisions to classical dispensationalism. Those revisions became widely accepted such that many graduates of dispensational schools in the '60s and '70s hardly knew what classical dispensationalism was. Many have not even been aware of the variety of views within revised dispensationalism. Nevertheless, revised dispensationalism is a distinctive form of the dispensational tradition, which through its modifications and the problems it was dealing with prepared the way for the eventual development of progressive dispensationalism.[105]

6. Gracious Considerations (1980–2000)

In the 1980s, some American dispensationalists—especially those associated with Dallas Theological Seminary as either faculty or alumni—began to promote several developments and changes in dispensationalism. Bateman points out that in the 1980s and 1990s, a new generation of dispensational scholars reconsidered Ryrie's former *sine qua non* of dispensationalism, especially the doxological purpose of God as a distinguishing mark of dispensationalism and the consistent employment of normal or plain (literal) interpretation.[106] Critics pointed out that not all dispensationalists have agreed that the doxological principle is the unifying theme of all Scripture, nor was this a doctrine held only by dispensationalists. Also, it has been demonstrated by many that the roots of dispensationalism were more complicated than simply a literal approach to the Bible. So during this period dispensationalists returned to the question of how the New Testament informs our reading of the Old and vice versa.[107]

Progressive Dispensationalism

From among these new attempts at reconciling the history of their own tradition with the criticism and insights of non-dispensationalists, the school of thought known as "progressive dispensationalism" emerged. The name refers to the movement's emphasis on the progressive nature of the dispensations, preferring to stress the positive development of God's plan through the ages rather than a pattern of test and failure.[108] This emphasis on the dispensations as more progressive stair steps rather than distinct, unrelated eras of testing itself was not new in dispensationalism. The German dispensationalist Erich Sauer had emphasized both the distinctive character of the dispensations as well as their "Stufencharakter" (i.e., characteristic of progressive advancement).[109] So, some of the changes associated with progressive dispensationalism can be viewed more as shifts in emphasis by some scholars within a diverse tradition of dispensational thinkers, not necessarily as entirely new developments.

Some of the more significant doctrinal and interpretational modifications advanced by progressive dispensationalism in contrast to other forms of the tradition involved the nature of the church's relationship to Israel and the people of God; the proper place and practice of "literal" interpretation; the present state of fulfillment of the biblical covenants, especially the Davidic and new covenants; and an understanding of the kingdom of God and the church as an inaugurated form of the coming messianic kingdom.[110] The question of whether Christ's present session at the right hand of the Father was in any way a partial inauguration of the promised Davidic reign of the Messiah, or, as most past dispensationalists held, the Davidic kingdom would not begin until Christ's return in the millennium, became a major mark of divergence of progressive dispensationalists from most of their theological siblings. However, it should be recognized that while most American dispensationalists had long insisted that Christ's reign as the Davidic King would not begin until His second coming,[111] In the 1950s Sauer had already taught that "in dieser Zeit . . . ist Christus im Himmel Priester und König zugleich" (in the present time . . . Christ is simultaneously priest and king in heaven), though the present priesthood and kingship of Christ is really known only to the believer.[112]

But more noticeable than some of the doctrinal and interpretational modifications was the tone of debate and dialogue among some dispensationalists. Prior dogmatism seemed to yield to a softer, more irenic tone both among dispensationalists with differing perspectives and emphases and between dispensationalists and non-dispensationalists. When progressive dispensationalism first arrived on the scene, it was perceived as a "bridge" between dispensational and nondispensational systems. In fact, the subtitle of the first book advancing the new pattern in 1993, *The Case for Progressive Dispensationalism* (by Robert Saucy), was *The Interface between Dispensational and Non-Dispensational Theology.* The author describes some of the changes among some dispensationalists that have aided in softening the differences:

> The changes in dispensationalism have been largely in the direction of a greater continuity within God's program of historical salvation. Instead of a strict parenthesis that has no relation with the messianic kingdom prophecies of the Old Testament, many dispensationalists now acknowledge the present age of the church as the first-stage partial fulfillment of these prophecies. Israel and the church are no longer viewed as representing two different purposes and plans of God, as some earlier dispensationalists taught; they are now seen as sharing in the same messianic kingdom of salvation history. These changes have obviously brought more congruence between dispensationalism and non-dispensationalism at many points.[113]

Progressive dispensationalism found more lines of continuity between Israel and the church, especially as it relates to the church's relationship to the new covenant. One non-dispensationalist, Ronald Henzel, argues that the classic view of the new covenant being entirely for Israel with no relationship to the church and the resultant "radical disjunction between Israel and the church" is "Dispensationalism's very cornerstone."[114] The disintegration of this "load-bearing wall" in progressive dispensationalism, says Henzel, gives traditional dispensationalists good reason to be alarmed, because it "will bring about the collapse of the house as they have known it."[115]

The Debate During the 1990s

And alarmed many were. Within dispensationalism, the developments and changes were not always well received. A flurry of articles, books, and debates ensued throughout the 1990s, often resulting in legitimate internal discussions, clarifications, and corrections, but sometimes resulting in polarization and fragmentation.[116] In 1995 Robert L. Thomas wrote, "Progressive dispensationalists view themselves as a continuation of the dispensational tradition, but realize they are moving toward nondispensational systems. The movement's desire for rapprochement with other theological systems has involved a hermeneutical shift in its understanding of Scripture."[117] However, many of the institutions, ministries, churches, and publishers have come to terms with both the historical and contemporary diversity within dispensationalism, allowing for various perspectives and emphases to coexist within the movement.

At the same time, broadly evangelical associations like the Evangelical Theological Society fostered a better understanding between dispensational and nondispensational theologians. As a result, much of the hard feelings, harsh words, misunderstandings, and misapprehensions that had divided orthodox Protestant evangelicals turned to mutual respect and a spirit of "unity in diversity" or "agreeing to disagree." Stanley J. Grenz noted in 1992, "I have left the dispensationalism bequeathed to me by my father and childhood church community. At the same time, I retain great respect for this tradition and for the positive contribution dispensationalism has made and continues to make to evangelicalism."[118] With a similar tone, Millard Erickson fairly presents what he views as both positive and negative aspects of dispensationalism in *A Basic Guide to Eschatology*.[119] And in the "Acknowledgments" of his calm, careful, but critical appraisal of dispensationalism, covenant theologian Vern Poythress remarks, "I am most grateful that in our day many dispensationalists and covenant theologians alike are showing themselves willing to lay aside past biases and acknowledge some of the insights that exist on the other side."[120]

7. New Millennial Anticipations (2000–)

Now in the early twenty-first century, dispensationalists seem to be increasingly reckoning with their own history as a movement, examining their present doctrinal and interpretational orientations, and looking to the future.[121] Younger dispensationalists seem to demonstrate a keen interest in correcting some of the extremes and excesses of their tradition's past. Others are recovering neglected emphases of some of its earlier teachers, which in turn contributes to the diversity of the movement. Many are finding helpful tools in this endeavor through Patristic and Reformation studies as well as engagement with broader biblical and theological traditions.

Many of these reorientations toward the future are accompanied by new "oughts" for the old "ism." For example, DeWitt suggests that dispensationalism as a theological tradition "will need to sharpen its scholarship, renew and modernize its pamphleteering, and above all develop a more comprehensive and dynamic ecclesiology."[122] R. Todd Mangum's plea is typical of the tone among many:

> Perhaps it is time to cease grasping for new *sina qua non's,* on either side. Efforts to show where the "line of division" is, beyond which one cannot cross without "succumbing" to the "other system," seems to manifest an unhelpful, "us-vs.-them" mentality. I suspect that this sort of drawing of lines in the sand is done primarily to reassure the more hard-line in one or the other constituency. But,

> such hard-line attitudes are exactly what wreaked such havoc on twentieth-century evangelicalism, and contributed greatly to the misunderstandings that have vexed both sides.[123]

Not all have entered the new millennium, however, with a feeling of contentment. Both irenic critiques and polemical attacks on dispensationalism from outside have continued.[124] And many "traditional dispensationalists" have continued to offer up critiques of the changes within dispensationalism.[125]

What is the future of the movement in light of its past and present? As we have learned repeatedly during the history of the church, forecasting the future is frequently a stupid and sometimes a dangerous thing.[126] However, I will conclude this already lengthy chapter with three thoughts on the near future of dispensationalism.

First, I believe the knots caused by the internal disputes between traditional (classical) dispensationalists and progressive dispensationalists will work themselves out, mostly because it is becoming increasingly obvious that dispensationalism has always been marked by unity and diversity. I doubt that one side will "win" the tug-of-war, especially since dispensationalism is more of a web of diverse perspectives in constant tension than a cable pulled in two directions. The result will most likely be a mutual forbearance of and appreciation for the past and present varieties of perspectives on issues like the relationship between Israel, the church, and the new covenant; the interpretation of particular prophecies; the status of Christ's Davidic reign; the degree of continuity and discontinuity between dispensations, and so forth.

Second, I believe dispensational theologians will need to come to terms with questions of compatibility between various theological systems and interpretations. In light of dispensationalism's history, the tradition cannot be naively contrasted with Reformed theology and Calvinism.[127] In its past, certain aspects of covenant theology—though not the entire system—have also been compatible with dispensational thought. Particular ecclesiological questions such as paedobaptism versus credobaptism, church polity, and sacramentalism are left completely unaddressed by dispensational distinctives, and theologians must continue to wrestle with these aspects of a fuller theological system. Also, dispensationalism will need to come to terms with its orientation and compatibility with developments known as "new covenant theology," which "attempts to combine strengths of dispensationalism and covenant theology and eliminate the weak points of the two."[128] I predict that this close nephew of dispensationalism will be the next great dialogue partner with dispensational theologians in the near future.

Finally, dispensationalists must come to terms with its global history, not just its North American history. Most historical treatments of the movement (including, to a large degree, my own) have been limited to American dispensationalism and especially the history of dispensationalists at or from Dallas Theological Seminary. Yet dispensationalism has parallel histories on other continents and countries and in other languages—histories that are unique to those particular cultures and even predate the advent of dispensationalism in America. Some attempt has been made to reckon with some of these non-English-speaking dispensational traditions in this chapter, but the scope and scale of such an endeavor is prohibitive. An account, analysis, and evaluation of global dispensationalism will provide helpful insights to the movement for the future.

RECAPITULATION: THE STORY OF DISPENSATIONALISM FROM SEEDS TO ORCHARD

Contrary to what this chapter may have led the reader to think, the story of dispensationalism is not in itself altogether complicated. Perhaps an agricultural illustration will helps us step back, take a deep breath, and summarize the panoramic scene I have been trying to describe.

We have seen that scattered seeds of the movement eventually known as dispensationalism can be found in historical antecedents, few of which ever made it to the seedling stage. The distinct theological species called dispensationalism itself eventually sprouted from the soils of nineteenth-century Europe, a ground fertile with theological—especially *eschatological and ecclesiastical*—discontent. Before the new strain had a chance to fully develop into a strong, mature, and stable theological system, it already began to diversify, adapting to its new environments, shedding some of its original characteristics and taking on new ones.

By the time dispensationalism made the leap across the Atlantic to North America, it had developed from an antidenominational, sectarian protest movement to an interdenominational reform movement. Then, as the varieties of dispensationalism formed firmer roots especially in the United States and cast their own runners far and wide, the movement grew away from what it perceived as the increasing darkness of the established denominations toward the brighter light of nondenominationalism.

In those circumstances in which dispensationalism especially flourished among parachurch organizations like Bible institutes, colleges, and seminaries, its once malleable green stems began to thicken into less flexible rinds or even inflexible bark. Some of these varieties succumbed to the elements, withering and dying away or shrinking into obscurity. Others grew into large orchards, bearing worldwide fruit. Some were uprooted or splintered in storms of controversy. Still others continued to quietly reproduce saplings after their own kind.

In all of its life stages, the story of dispensationalism is not one of a uniform movement that developed and matured through distinguishable progressive "ages." It is rather a story of a general consensus on certain key points in the midst of ongoing diversification, which resulted in a movement characterized by both unity and diversity. The story is not one of large-scale evolution or devolution of a monolithic tradition as a whole. It is instead a story of continual expansion, variation, and adaptation.

So, though we can speak in terms of *dispensationalism* as a definable and distinguishable theological movement, we must in some ways also speak of *dispensationalisms* as distinct varieties within a larger species. It is a movement that continues to grow, reproduce, and develop to this day.

NOTES

1. E.g., Oswald T. Allis, *Prophecy and the Church* (Philadelphia: Presbyterian and Reformed, 1969); Clarence B. Bass, *Backgrounds to Dispensationalism* (Grand Rapids: Baker, 1978). This critique has not always been leveled with the kind of impartial interest one would hope from historical inquiry (e.g., John Gerstner, *Wrongly Dividing the Word of Truth: A Critique of Dispensationalism* [Brentwood, TN: Wolgemuth and Hyatt, 1991]).
2. See Charles C. Ryrie, "Update on Dispensationalism," ed. Wesley R. Willis, John R. Master, and Charles C. Ryrie, *Issues in Dispensationalism* (Chicago: Moody, 1994), 16–20.
3. This is especially evident in Blaising's sympathetic essay that employs the designations *classical dispensationalism, revised dispensationalism,* and *progressive dispensationalism;* Craig A. Blaising and Darrell L. Bock, *Progressive Dispensationalism* (Wheaton: Victor, 1993; repr., Grand Rapids: Baker, 2000), 21–56.
4. Ryrie, "Update on Dispensationalism," 20–26. Ryrie begins his discussion of the development of "progressive dispensationalism" with the following: "On the theological scene there has appeared today an aberration from what has been considered normative dispensational teaching" (ibid., 20).
5. Cf. Ben Witherington III, *The Problem with Evangelical Theology: Testing the Exegetical Foundations*

of Calvinism, Dispensationalism, and Wesleyanism (Waco, TX: Baylor University Press, 2005), 94–96.

6. Max Wiley, "Historical Antecedents of Dispensationalism" (ThM thesis, Dallas Theological Seminary, 1960); Larry V. Crutchfield, "The Early Church Fathers and the Foundations of Dispensationalism," in *An Introduction to Classical Evangelical Hermeneutics*, ed. Mal Couch (Grand Rapids: Kregel, 2000), 87–94.
7. See Craig A. Blaising, "Developing Dispensationalism, Part 1: Doctrinal Developments in Orthodoxy," *Bibliotheca Sacra* 145 (1988): 133–40.
8. Cox imprecisely refers to dispensationalism as "a comparatively new doctrine" (William E. Cox, *An Examination of Dispensationalism* [Phillipsburg, NJ: Presbyterian and Reformed, 1979], viii), though he also refers to "cardinal doctrines of dispensationalism" (ibid., vii).
9. Millard J. Erickson, *A Basic Guide to Eschatology: Making Sense of the Millennium* (Grand Rapids: Baker, 1998), 122.
10. Contra Gerstner's exaggerated misunderstanding (*Wrongly Dividing the Word of Truth*, 18), dispensationalism itself does not uniquely deviate from or contribute to classic orthodox Protestant positions on theology proper, trinitarianism, christology, pneumatology, bibliology, anthropology, angelology, hamartiology, soteriology, or sanctification. Though some have attempted to construe a unique dispensational perspective on elements of these doctrines (John F. Walvoord, "The Augustinian-Dispensational Perspective," in *Five Views on Sanctification*, Counterpoints, ed. Stanley N. Gundry [Grand Rapids: Zondervan, 1987], 197–226), it cannot be demonstrated that the doctrinal reach of dispensationalism extends in any unique or significant way beyond the realms of ecclesiology and eschatology.
11. Foundational piers of dispensationalism include: (1) a pronounced distinction between Israel and the church; (2) a strong discontinuity between past, present, and future eras; (3) a future earthly fulfillment of Old Testament promises to national Israel; (4) an abrogation of the law of Moses for the church; and (5) the birth of the church at Pentecost and the completion of the church at the rapture. Some might quibble about whether foundational doctrines should be added or removed from this list (cf. Blaising and Bock, *Progressive Dispensationalism*, 13–21; and Charles C. Ryrie, *Dispensationalism Today* [Chicago: Moody, 1965], 43–47; also Charles C. Ryrie, *Dispensationalism*, rev. ed. [Chicago: Moody, 2007], 45–48). It is also important to point out that upon these foundational piers, several distinctive "support beams" that have been erected are not necessarily required by the pattern. These include the relationship between the King of God, the church, and the millennium; the relationship between the church and the new covenant; whether the present session of Christ is primarily priests, kingly, or a combination; the relationship of the Sermon on the Mount to the church or to the millennial age; and how literally we should expect Old Testament prophecies to be fulfilled in the future. Upon these support beams dispensationalists with various interests, emphases, and agendas have continuously constructed, demolished, remodeled, redecorated, expanded, and developed a variety of different forms of "dispensationalism." As such, the history of dispensationalism is both a history of unity and continuity with regard to immovable piers and a history of diversity, discontinuity, and even internal conflict with regard to the adjustable beams.
12. Dispensationalism shares common ground with other orthodox, Protestant, evangelical traditions (cf. Blaising and Bock, *Progressive Dispensationalism*, 11; George M. Marsden, *Understanding Evangelicalism and Fundamentalism* [Grand Rapids: Eerdmans, 1990], 41). The vast majority of its adherents have held to classic orthodox theology (the Christocentric Trinitarian creation-redemption narrative summarized in the Nicene-Constantinopolitan Creed and the definition of Chalcedon). They have generally embraced Protestant principles of *sola Scriptura, sola gratia, sola fide, solus Christus,* and *soli Deo gloria*. They have vigorously defended the inspiration and accuracy of conservative evangelicalism. They also occupy a tract of land within the territory of "premillennialism," though not all premillennialists have been dispensationalists (cf. Craig L. Blomberg and Sung Wook Chung, eds., *A Case for Historic Premillennialism: An Alternative to "Left Behind" Eschatology* [Grand Rapids: Baker, 2009]).
13. In keeping with the theme of this chapter, I have titled the seven stages in the history of dispensationalism with terms slightly reminiscent of the seven dispensations of twentieth-century dispensational

schemes. Often: *innocence, conscience, government, promise, law, grace*, and *millennium*, or variations on those terms.

14. John Shute Barrington, *Miscellanea Sacra*, vol. 1 (London: Chandler, 1725), xxxiii–xxxiv.

15. John Shute Barrington, *An Essay on the Several Dispensations of God to Mankind, in the Order, in Which They Lie in the Bible* (London: Gray, 1728), 1, 2.

16. See Scott Aniol, "Was Isaac Watts a Proto-Dispensationalist?" (A paper presented to the Southwest region of the Evangelical Theological Society, March 2, 2013, Dallas, Texas); cf. Charles C. Ryrie, *Dispensationalism*, rev. ed. (Chicago: Moody, 1995), 67, 77. It is true, however, that Watts (as well as many others prior to Darby) held to some of the unique doctrines and interpretations that would later make up the pattern known today as dispensationalism.

17. Watts briefly defined dispensations as "the appointed moral rules of God's dealing with mankind considered as reasonable creatures, and as accountable to him for their behaviour, both in this world and in that which is to come." Isaac Watts, *Harmony of All the Religions which God Ever Prescribed; Containing a Brief Survey of the Several Public Dispensations of God toward Man, or His Appointment of Different Forms of Religion in Successive Ages*, in *The Works of the Revered and Learned Isaac Watts*, vol. 4 (London: Barfield, 1810; repr., New York: AMS, 1971), 7.

18. According to Watts, "a due survey of these dispensations . . . may enable us to understand many parts of the Bible much better, since it will happily account for many difficulties in the Old Testament and the New, which seem to me very hard to be solved in any other way, to the satisfaction of a diligent enquirer" (Watts, *Harmony of All the Religions*, 40).

19. He continues, "I cannot but recommend the serious consideration of it to those who are resolved to follow the same method of study, and read the scriptures, to learn from thence the articles of our Christian faith and practice. Let them, like the noble *Bereans, search the scriptures, and see whether* this representation of divine things does not come very near to the truth, and make scripture more easy to be understood by shewing the connexion and consistence of every part of it with all the rest" (ibid.).

20. Anonymous review of George Townsend, *The New Testament, Arranged in Christological and Historical Order; with Copious Notes on the Principal Subjects of Theology*, 2 vols. (London: Rivingtons, 1822). In *The Congregational Magazine* N.S. 10.26 (February 1827): 86.

21. John Taylor, *A Scheme of Scripture-Divinity Formed upon the Plan of the Divine Dispensations; with a Vindication of the Sacred Writings* (London: Waugh and Fenner, 1762). This was made a textbook in his academic instruction at the Warrington Academy (John Kenrick, *A Biographical Memoir of the Late Charles Wellbeloved* [London: Whitfield, 1860], 100).

22. Jonathan Edwards, *The History of Redemption, Comprising a Summary of the History of the Jews up to the Destruction of Jerusalem* (London: Religious Tract Society, 1836). This work is not to be confused with that of John Edwards (1637–1716), whose *Compleat History or Survey of all the Dispensations and Methods of Religion, from the Beginning of the World to the Consummation of All Things* (London: Brown and Co., 1699) is characterized by Ryrie as a forerunner of dispensationalism as a system (Ryrie, *Dispensationalism*, 66).

23. George Chandler, *The Scheme of Divine Revelation Considered*, Bampton Lectures, 1825 (Oxford: Oxford University Press, 1825), xix–xx.

24. Ibid., 2.

25. "Review of Townsend," 86.

26. Ibid. He mentioned three: (1) Taylor's *Scheme of Scripture Divinity*, (2) Edwards's *History of Redemption*, and (3) Watts's *Harmony of All the Religions*.

27. Larry V. Crutchfield, *The Origins of Dispensationalism: The Darby Factor* (Lanham, MD: University Press of America, 1992), preface.

28. John Nelson Darby, Letter to Gillette, from Lausanne (1843) in *Letters*, vol. 1, no. 29.

29. John Nelson Darby, Letter to G. V. Wigram, from Lausanne (Feb. 3, 1841), in *Letters*, vol. 1, no. 21.

30. E. Schuyler English, "E. Schuyler English Looks at Dispensationalism," *Christian Life* 17 (September 1956): 24.

31. Benjamin Wills Newton, *Thoughts on the Apocalypse* (London: Hamilton, 1846), 2–6.

32. Ibid., 116.

33. See Jonathan David Burnham, *A Story of Conflict: The Controversial Relationship between Benjamin Wills Newton and John Nelson Darby* (Carlisle, UK: Paternoster, 2004).

34. John Nelson Darby, *An Examination of the Statements Made in the Thoughts on the Apocalypse by B. W. Newton and an Enquiry How Far They Accord with Scripture* (Plymouth: J. B. Rowe, 1848), 1.

35. Ibid., 2.

36. Kraus notes, "Probably the two most popular writers, and the widest read by American ministers, were William Trotter and Charles Henry Mackintosh, although the writings of William Kelly and Darby also circulated widely" (C. Norman Kraus, *Dispensationalism in America: Its Rise and Development* [Richmond: John Knox, 1958], 48).

37. William Trotter, *Plain Papers on Prophetic and Other Subjects*, 3rd rev. ed. (London: Theobald, 1854), i.

38. Darby wrote, "The church is not earthly. . . . It was hid in God from the foundation of the world (Eph. 3), and the prophets do not speak of it" (Letter to Major Lancey [May 1, 1848], in *Letters*, vol. 1, no. 66).

39. Trotter, *Plain Papers on Prophetic and Other Subjects*, 7.

40. Ibid., 81–82.

41. Ibid., 15.

42. Ibid., 19.

43. Though much has been made of an "anthropological dualism" and a "heavenly versus earthly people" in criticisms of dispensationalism, for Trotter such a "dualism" was really a covenantal and prophetic distinction: "That which, above all else, marks the difference between the church and Israel, and indeed we may say between the church and the entire population of the millennial earth, is, that the church is blessed *in* Christ and *with* Christ:—Israel and the millennial nations will be blessed *by* him, and *under his sway*" (ibid., 322).

44. Ibid., 406.

45. Ibid., 406–8.

46. Michael D. Stallard, *The Early Twentieth-Century Dispensationalism of Arno C. Gaebelein*, Studies in American Religion, vol. 77 (Lewiston, ME: Edwin Mellen, 2002), 247.

47. Émile Guers, *Israel aux Derniers Jours de l'économie actuelle, ou, Essai sur la restauration prochaine de ce peuple, suivi d'un fragment sur le millénarisme* (Genève: Émile Beroud, 1856), 5.

48. Émile Guers, *Le littéralisme dans la prophétie: Lettres a M. Le Pasteur F. Bertholet-Bridel* (Genève: Émile Beroud, 1862), 4.

49. Ibid., 15–18.

50. Ernst Eylenstein, "Carl Brockhaus: Ein Beitrag zur Geschichte der Entstehung des Darbyismus in Deutschland," *Zeitschrift für Kirchengeschichte* 46.9 (1927): 280–83; Rolf-Edgar Gerlach, *Carl Brockhaus—Ein Leben für Gott und die Brüder* (Wuppertal: R. Brockhaus, 1994), 69–74.

51. Eylenstein, "Carl Brockhaus," 283–88.

52. Ibid., 293–95.

53. Ibid., 290.

54. Ibid., 295–300.

55. Crutchfield rightly notes, "No dispensationalist who is aware of the fact can deny that Darby played a key role in the systematization and promotion of dispensational concepts" (Crutchfield, *Origins of Dispensationalism*, 1).

56. Ibid., 13.

57. Gary Dorrien, *The Remaking of Evangelical Theology* (Louisville: Westminster John Knox, 1998), 15, notes, "The Bible conference movement on which fundamentalism was mainly founded was dominated by dispensationalists. Over the next generation, dispensationalist fundamentalism was championed by such [D. L.] Moody associates as Erdman, Gordon, Torrey, James M. Gray, C. I. Scofield, George Needham, and A. C. Dixon."

58. Scott M. Gibson, *A. J. Gordon: American Premillennialist* (Lanham, MD: University Press of America, 2001), 73.

59. Lefferts A. Loetscher, "Foreword," in Kraus, *Dispensationalism in America*, 7.

60. Little is known today of W. A. Parlane, who was a layperson from Collingwood, Ontario, associated with the Niagara Bible Conferences, and thus a friend of early premillennialists and dispensationalists (cf. Nathaniel West, *The Thousand Year Reign of Christ*, reprint ed. [Grand Rapids: Kregel, 1993], xvi; S. R. Briggs, ed., *The Second Coming of Our Lord: Being Papers Read at a Conference Held at Niagara, Ont., July 14th to 17th, 1885* [Toronto: Willard Tract Depository, 1885], 3).

61. In chapters 7–9, Scofield articulated his views on the old and new natures of the believer (chapter 7), the believer's sanctification (chapter 8), and the past, present, and future aspects of salvation (chapter 9). Though some have attempted to construe a uniquely dispensational soteriology and sanctification from Scofield's theology, these perspectives of Scofield have never been regarded as essential aspects of the pattern of doctrines and interpretations that mark dispensationalism.

62. C. I. Scofield, *Rightly Dividing the Word of Truth* (Findlay, OH: Fundamental Truth, 1947), 6.

63. Dispensationalist Charles Henry Mackintosh (1820–1896), who heavily influenced American dispensationalists like D. L. Moody (1837–1899), and A. C. Gaebelein (1861–1945) wrote in 1867, "What is the precise period to which the formation of the Church is confined? The answer is simple, viz.: From the time that Christ took His seat at the right hand of God, and sent the Holy Ghost from on high to baptize believers into one body, until the time when He shall leave it to meet His Church in the air. . . . This, be it long or short, is, properly speaking, the Church period" (Charles Henry Mackintosh, *Occasional Papers* [London: W. H. Broom, 1867], 49).

64. Cf., e.g., Watts, *Harmony of All the Religions,* 31.

65. Scofield, *Rightly Dividing the Word of Truth*, 7.

66. Ibid., 13.

67. Ibid., 17, 28.

68. These are the judgment of the cross, the judgment of sin in the life of a believer, the judgment seat of Christ after the rapture, the judgment of the nations during the tribulation, and the judgment of the wicked after the millennium (ibid., 29–33).

69. Ibid., 34.

70. W. A. Parlane, *Elements of Dispensational Truth* (Collingwood, Canada: n.p. 1894), v.

71. Ibid., 3.

72. Ibid., 4.

73. Ibid., 4–5.

74. Ibid., 13.

75. Ibid., 25.

76. Ibid., 14–15.

77. Ibid., 50. With regard to the book of Revelation, Parlane wrote, "It is said, and with truth, that this book is a book of symbols;—granted,—but the symbols are symbolic of something, and the word does not always leave us in doubt as to their meaning" (ibid., 32).

78. Ibid., 21–24. He explicitly rejected the charge that a pretribulation rapture implied two second comings (ibid., 24).

79. Ibid., 39–46.

80. Dale S. DeWitt, *Dispensational Theology in America during the Twentieth Century: Theological Development and Cultural Context* (Grand Rapids: Grace Bible College, 2002), 43.

81. Ronald M. Henzel, *Darby, Dualism, and the Decline of Dispensationalism: Reassessing the Nineteenth-Century Roots of a Twentieth-Century Prophetic Movement for the Twenty-First Century* (Tucson: Fenestra, 2003), 3.

82. Kraus, *Dispensationalism in America,* 33.

83. Crutchfield, *The Origins of Dispensationalism,* 14; R. Todd Mangum and Mark S. Sweetnam, *The Scofield Bible: Its History and Impact on the Evangelical Church* (Colorado Springs: Paternoster, 2009), 195.

84. John D. Hannah, *An Uncommon Union: Dallas Theological Seminary and American Evangelicalism* (Grand Rapids: Zondervan, 2009), 18–19, 115.

85. Ibid., 81.

86. C. A. Chader, *God's Plan through the Ages: An Evangelical Exposition Neither Adventistic nor Russellistic,* 2nd ed. (Grand Rapids: Zondervan, 1940), vii. The author noted in the introduction to the second edition that his book "has been adopted by the American Prophetic League of Los Angeles . . . as its text-book on Dispensational Truth" (ibid., viii).

87. Ibid., 14. These ages are: (1) Innocence (from creation to the Fall), (2) Conscience (from the Fall to the flood), (3) Human Government (from the flood to the Tower of Babel and call of Abraham), (4) Promise (from the call of Abraham to the exodus from Egypt), (5) Law (from the exodus to Christ), (6) Grace (from Christ to the Second Advent), (7) Tribulation (from the coming of Christ for His Bride to the coming with His saints), and (8) Millennium (from Armageddon to the last rebellion against God).

88. On the international scene, one should also consider the popular influence of Erich Sauer, *Der göttliche Erlösungsplan von Ewigkeit zu Ewigkeit: Eine prophetische Karte mit erklärendem Text* (Wuppertal: Brockhaus, 1950), based on his earlier works promoting his perspective of "Offenbarungsgeschichte" (Erich Sauer, *Das Morgenrot der Welterlösung: Ein Gang durch die alttestamentliche Offenbarungsgeschichte,* 4th ed. [Gütersloh: Evangelischer Verlag, 1947]).

89. See Erich Sauer, *50 Jahre Missionshaus Bibelschule Wiedenest* (Wiedenest: Bibelschule Wiedenest, 1955), and Horst Afflerbach, *Die Heilsgeschichtliche Theologie Erich Sauers,* STM 16 (Wuppertal: R. Brockhaus, 2006), 65–77.

90. Hannah, *An Uncommon Union,* 130.

91. Significant works by Walvoord include, in chronological order: *The Return of the Lord* (Findlay, OH: Dunham, 1955); *The Rapture Question* (Findlay, OH: Dunham, 1957); *The Millennial Kingdom* (Findlay, OH: Dunham, 1959); *Israel in Prophecy* (Grand Rapids: Zondervan, 1962); *The Church in Prophecy* (Grand Rapids: Zondervan, 1964); *The Revelation of Jesus Christ: A Commentary* (Chicago: Moody, 1966); *The Nations in Prophecy* (Grand Rapids: Zondervan, 1967); *Daniel, the Key to Prophetic Revelation* (Chicago: Moody, 1971); *Armageddon, Oil, and the Middle East Crisis: What the Bible Says about the Future of the Middle East and the End of Western Civilization* (Grand Rapids: Zondervan, 1974); *The Blessed Hope and the Tribulation: A Biblical and Historical Study of Posttribulationism* (Grand Rapids: Zondervan, 1976).

92. For example, see Charles F. Baker, *A Dispensational Theology* (Grand Rapids: Grace Bible College, 1971); W. W. Barndollar, *The Validity of Dispensationalism* (Johnson City, NY: Baptist Bible Seminary, 1964); Lewis Sperry Chafer, *Dispensationalism,* rev. ed. (Dallas: Dallas Theological Seminary, 1951); Clarence E. Mason, *Dispensationalism Made Simple* (Arnold, MO: Shield, 1976); J. Dwight Pentecost, *Things to Come* (Grand Rapids: Zondervan, 1958); J. Dwight Pentecost, *Prophecy for Today: The Middle East Crisis and the Future of the World* (Grand Rapids: Zondervan, 1961); Charles C. Ryrie, *The Basis of the Premillennial Faith* (New York: Loizeaux, 1953); Charles C. Ryrie, *The Bible and Tomorrow's News: A New Look at Prophecy* (Wheaton: Scripture Press, 1969); Chester E. Tulga, *The Case for Dispensationalism* (Somerset, KY: Eastern Baptist Institute, 1962).

93. For example, see S. E. Anderson, *Scofieldism Upgraded* (Glenwood, IL: Fundamental Publishers, 1973); Greg L. Bahnsen and Kenneth L. Gentry, Jr., *House Divided: The Break-Up of Dispensational Theology* (Tyler, TX: Institute for Christian Economics, 1989); Bass, *Backgrounds to Dispensationalism*; Cox, *An Examination of Dispensationalism*; Jesse Wilson Hodges, *Christ's Kingdom and Coming: With an Analysis of Dispensationalism* (Grand Rapids: Eerdmans, 1957); Kraus, *Dispensationalism in America*; Dave MacPherson, *The Unbelievable Pre-Trib Origin* (Kansas City, MO: Heart of America Bible Society, 1973); John Zens, *Dispensationalism: A Reformed Inquiry into Its Leading Figures and Features* (Phillipsburg, NJ: Presbyterian and Reformed, 1978).

94. H. A. Ironside, *Wrongly Dividing the Word of Truth: Ultra-Dispensationalism Examined in the Light of Holy Scripture* (Oakland, CA: Western Book and Tract, 1938).

95. See Hannah, *An Uncommon Union*, 115.

96. Ryrie, *Dispensationalism Today*, 43–47. Cf. *Dispensationalism* (2007), 38–41.

97. Toussaint noted that of Ryrie's three *sina qua nons*, "the most important is the distinction between Israel and the church." Stanley D. Toussaint, "Israel and the Church of a Traditional Dispensationalist," in ed. Herbert W. Bateman IV, *Three Central Issues in Contemporary Dispensationalism: A Comparison of Traditional and Progressive Views* (Grand Rapids: Kregel, 1999), 227.

98. Notably, many earlier dispensationalists could not be described as entirely consistent in their hermeneutic. Henzel suggests, "Contrary to the conventional understanding of Darby's system within traditional Dispensationalism, it was not based on the principle of a consistent literal hermeneutic for prophecy. Darby himself never committed to that procedure as his successors did, and in fact prescribed *symbolic* interpretation for prophecies that concerned Gentiles, who now form the majority of the Church (God's "heavenly" people)." Henzel, *Darby, Dualism, and the Decline of Dispensationalism*, 124–25.

99. Apparently in distinction from Anglican dispensationalist W. H. Griffith Thomas's 1919 claim that "the supreme theme of the Bible is, beyond all question, the will of God as therein revealed. From first to last the dominant and dominating thought is the knowledge and obedience of what God has revealed and recorded as His purpose for men" (W. H. Griffith Thomas, "The Lord's Coming and the Supreme Theme of the Bible," *The Christian Workers Magazine* 20.2 [October 1919]: 95).

100. Anderson, *Scofieldism Upgraded*, 11–12.

101. Herbert W. Bateman IV, "Dispensationalism Yesterday and Today," in Bateman, ed., *Three Central Issues in Contemporary Dispensationalism*, 23–34.

102. See Blaising and Bock, *Progressive Dispensationalism*, 37–38.

103. Toussaint, "Israel and the Church of a Traditional Dispensationalist," 228–29.

104. Ibid., 229.

105. Blaising and Bock, *Progressive Dispensationalism*, 46.

116. Bateman, "Dispensationalism Yesterday and Today," 34–42.

107. Bateman himself identifies several "schools" of thought on the issue of the relationship between the New Testament and the Old (ibid., 38–42).

108. Blaising and Bock, *Progressive Dispensationalism*, 48–49.

109. Sauer, *Morgenrot der Welterlösung*, 223. The influence of Sauer on progressive dispensationalism is acknowledged in a footnote of Blaising and Bock, *Progressive Dispensationalism*, 307.

110. See description in Blaising and Bock, *Progressive Dispensationalism*, 46–56.

111. Parlane, *Elements of Dispensational Truth*, 13; Trotter, *Plain Papers on Prophetic and Other Subjects*, 448–60.

112. Erich Sauer, *Gott, Menschheit und Ewigkeit*, 2nd ed. (Wuppertal: R. Brockhaus, 1955), 63–64.

113. Robert L. Saucy, *The Case for Progressive Dispensationalism* (Grand Rapids: Zondervan, 1993), 9.

114. Henzel, *Darby, Dualism, and the Decline of Dispensationalism*, 4.

115. Ibid., 4–5.

116. Cf., for example, Master and Willis, eds., *Issues in Dispensationalism.*

117. Robert L. Thomas, "The Hermeneutics of Progressive Dispensationalism," *The Masters Seminary Journal* 6.2 (Spring 1995): 79.

118. Stanley J. Grenz, *The Millennial Maze: Sorting out Evangelical Options* (Downers Grove, IL: InterVarsity, 1992), 11.

119. Erickson, *A Basic Guide to Eschatology,* 122–24.

120. Vern Sheridan Poythress, *Understanding Dispensationalists,* 2nd ed. (Phillipsburg, NJ: Presbyterian and Reformed, 1994), 5.

121. DeWitt, *Dispensational Theology in America* (2002); Stallard, *The Early Twentieth-Century Dispensationalism of Arno C. Gaebelein* (2002).

122. DeWitt, *Dispensational Theology in America,* 43.

123. R. Todd Mangum, *The Dispensational-Covenant Rift: The Fissuring of American Evangelical Theology from 1936 to 1944* (Waynesboro, GA: Paternoster, 2007), 211.

124. John H. Gerstner, *Wrongly Dividing the Word of Truth: A Critique of Dispensationalism,* ed. Don Kistler, 2nd ed. (Morgan, PA: Soli Deo Gloria, 2000); Sam Storms, *Kingdom Come: The Amillennial Alternative* (Geanies House, UK: Christian Focus, 2013).

125. E.g., Ron J. Bigalke, Jr., *Progressive Dispensationalism: An Analysis of the Movement and Defense of Traditional Dispensationalism* (Lanham, MD: University Press of America, 2005).

126. Cf. Francis X. Gumerlock, *The Day and the Hour: A Chronicle of Christianity's Perennial Fascination with Predicting the End of the World* (Powder Springs, GA: American Vision, 2000).

127. The fact is, the great majority of early American dispensationalists were Calvinists, coming from Presbyterian, Congregationalist, Anglican, or Calvinist Baptist denominations (Kraus, *Dispensationalism in America,* 59–60).

128. Dennis M. Swanson, "Introduction to New Covenant Theology," *The Masters Seminary Journal* 18.1 (2007): 149.

4

The Hermeneutic of Dispensationalism

NATHAN D. HOLSTEEN

"I love the game of football," my Aberdonian friend said to me one day. Now if you are an American reader, this statement may conjure up mental images of Peyton Manning and the Denver Broncos' amazing passing attack (or, for some of us older readers, it might be Joe Montana—or even Johnny Unitas). Having lived in Scotland for a couple of years at the time my friend said this to me, however, I had not a single mental flash of Troy Aikman and the Dallas Cowboys. I already knew that when a Scotsman says *football,* he means the same thing Americans mean when they say *soccer.* And when an American says *football,* that's what Scotsmen call *American football.*

It all sounds a little confusing when written down like this, but it's really a most natural thing: people use different terms to refer to the same thing. And people use the same term to refer to different things.

A similar phenomenon is part of the discussion we are going to encounter in this chapter. As we discuss hermeneutics, and more specifically the *literal hermeneutic,* we are going to discover that careful attention to how different folks use that term will take us a good distance toward understanding the real issues in some common disagreements. And if, at the end of the day, you still like *football* more than *American football,* you're probably in good company: people tell me that most of the world's inhabitants agree with you.

The purpose of this chapter is to locate dispensationalism on the broader map of Christian approaches to the reading of Scripture. Or, to put it another way, I intend to answer the question, What is the hermeneutic of dispensationalism?

But this question, which appears to be straightforward at first glance, turns out to be exceedingly difficult. A number of questions arise with a second glance: What is a hermeneutic? What is dispensationalism? How are the two related? In the process of wading through these questions, I believe we will find that dispensationalism *is* a hermeneutic—but a hermeneutic with sufficient breadth to explain the variety of perspectives we find within dispensationalism today.

WHAT IS A HERMENEUTIC?

The place to start, then, seems obvious. Before we can decipher the hermeneutic of dispensationalism, we must wrestle first with the concept of a hermeneutic in general. This, as it turns out, is no small feat. There is no universal agreement on the relationship between three ideas that show up with regularity in conversations on the reading of Scripture: hermeneutics, interpretation, and exegesis.

The simplest approach is to equate the first two—to say, hermeneutics *is* interpretation. And this approach finds support from many quarters in the world of Christendom. For example, Schökel, in his influential work *A Manual of Hermeneutics,* suggests that "hermeneutics [is] the theory of the activity of understanding and interpreting texts."[1]

Notice, however, that our simple equation just got a little more complicated. Hermeneutics is not identical to interpretation; even in the most simplified approaches, hermeneutics is the theory that stands behind the activity of interpretation.

Thiselton, one of the most respected voices in the field of Christian hermeneutics, agrees.

> Finally, whereas *exegesis and interpretation* denote the *actual processes* of interpreting texts, *hermeneutics* also includes the second-order discipline of asking critically *what exactly we are doing when we read, understand, or apply* texts. Hermeneutics explores *the conditions and criteria* that operate to try to ensure responsible, valid, fruitful, or appropriate interpretation.[2]

Without belittling in any way the massive and significant discussions that take place in the world of Schökel and Thiselton, I think we are justified in offering a summary at this point. *A hermeneutic* is a specific approach to the interpretation of texts (in this case, of course, we are interested in Scripture); *hermeneutics* is the study of various ways of approaching the interpretation of texts.

HERMENEUTICS AND CHRISTIANITY

Christendom has brought forth a profusion of approaches to the interpretation of Scripture.[3] And while the variety is staggering, it seems safe to characterize the lot as a toddler on a tether. A hermeneutic here struggles to see how far she can get from her parent, while a hermeneutic there is content to walk right by his parent's side. No matter how far away a hermeneutic may roam, the distance is limited—and the toddler remains clearly connected to the parent.

In this imagery, the parent represents an irresistible force in biblical hermeneutics, and that irresistible force is the concept of authorial intent.

I can already hear the outcry. Yes, I know that the concept of authorial intent has been attacked from virtually every angle. Yes, I know that any affirmation of authorial intent results in the charge that whoever defends authorial intent has lost all cognitive function. But I'm willing to take the risks associated with this claim because I think that exploring the author's intent is the only satisfactory explanation for the historical and theological data available to us.

Authorial Intent

So what is this disputed concept? What does "authorial intent" mean when it shows up in a discussion of biblical hermeneutics? According to E. D. Hirsch, authorial intent can be summed up as "the sensible belief that a text means what its author meant."[4]

And yet it must be admitted that this sensible idea runs into a number of difficulties, especially when applied to Scripture. What does the Christian do with the concept of dual authorship? Are we looking for the intent of the human author, or for the intent of the divine author? Are those two intents distinct or identical? How does each individual part of Scripture fit into the canonical whole—a whole of which none of the human authors was completely aware? Precisely because the Christian affirms the doctrine of inspiration, the Christian reaps difficulty in applying a simple and intuitive hermeneutic.

Further challenges to authorial intent have arisen from a number of directions. One of the most famous is the impact of speech-act theory.[5] In wrestling with the concepts of locutionary, illocutionary, and perlocutionary acts, some have found reason to dispense entirely with authorial intent. At the same time, it still seems to me that these challenges to authorial intent, while perhaps stretching the tether, ultimately validate the very principle of authorial intent—even if that principle must be articulated in ways that address the challenges already mentioned.

As a matter of fact, this is what both Vanhoozer and Wolterstorff do—although in slightly different ways.[6] Wolterstorff clearly says, "My main aim in these chapters is to defend the integrity and legitimacy of authorial-discourse interpretation."[7] And when one asks what authorial-discourse interpretation is, Wolterstorff's answer, in the same context, is simply the practice of reading a text so that one can find out what the author of the text was saying thereby. More specifically, Wolterstorff describes his own approach as "that particular interpretative practice which assumes that the Christian Bible as a whole is a medium of divine discourse and then, when confronted with a particular passage, seeks to discern what God was saying by way of that passage from the whole."[8] This, from all appearances, is indeed an affirmation of authorial intent—but chastened and modified in response to certain criticisms. "Ricoeur was right," Wolterstorff says, "to look for a practice of interpretation located in the space between Romanticism and structuralism. But what occupies that space is not the practice of textual sense interpretation but the practice of authorial-discourse interpretation—a specific version of this being the practice of reading sacred texts to discern divine discourse."[9]

One final point: Wolterstorff is careful to ensure that his interpretive approach is connected conceptually—tethered intentionally, if you will—to the irresistible force in scriptural interpretation. While he admits that there are a number of other interpretive approaches, the one he defends "was the dominant interpretative practice in the Christian community for about 1500 years."[10] It seems inescapable. Wolterstorff views himself as a proponent of authorial intent—although his affirmation is shaped by elements of speech-act theory.

David Williams, speaking from within the Roman Catholic tradition, agrees with the assertion that authorial intent is historically the irresistible force in the interpretation of Scripture, and in spite of trends in the field of hermeneutics, authorial intent is experiencing something of a resurgence. He writes,

> Among [the parameters of discussion of the Bible as Scripture] one finds a firm attachment to recovery of authorial intention as a major interpretive goal. To take but one example, there is a consistent understanding, which runs throughout the last sixty years of Catholic teaching, that the communicative intention of the author grounds the literal sense of Scripture and that this literal sense must be the foundation of exegesis.[11]

Indeed, authorial intent is historically the principle to which all biblical hermeneutics are tethered. It may even be fair to say that those hermeneutics that flatly reject the principle of authorial intent seem to be toddlers straining at the tether while claiming that it doesn't even exist. Such hermeneutics are self-refuting, insofar as they make use of the hermeneutic of authorial intent in order to deny its validity.

So why are we having this entire discussion on authorial intent? The simplest answer is this: While we have not yet arrived at a dispensational hermeneutic, we will find once we get there that it occupies a portion of the same space that Christian approaches to Scripture have occupied throughout history—at least until the Enlightenment—and that the hermeneutic of dispensationalism is in good company.

The Question of Dual Authorship

Being in good company, however, does not mean that there are no questions still to be discussed. As mentioned in brief earlier, one of the driving questions that arises from a discussion of authorial intent is the question of the dual authorship of Scripture. Christians throughout history have affirmed that God speaks in Scripture (thus, for example, the title of Nicholas Wolterstorff's work, *Divine Discourse*). But when a Christian affirms the doctrine of inspiration, this brings into the discussion the role of the human author, and the historical situation in which that author wrote. Teasing out the precise role of each author remains a challenge for anyone who affirms authorial intent.[12]

While the challenge of dual authorship remains a topic worth discussing—and especially for those within the evangelical fold—it is unfortunately beyond the scope of this chapter. Suffice it to say that this challenge does not overturn a hermeneutic tied to the principle of authorial intent.

Grammatical-Historical Interpretation

Another term that appears frequently in discussions of hermeneutics is *grammatical-historical interpretation.* Growing out of a desire to find the author's intended meaning as an approach to Scripture, the term grammatical-historical interpretation is not, strictly speaking, a hermeneutic, although it is often treated as one. Nor is it, strictly speaking, an approach to reading Scripture—and therefore it is not a hermeneutic. Instead it is a description of method in pursuing the meaning of a text, or a description of the process used in finding the meaning of a text. As Thiselton taught us (see above), this distinguishes the grammatical-historical method from a proper hermeneutic.

So what hermeneutic, properly speaking, employs the grammatical-historical method? Most scholars agree that the hermeneutic most likely to employ the grammatical-historical method is the hermeneutic of authorial intent (in any of its historical or modified forms). This is affirmed by Blomberg when he writes, "The grammatico-historical method, on the other hand, refers to studying the biblical text, or any other text, in its original historical context, and seeking the meaning its author(s) most likely intended for its original audience(s) or addressees based on the grammar and syntax."[13]

What we have found so far is this: for the majority of Christian history, the dominant approach to the reading of Scripture has revolved around the concept of authorial intent. Although that principle certainly has seen its challenges (and rightly so), it is by no means completely discredited. In chastened form, it has made a comeback in many areas of Christian thought. But this is not the entire picture. It can legitimately be argued that one part of Christendom never really abandoned the principle of authorial intent—and that part is conservative evangelicalism. As Lundin has rather pointedly stated (perhaps overstated), "The conviction of E. D. Hirsch [is] a belief widely held among conservative biblical scholars."[14]

THE REFORMED TRADITION AND THE COVENANT HERMENEUTIC

Having narrowed the scope of our hermeneutical conversation to the field of conservative evangelicalism, we are now in a position to see the relationships between a dispensational hermeneutic and nondispensational (yet conservative and evangelical) hermeneutic. The first step in this process, at least historically, is to trace the development and shape of the Reformed tradition—for in it we encounter the concept of the covenant hermeneutic.

Before we proceed any further, it is worth pausing to reflect on the significance of what has just been said. Both dispensationalism and covenant theology share the same conviction about God's speaking in Scripture. They also share the same conviction about the need to find God's intended meaning in Scripture (and so both traditions say the same kinds of things about authorial intent and the need to express authorial intent in a way that is chastened). So the two traditions are certainly very close to one another with respect to their positions on the broader map of Christian hermeneutics. But—and this will surprise no one—there are yet differences that create a measurable conceptual distance between the two hermeneutics. It is to a discussion of these differences that we now turn.

For some, the covenant hermeneutic is synonymous with Reformed theology. This is actually a bit of an overstatement, as not all Reformed theology is covenant theology.[15] But the point is well made—the covenant hermeneutic does indeed exhibit a very close relationship with covenant theology. As J. I. Packer has written, "What is covenant theology? The straightforward, if provocative answer to that question is that it is what is nowadays called a hermeneutic—that is, a way of reading the whole Bible that is itself part of the overall interpretation of the Bible that it undergirds."[16]

Now this is interesting. Packer calls covenant theology itself "a hermeneutic." While I concur, this claim raises an interesting question. Where did this covenant hermeneutic come from?

The short answer, historically, is that the covenant hermeneutic arose out of the reformation/post-reformation discussions focused on God's sovereignty. To be even more specific, Weir suggests that covenant theology (at least that form of covenant theology that features a pre-lapsarian covenant with Adam) "had its origins in the predestinarian discussions which took place during the sixteenth century."[17]

This observation opens up new avenues of understanding the covenant hermeneutic. Historically, discussions about God's sovereignty led to affirmation of predestination—the idea that God's choice lies behind all of salvation, and that only those chosen by God for salvation will experience salvation. But this predestinarian discussion led further to a discussion of the covenants that undergird salvation—ultimately to a pre-lapsarian covenant of works and a post-lapsarian covenant of grace.[18]

The development of a pre-lapsarian and post-lapsarian covenant schema leads directly to another building block in the covenant hermeneutic: the unity of the covenant. This is the idea that all the saved (or elect) will be saved in precisely the same way: in accordance with the terms of the covenant of grace. But there is only *one* covenant of grace. This is precisely why covenant theologians speak of "the paramount importance of the unity of the covenant in Reformed theology."[19]

Following the logic of covenant theology one step further, it becomes apparent that since there is only one covenant of grace, there can be only one people of God. All of the elect are to be considered as one body, and this claim functions as an *a priori* insofar as the interpretation of Scripture goes. As a matter of fact, this may be the most compelling feature of the covenant hermeneutic: the unity of the covenant, with the result that there can be only one people of God. As Adams writes, "Each succeeding age, in perfect harmony with, and progressing naturally from, the previous one, reveals reasonable progression in the ongoing . . . divine plan of the ages. Each age has its own peculiar hue and intensity, blending with (but not overlapping) the colors each lends to the heavenly canvas. Through it all runs the unifying theme of the Covenant of Grace."[20]

Perhaps the clearest summary comes once again from Packer, who writes, "The Word of God is not properly understood till it is viewed within a covenantal frame." And further, "The unifying strands that bind together the books of the Bible are, first, the one covenant promise, sloganized as '. . . I will be your God, and you shall be my people,' which God was fulfilling to his elect all through his successive orderings of covenant faith and life."[21]

So that's it. The covenant hermeneutic is a way of reading Scripture that insists the only way to read Scripture is through a covenantal frame—and that covenantal frame teaches that there is one covenant of grace, so there can only be one people of God, and that one people of God is all the elect through all the ages. The consequence is simply this: any promises made to Israel in the Old Testament can legitimately, by means of this hermeneutic, be fulfilled to the saints of the New Testament. If the promises don't seem to line up very well because they look like "sensuous, earthly forms,"[22] then we must look at those promises again; we must find a spiritual reading that allows the fulfillment of those promises to be seen in ways that fit the spiritual blessings poured out on the New Testament church. This is precisely because of the principle of unity. The covenant hermeneutic is indeed a hermeneutic of unity: there is one predestination, there is one covenant, there is one salvation, and therefore there is one people of God.

To recapitulate, then: the covenant hermeneutic is a way of reading Scripture that starts with the pursuit of authorial intent, and then applies a theological dictum—the unity of the covenant of grace—in the pursuit of the divine message of Scripture.

A LITERAL TURN: THE DISPENSATIONAL HERMENEUTIC

The same traditional attraction to the principle of authorial intent gave rise to another distinct hermeneutic. While the seeds of this hermeneutic—like the seeds of the covenant hermeneutic—may be traced, at least in snippets, to earlier stages in Christian history, its developed form—again like the covenant hermeneutic—appeared after the Reformation. This approach to the reading of Scripture we might call the dispensational hermeneutic.

In the pages that follow, I shall explain the elements that distinguish the dispensational hermeneutic from the covenant hermeneutic. This is because the dispensational hermeneutic arose, at least in developed form, in a time when the covenant hermeneutic had already become well-entrenched. It has always been somewhat natural to identify the dispensational hermeneutic by means of its differences from the covenant hermeneutic, and that approach does produce a valuable discussion. But I see the two differing hermeneutics as variations on a theme—there is much in common between the two, and they even share the goal of determining God's intended message in Scripture—and a more helpful approach is to start not with the differences between the two, but with the theological foundations of the dispensational hermeneutic.

Further, I should note up front that I am *not* suggesting that any of these affirmations are missing from the covenant hermeneutic. Instead, it seems to be a matter of *emphasis*. For example, dispensationalists typically do not deny the unity of the people of God. But that unity does not form the foundation of the dispensational hermeneutic; that unity grows out of the variegated plan of God as Scripture is read in a more literal fashion.[23] Ladd hints at a similar understanding of the boundary between a dispensational heremeneutic and a nondispensational hermeneutic when he writes:

> Here is the basic watershed between a dispensational and a nondispensational theology. Dispensationalism forms its eschatology by a literal interpretation of the Old Testament and then fits the New Testament into it. A nondispensational eschatology forms its theology from the explicit teaching of the New Testament. It confesses that it cannot be sure how the Old Testament prophecies of the end are to be fulfilled, for (a) the first coming of Christ was accomplished in terms not foreseen by a literal interpretation of the Old Testament, and (b) there are unavoidable indications that the Old Testament promises to Israel are fulfilled in the Christian church.[24]

The Nature of Revelation

Perhaps the first topic that needs to be addressed in analyzing the dispensational hermeneutic is the nature of divine revelation. As I mentioned earlier, both the covenant hermeneutic and the dispensational hermeneutic affirm that the goal of reading Scripture is to identify the meaning intended by God. This common affirmation drives both hermeneutical approaches, but due to other theological emphases, it drives them in slightly different directions. The dispensationalist is likely to emphasize the perspicuity, or clarity, of the divine message. Actually, the dispensationalist is likely to articulate a point about the divine message that goes a half-step further: *God's message can be understood by those to whom it is originally given.* Or, to say it another way, God does not normally reveal Himself or His plan in ways that are completely incomprehensible. Now, of course there are elements of the divine message that exceed our comprehension—elements around which we simply cannot wrap our finite minds. How this affirmation takes shape in the dispensational hermeneutic we will examine shortly.

Excursus: The Irony of the Reformed Doctrine of Perspicuity

It should be noted very clearly at this point that the perspicuity of the divine message is explicitly affirmed by the Reformed tradition. For example, the Westminster Confession, chapter 1, states that "all things in Scripture are not alike plain in themselves, nor alike clear unto all; yet those things which are necessary to be known, believed, and observed, for salvation, are so clearly propounded and opened in some place of Scripture or other, that not only the learned, but the unlearned, in a due use of the ordinary means, may attain unto a sufficient understanding of them."

But this affirmation, upon closer inspection, leads the covenant hermeneutic into a deep irony. Namely, this understanding of perspicuity must necessarily exclude the message of the Old Testament prophets. For they prophesied to the children of Israel about a time of purification for Israel, and a time of restoration for Israel, and a coming kingdom for Israel during which Jerusalem itself would be rebuilt and adorned—but according to the covenant hermeneutic *none of these promises can be understood without the hermeneutical key, which is Christ as revealed in the New Testament.*

In other words, Old Testament Israel had precisely *no chance* of understanding the true meaning of the prophets' message. For Old Testament Israel, then, the message of the prophets as found in Scripture was *irretrievably imperspicuous.*

This is one reason dispensationalists are not enchanted by the apparent simplicity of the covenant hermeneutic: it leads to real difficulty in accounting for the entirety of Scripture. The simplicity of a theologically determined unity results in hermeneutical bifurcation—a dividing into two branches.

The Progress of Revelation

Beyond perspicuity, dispensationalists in a discussion of divine revelation are also likely to affirm the incremental nature of revelation. This second affirmation might show up in a form something like this: *God's revelation of Himself and His plan takes place progressively throughout history.* As a matter of fact, this observation is so prevalent it even has a name—progressive revelation. Again, this is not an affirmation unique to the world of dispensationalism, but dispensationalists are likely to put greater emphasis on it.

Logically, affirming progressive revelation flows out of the previous affirmation. For if God's message to humanity is understandable by those who receive it, the idea of progressive revelation best fits the content of revelation recorded in Scripture.

One example of this should be sufficient to demonstrate the logical connection. The earthly ministry of Jesus is described in the Old Testament—but that description contains elements that are hard to reconcile in prospect. How do prophecies of the suffering servant fit with prophecies of a glorious kingdom rule? This question is easy to answer in retrospect (there are two comings of our Lord—one in humility and one in glorious power), but very difficult to assemble beforehand. (Just ask the disciples of our Lord during His earthly ministry!) The biblically necessary conclusion that the Old Testament prophecies conflate aspects of our Lord's first and second comings demonstrates the power of the principle called progressive revelation.

THE DISPENSATIONAL HERMENEUTIC SUMMARIZED

These two principles on the nature of revelation and the progress of revelation are sufficient to summarize the path to a dispensational hermeneutic. If one affirms that Scripture can be understood by those to whom it was originally given, one is well on the way to a hermeneutic of consistent literalism. And if one affirms the principle of progressive revelation, that hermeneutic of consistent literalism is buttressed.

What I am arguing so far is this: The dispensational hermeneutic is a commitment to literalism, but as we have seen it is a commitment to literalism that is distinct from the literalism of the covenant hermeneutic. It is, in this light, fair to characterize the hermeneutic of dispensationalism as a (more) consistent literalism.

What is more, a more complete investigation of this theme of literalism will lead us to an understanding of unity and diversity within the ranks of dispensationalism, for the principle of literalism itself will serve as the unifying factor, whereas various dispensationalists' answer to the question "how far can we push a literal hermeneutic?" will serve to clarify the diversity within dispensationalism. It is to a discussion of this unity and diversity that we now turn.

UNITY IN DISPENSATIONAL HERMENEUTICS: LITERALISM

So what exactly is this literal hermeneutic? While any attempt to answer this question will likely provoke a number of additional questions, we must at least attempt an answer in the interests of clarity. So here goes: *A literal hermeneutic is an approach to Scripture that finds the meaning of the text in the plain or normal sense of the text in its context.* (Notice that we have circled around again to the idea of grammatical-historical interpretation.)[25]

A literal hermeneutic allows for the presence of images and figures of speech, for such devices still function to convey a meaning that is literally determined.

While this (or any other attempt, for that matter) can certainly be improved, it might be wise to forestall any huge argument at this point by recognizing again that the vast majority of evangelicals do not need a tutorial on literal interpretation, because this is the way they normally approach Scripture.

Take, for example, evangelical readings of John 1:1, "In the beginning was the Word, and the Word was with God, and the Word was God." We evangelicals might argue about the exact nature of the term "Word." Some of us might see it as a name or title, whereas others might see it as some other kind of figure. But the truth is, we all agree that in this context it refers to the eternal Son of God—the person of the Trinity who became flesh in the person of Jesus.

So what keeps this understanding from moving into what we might call a "spiritualizing hermeneutic"? The answer is that the normal rules of language, functioning along with the contents of the passage itself, in its various contexts, make it clear that the Word in John 1:1 is to be understood as the divine Son in human flesh. After all, John 1:14 says, "and the Word became flesh, and dwelt among us." But why do we claim that the Word is a divine person? Well, the short answer is because we read John 1:1 literally. It says, "The Word was God." This is not read as a figure of speech, but literally.

By the way, it is worth pausing to recognize what just happened here. We just discovered that many evangelicals are going to agree wholeheartedly on our approach to a huge number of scriptural passages. That is precisely why a dispensationalist might be very happy with a commentary on the gospel of John that is written by a covenant theologian—or why a covenant theologian might be very happy with a dispensationalist's commentary on Luke.[26] Make no mistake. We will always find details upon which we will disagree—but for much of Scripture these disagreements are *not* due to the issue of literalism. Evangelicals read Scripture literally, for the most part. The interesting observation, at least for the purposes of this essay, is *when, where, and why* some evangelicals abandon a literal approach to Scripture. I am arguing that the unifying factor in dispensationalism is indeed a systemic commitment to literal interpretation.

I recognize that this claim may indeed create some tension with the expressed views of two scholars whom I respect greatly. In *Progressive Dispensationalism*, Blaising and Bock carefully set out their reasons for distancing their views on interpretation, literalism, and the grammatical-historical method from the corresponding views found within revised dispensationalism.[27] But I think any perceived tension between what I am suggesting here and what Blaising and Bock have argued elsewhere is just that: a perceived tension without substance. This is because I am arguing for the unifying effects of literalism while specifically and intentionally focusing on the *systemic* roots of that principle rather than the success rate in applying that principle to every passage in Scripture.

So I say it again: a literal hermeneutic is what creates unity within the variety of dispensational readings of Scripture. But that literal hermeneutic is here understood to be the rejection of a systemically mandated abandonment of literalism for significant portions of Scripture.

One last word: I believe that this approach is also consistent with the self-description of non-dispensationalists as well. A number of reputable authors could be cited, but for the sake of brevity we will content ourselves with but a few.

We have the testimony of J. I. Packer and Willem VanGemeren (noted earlier), but even more recent non-dispensationalists end up (maybe unwillingly?) supporting this claim. Kim Riddlebarger, in his landmark work *A Case for Amillennialism,* cites with approval an older Reformed writer who explains how an amillennialist can tell what interpretive rules to follow when the amillennialialist "reject[s] the literal method of interpretation as the universal rule for the interpretation of all prophecies."[28] Consequently, even though Riddlebarger later claims that a Reformed approach to Scripture is "literal" while the dispensational approach is "literalistic," it becomes quite clear that he has redefined literalism. Note his words: "It is amillenarians, not dispensationalists, who interpret prophecy literally in that *they follow the literal sense of how the writers of the New Testament interpret Old Testament prophecy*" (emphasis added).[29]

Indeed, it looks entirely defensible to say that a literal hermeneutic is the unifying factor in various dispensational approaches to Scripture. But that brings us to an even larger question: What factors account for the diversity of dispensational approaches to Scripture?

DIVERSITY IN DISPENSATIONAL HERMENEUTICS: THE LIMITS OF LITERALISM

The bad news is this: We cannot hope to begin to discuss all of the factors that contribute to the diversity of approaches to Scripture within the world of dispensationalism. We simply do not have the space to do so. But the good news is this: Having approached the subject as we have, there is a plausible and defensible concept that can help us summarize the development of diversity. Namely, the pursuit of a literal hermeneutic binds various dispensational approaches to Scripture together; noting *when, where, how, and why* various dispensationalists modify that approach will help us understand the variety of approaches within dispensationalism. To say it a different way, the varieties within dispensationalism are identified by how the principle of literalism is adapted, modified, or rejected.

Let's adopt the taxonomic structure suggested by Blaising and Bock—at least for the sake of discussion—and envision dispensationalism in three major movements: classic, revised, and progressive.[30] Even without "taking sides," it becomes crystal clear that the revised versus progressive debate does indeed revolve around different understandings of what it means to pursue a literal hermeneutic. If we take Blaising and Bock's perspective, revised dispensationalism is a system tied to a too-simple understanding of the literal hermeneutic. Blaising says, "Hermeneutics has become much more complex today than when Charles Ryrie affirmed literal interpretation as the 'clear, plain, normal' method of interpretation."[31] Clearly Blaising and Bock intend to offer, as part of their system, a more developed and nuanced approach to the literal hermeneutic.

So what are some of these differences of opinion on the literal hermeneutic? Without going into great detail (that would require a series of additional essays), we can very easily highlight a few of them. In this context, it is highly instructive to consider the list of items that cause Blaising and Bock to suggest amendments to Ryrie's kind of hermeneutic. While this list is not intended to be exhaustive, I certainly hope that it will be illustrative.[32]

Some of the elements that Blaising and Bock suggest are these: the role of preunderstanding in interpretation, developments in understanding how readers approach texts, developments in wrestling with the implications of the Bible's inspiration, developments in understanding how the literary context shapes interpretation, and developments in understanding how the theological context shapes interpretation. This, in essence, is why Blaising and Bock suggest that Ryrie's grammatical-historical approach to a literal hermeneutic might be improved by making it a grammatical-historical-literary-theological approach to a literal hermeneutic.

One difference highlighted by Blaising and Bock has to do with the role of the canon in shaping the interpretation of any given passage. In other words, how do inter-textual connections within the canon affect our reading of a passage? As most can quickly see, this is an extremely relevant question—but dispensationalists can sometimes disagree on exactly how to answer this responsibly. Some consider this a threat to the purity of the literal hermeneutic, whereas others see it as the only responsible way to pursue the literal hermeneutic. This difference leads to variety within dispensational interpretations of Scripture.

Another difference that Blaising and Bock mention might be called the question of theological interpretation. Again, the same kind of question arises. How do related theological principles affect our reading of any given passage of Scripture? And again, dispensationalists differ on the answer to this question, leading to more variety.

I am not trying to resolve this debate, nor to mediate a resolution. I am simply observing that Blaising and Bock identify explicitly their reservations about Ryrie's version of a literal hermeneutic. It needs, they explain carefully, to be amended in certain specific respects. The result, they insist, is a *more appropriate literal hermeneutic.*

On the other hand, if we consider Ryrie's perspective, we find once again an affirmation—from the other side of the debate—that the issue is disagreement on what a literal hermeneutic actually is. Progressive dispensationalism has departed from the traditional view of a literal hermeneutic. Ryrie writes, "Clearly, progressive dispensationalists are distancing themselves from the consistent literal hermeneutics of normative dispensationalism by introducing 'complementary hermeneutics.' "[33]

Everyone agrees. The central factor accounting for the variety within dispensationalism is the variety of perspectives on the literal hermeneutic.

At the end of the day, our principle seems secure: The literal hermeneutic giveth, and the literal hermeneutic taketh away. It provides a degree of unity for dispensationalism, and it also demonstrates the primary factor in creating variety within dispensationalism.

A TEST CASE: THE PLACE OF CHRIST IN DISPENSATIONAL HERMENEUTICS

An interesting opportunity to test the accuracy of this discussion on the unity and diversity of dispensational hermeneutics arises when we consider the place of Christ in hermeneutics. One very popular approach to reading Scripture is known as the "Christological hermeneutic." Put simply, this hermeneutic affirms that Christ is the key to understanding the Scriptures. Further, this very question is raised by the doctrinal statement of Dallas Theological Seminary (DTS), which reads, in part, "We believe that all the Scriptures center about the Lord Jesus Christ in His person and work in His first and second coming, and hence that no portion, even of the Old Testament, is properly read, or understood, until it leads to Him."[34]

Using the claims previously made in this essay as a guide, we should expect dispensational perspectives on the question of the place of Christ in hermeneutics to display a degree of variety based on *when, where, how, and why* a given dispensational perspective modifies the basic literal hermeneutic.

Indeed, this seems to be a very reasonable description of the variety that we actually find within dispensationalism on this topic. Some dispensationalists, embracing a more robust vision of the roles of theology and canon in hermeneutics, seem willing to affirm that the person and work of Christ factor into the hermeneutical approach to every passage in Scripture. Others, conversely, argue that Christ is simply the central figure in the Bible story—and as a result the role of Christ in hermeneutics is not so much to shape the interpretation of any given passage but rather to anchor that passage's place in the overall story by identifying the passage's relationship to the central character. This view, in other words, denies that Christ gives shape to the reading of any given passage; rather, every given passage contributes to the shape of the overall story—the central figure of which is Christ. Notice that this view is discernibly less eager to accept modifications to the traditional literal hermeneutic, and as such may be assigned a place a little closer to the center point. Given the history of the DTS doctrinal statement, this assessment makes sense. The framers of the statement, writing long before the development of progressive dispensationalism, chose to articulate their view by saying that all passages in Scripture "lead to Him."[35] The very choice of the word "lead" appears to put some distance between the thought of the statement and a stronger version of the Christological hermeneutic.

Numerous additional nuances in describing the place of Christ in hermeneutics could be investigated, but it seems reasonable to observe that our central claim has displayed significant diagnostic accuracy in wrestling with the concept of a Christological hermeneutic in dispensationalism.

CONCLUSION

There is still plenty of room for disagreement between non-dispensationalists and dispensationalists. Whose hermeneutic is more appropriate in the light of Scripture? And even within dispensationalism, we are still going to find discussion regarding what understanding of the literal hermeneutic is the most reasonable. Those discussions, in my view, are worthwhile. Brothers and sisters who disagree ought to discuss openly their differences.

What I have argued, however, is this. Dispensationalism and its distinctive hermeneutical approach occupies a legitimate place in the catalogue of Bible-believing, Christian approaches to Scripture. It is a child of the Reformation, and honors the basic reformation approach to Scripture. In its unique implementation of a literal hermeneutic, however, dispensationalism distinguishes itself from nondispensational approaches to Scripture, and finds a unifying theme that, despite disagreement from some within the dispensational fold, binds dispensationalists together. The *systemic* connections of the literal hermeneutic within dispensationalism ensure that.

Further, the very mention of the literal hermeneutic brings disagreement—even within dispensationalism. But as it turns out, this disagreement does not fracture dispensationalism; it creates variety within dispensational interpretation as various dispensationalists seek to define and implement the literal hermeneutic.

Fans of American football are unified, in some sense, by that affinity. And that unity is not fractured as different groups of American football fans propose slightly different understandings of excellence in American football. I sincerely wish (but I know that I cannot do so with conviction) that I could define excellence in American football as *having a big blue star on your helmet.*

Notes

1. Luis Alonso Schökel, *A Manual of Hermeneutics* (Sheffield: Sheffield Academic Press, 1998), 13.
2. Anthony C. Thiselton, *Hermeneutics* (Grand Rapids: Eerdmans, 2009), 4. Emphasis in the original.
3. One need only look at a book like *Biblical Hermeneutics: Five Views,* ed. Stanley E. Porter and Beth M. Stovell (Downers Grove, IL: InterVarsity, 2012) to find abundant evidence for this claim. In a wonderfully helpful work aimed primarily at the evangelical world, we find five distinct views, each of which represents an entire spectrum of unique approaches to interpretation.
4. E. D. Hirsch, Jr., *Validity in Interpretation* (New Haven, CT: Yale University Press, 1967), 1.
5. Virtually any book on biblical interpretation, if it is aimed at the evangelical world, will have something to say about speech-act theory. See, for example, Part 2 in Kevin J. Vanhoozer, *Is There a Meaning in This Text?* (Grand Rapids: Zondervan, 1998), or Vanhoozer's chapter, "The Semantics of Biblical Literature: Truth and Scripture's Diverse Literary Forms," in *Hermeneutics, Authority, and Canon,* ed. D. A. Carson and John D. Woodbridge (Grand Rapids: Zondervan, 1986).
6. The example of Wolterstorff raises one of the most delightful occasions for celebrating the diversity of views on biblical hermeneutics. Wolterstorff is criticized by Grenz and Franke for remaining "at least at times—too closely focused on the author who produced the text, rather than on the text itself being canon" (Stanley J. Grenz and John R. Franke, *Beyond Foundationalism: Shaping Theology in a Postmodern Context* [Louisville, KY: Westminster John Knox Press, 2001], 74), while Lundin, in introducing a volume to which Wolterstorff contributed a chapter, says, "Not one of these authors would share the conviction of E. D. Hirsch—a belief widely held among conservative biblical scholars—that the goal of textual interpretation is the recovery of the intention of the text's author. Such a view implies that it is possible for interpreters to set aside fully their own assumptions and understandings" (Roger Lundin, *Disciplining Hermeneutics* [Grand Rapids: Eerdmans, 1997], 21).
7. Nicholas Wolterstorff, *Divine Discourse* (Cambridge: Cambridge University Press, 1995), 136.
8. Ibid., 134.
9. Ibid., 155.
10. Ibid., 135.
11. David M. Williams, *Receiving the Bible in Faith: Historical and Theological Exegesis* (Washington, D.C.: Catholic University of America Press, 2004), 6. The resurgence is also demonstrated by evangelicals such as Craig Blomberg, who writes, "Most of what writers like E. D. Hirsch Jr. have meant in insisting on interpretation according to authorial intent refers to those dimensions of a writer's designs that are disclosed in the actual text he or she produced, especially when one can locate the text in its original historical context and analyze the sociocultural settings and contexts in which it was composed" (Craig L. Blomberg, "The Historical–Critical/Grammatical Response," in *Biblical Hermeneutics: Five Views,* ed. Porter and Stovell, 138).
12. This very challenge explains the existence of articles such as Elliott Johnson, "Dual Authorship and the Single Intended Meaning of Scripture," *Bibliotheca Sacra* 143 (1986): 218–27.
13. Blomberg, "The Historical-Critical/Grammatical Response," 27.
14. Lundin, *Disciplining Hermeneutics,* 21.
15. See on this point Stephen R. Spencer, "Reformed Theology, Covenant Theology, and Dispensationalism," in *Integrity of Heart, Skillfulness of Hands: Biblical and Leadership Studies in Honor of Donald K. Campbell,* ed. Charles H. Dyer and Roy B. Zuck (Grand Rapids: Baker, 1994), 238–54.
16. J. I. Packer, "Introduction: On Covenant Theology," in Herman Witsius, *The Economy of the Covenants between God and Man* (repr., Escondido, CA: The den Dulk Christian Foundation, 1990), 1.
17. David A. Weir, "*Foedus Naturale*: The Origins of Federal Theology in Sixteenth Century Reformation Thought" (PhD diss., University of St. Andrews, 1984), 188.

18. Again, Weir's work is helpful in tracing the development of a covenant schema. See especially chapters 3 and 4 in Weir, "*Foedus Naturale*."

19. Willem A. VanGemeren, "Israel as the Hermeneutical Crux in the Interpretation of Prophecy," *Westminster Theological Journal* 45 (1983): 134.

20. Jay Adams, *The Time Is at Hand* (Philadelphia: Presbyterian and Reformed, 1970), 41. Cited by Willem A. VanGemeren, "Israel as the Hermeneutical Crux in the Interpretation of Prophecy (II)," *Westminster Theological Journal* 46 (1984): 265.

21. J. I. Packer, "Introduction: On Covenant Theology," in Witsius, *The Economy of the Covenants between God and Man*, 5, 7.

22. Herman Bavinck, John Bolt, and John Vriend, *Reformed Dogmatics: Holy Spirit, Church, and New Creation*, vol. 4 (Grand Rapids: Baker, 2008), 659. To be fair, Bavinck sees in these forms of expression an image of something heavenly.

23. Note again that both the covenant hermeneutic and the dispensational hermeneutic feature a robust commitment to literalism in interpretation. What sets them apart is their respective *systemic approach* to literalism. The covenant hermeneutic jettisons literalism wherever the unity of predestination, the unity of the covenant, the unity of salvation, or the unity of the people of God is perceived to be threatened. The dispensational hermeneutic, on the other hand, does not jettison a literal hermeneutic for any *systemic* principle; it affirms the literal hermeneutic while admitting that the literal hermeneutic allows for a variety of perspectives on the use of imagery and figure in any given passage.

24. George Eldon Ladd, "Historic Premillennialism," in *The Meaning of the Millennium: Four Views*, ed. Robert G. Clouse (Downers Grove, IL: InterVarsity, 1977), 20–21.

25. It is commonplace in evangelicalism to draw some kind of firm connection between a literal hermeneutic and the grammatical-historical method of interpretation. The example of William B. Tolar is illustrative: "No element of interpretation is more important to an accurate understanding of the Bible than is the grammatical-historical method. It is the *sine qua non* for any valid understanding of God's Word. Without an honest, careful, intelligent use of grammatical and historical knowledge, there is little or no hope for a correct interpretation of documents written in foreign languages within several different ancient historical contexts. To fail to use proper grammatical rules or to ignore those historical contexts is most certainly to guarantee failure in understanding the writers' intended meanings. . . . It is a moral imperative for the interpreter to do his or her best to understand the text correctly so as to discover the meaning placed there by the original author. Anything less is intellectually dishonest and spiritually immoral and unworthy of a person of integrity." Tolar, "The Grammatical-Historical Method," in Bruce Corley, Steve Lemke, and Grant Lovejoy, *Biblical Hermeneutics*, 2nd ed. (Nashville: Broadman & Holman, 2002), 21.

26. Yes, I chose that one intentionally. This should be construed as a thinly veiled reference to my colleague's outstanding work on Luke (see the two-volume commentary on the gospel of Luke written by Darrell L. Bock). But you already knew that, since you are attuned to issues of context . . .

27. See chapter 1, "The Extent and Varieties of Dispensationalism," in Craig Blaising and Darrell Bock, *Progressive Dispensationalism* (Grand Rapids: Baker, 1993). In this chapter, Blaising disputes the claim that consistent literalism is a distinguishing feature of dispensationalism (or at least the forms of dispensationalism that existed prior to progressive dispensationalism). Further, Blaising disagrees with the way revised dispensationalism made use of the term "literal interpretation," claiming that it was used in such a way that it applied only to the system of revised dispensationalism in the first place. While Blaising's observations are, as usual, perceptive, I do not see his argument as a challenge to what I am saying. My reasons are these: (1) Blaising was, contextually, trying to carve out an acceptable "concept space" for the then-new idea of progressive dispensationalism. It is normal to accentuate differences in order to show the uniqueness of a new idea. As a result, some of his arguments are a little overstated. (One example is his claim that neither classical nor revised dispensationalism was "consistently literal" in its interpretation of Scripture. However, Ryrie clearly used the phrase as a description of revised dispensationalism in contrast to a covenant hermeneutic—and even some covenant theologians will admit that this is a reasonable description.) (2) Literalism considered in

this light—an approach that is either systemically affirmed (as in dispensationalism) or systemically denied in certain places (as in the covenant hermeneutic)—is still a common feature in all forms of dispensationalism. It is rather instructive to find Blaising exulting (and justifiably so, from his perspective) that consistent "grammatical-historical interpretation . . . is much closer to being realized in the hermeneutics of progressive dispensationalism" (*Progressive Dispensationalism,* 44). Evidently, from the perspective of all forms of dispensationalism, the literal approach to Scripture is considered key—even though Blaising is correct in questioning exactly what different dispensationalists mean by "literal."

28. Kim Riddlebarger, *A Case for Amillennialism* (Grand Rapids: Baker, 2003), 37.
29. Ibid., 41.
30. I will not pause to define or defend this structure here. You can find it in chapter 1 of Blaising and Bock, *Progressive Dispensationalism.* The point I am making stands even without a deep understanding of this taxonomic structure.
31. Blaising and Bock, *Progressive Dispensationalism,* 43.
32. All of these items are drawn from Blaising and Bock, *Progressive Dispensationalism*, Part Two: Hermeneutics.
33. Ryrie, *Dispensationalism* (2007), 100.
34. *DTS Doctrinal Statement,* "Article I: The Scriptures." See http://www.dts.edu/about/doctrinal statement.
35. The current form of the DTS doctrinal statement dates, at least in this particular area, to the original 1924 doctrinal statement prepared by Lewis Sperry Chafer and others for the board of the Evangelical Theological College. Apparently, in the process of preparing the statement, Chafer consulted such figures as W. H. Griffith Thomas, R. A. Torrey, and A. C. Gaebelein. See John D. Hannah, *An Uncommon Union* (Grand Rapids: Zondervan, 2009), 87–88. The full text of the 1924 doctrinal statement is presented in an appendix starting on page 299 of *An Uncommon Union.*

5

God's Plan for History Prior to Christ

EUGENE H. MERRILL

To say that God the Creator has a plan is almost a tautological statement. Put another way, the very notion of a personal God who has no rationale for what He has brought into being is a logical and theological absurdity.

The technical term to describe divine (or any other) purpose, especially one in flux, is "entelechy," a term suggesting a deliberate course of action that leads to a certain and comprehensible end. Since we as human beings track the progress of the implementation of plans within temporal frameworks, that is, in chronological and historical categories, the working out of the plan of God must be viewed similarly, although, of course, without human limitations.

The approach here, then, is diachronic, an approach that seeks to discover God's plan for history in the Old Testament era, before the Christ appeared, and as it was progressively revealed by God and recorded in the sacred texts inspired by Him.

The progress of the outworking of the divine plan may also be described in terms of dispensations, that is, God's various ways in various times of moving His purposes forward. At least six of these are isolated in this chapter: (1) the dispensation of the creation mandate, (2) the dispensation of human government,

(3) the dispensation of grace, (4) the dispensation of law, (5) the dispensation of messianic redemption, and (6) the dispensation of eschatological renewal of all things.

These periods will be defined by the scope of the origination of the texts themselves and not by the eons of time they presuppose and describe, for the meaning of persons and/or events is not to be found primarily in them as points of data or "facts" but in their interpretation by the prophets and poets who composed and compiled the accounts of the Old Testament canon—the only reliable witnesses to the divine purpose. Thus, our task is to trace the contours of the plan from its most ancient expression in the Mosaic Torah (ca. 1400 BC) through the writings of the Chronicler (ca. 400 BC), the span of an entire millennium. Canonically speaking, the approach will be to consider the three sections of the Hebrew Bible *seriatim*: Torah, Prophets, and Writings. Special attention will be given to the matter of continuity and discontinuity in the sequence of the various dispensations.

THE ORIGIN OF THE PLAN

Its Revelation

The first of the dispensations consisted of the so-called creation mandate, expressed as an imperative in the five words God spoke to humankind according to the Old Testament accounts: "Bear fruit, *and* multiply, *and* fill the earth, *and* subdue it, *and* rule over [its created beings]" (Gen. 1:28).[1] God's plan is thus articulated in such a manner as to include humankind in partnership with Him as "lords over all the manor." This is more finely set forth in the description of mankind as the image of God (v. 26), that is, the very representation of God on the earth.[2] How this should work out ideally is voiced in Jesus' model prayer: "Your will be done on earth as it is in heaven" (Matt. 6:10 HCSB).

Its Disruption

The dispensation of creation and the Edenic world in which mankind was placed required nothing more or less than obedience on the part of humans. The first practical test to determine man's willingness and ability to implement the plan of God was in the microcosmically tiny space of the garden where God placed the first man with the explicit command to "work it" and "watch over it" (Gen. 2:15 HCSB).[3] Instead, both man and woman submitted to the allurements of the serpent over which they had been granted dominion (Gen. 1:28). They exercised their own free will in opposition to the plan of God, thus alienating mankind from God and invoking upon themselves and all creation the harmful consequences that naturally followed such egregious disloyalty to God and to the gracious covenant He had granted and that bound them together (Gen. 3:14–19).[4]

The command to be fruitful and to multiply would remain in effect but it would now be implemented through the woman's multiplied pain in childbirth and her loss of independent dominion (Gen. 3:16). As for the man, he would continue to work the soil but with backbreaking toil all the days of his life until he fell exhausted at last and became a part of the very ground from which he was created (vv. 17–19).[5] This turn of events portended and required a new dispensational avenue. The curse therefore must not be understood as the undoing of the divine plan, as an irredeemable rupture between God and His creation, in particular between Him and humankind. Man still stood as the image of God through whom He would carry out His creation purposes albeit with alterations consistent with man's fallen state.

GOD'S RESPONSE AND HIS ETERNAL PLAN IN ALTERED FORM

The Noahic Covenant

The Continuation of God's Plan

Man's fall from his lofty position as the unmarred image of God resulted in universal calamity. All of Adam and Eve's descendants, like them, were forced now to make their way through mortal life both as inveterate sinners and as slaves to the environment over which they had been created to reign. Their plight is summed up early on in the flood narrative: "Yahweh saw that human wickedness was great [lit., had multiplied][6] throughout the Earth and that every inclination of his thoughts was only wicked all the time" (Gen. 6:5; author's translation[7]). Adam's sin had forced his expulsion from the garden; its multiplication, like a deadly virus, now called for expulsion from the whole earth itself in a mighty universal, cataclysmic event. However, just as Adam and Eve still remained within the orbit of God's plan for history, so Noah and his immediate family became the seedbed of a continuation of that plan, a gracious and necessary continuation if the creation purposes of God were to remain intact.[8]

The continuation of the plan through Noah is abundantly clear. A covenant with Adam is at least inferred (Gen. 6:18, "My covenant"); with Noah it is explicitly stated: "I am establishing my covenant with you" (9:8). That this is a reaffirmation of the creation mandate given to Adam is put beyond doubt by the almost identical wording between Genesis 1:28 and 9:1: "Be fruitful, multiply, and fill the earth." However, the crippling effects of the fall are now much in evidence and thus a new dispensation comes to pass, one that shifts the innate dominion of humankind over creation to one imposed by his superior status. Adam was told he would have unfettered dominion over all things as the vicegerent of God, but Noah and all who followed him would rule only by superior force and intelligence. Adam had yielded to the serpent, over which he should have had mastery, but from then on mankind's exercise of authority would be uneasy because there would be inherent fear and distrust between human beings and the lower animal world, so much so that man could and would even become carnivorous (Gen. 9:2–3).

The Establishing of an Institutional Government

Another aspect of the Noahic covenant—and a hallmark of its concessionary nature—was the establishment of institutional government, the central feature of a new dispensation, that of government. Direct rule by God could no longer be retained because of the unbridgeable chasm between His holiness and man's sinfulness and would be supplanted by indirect and intermediary political systems that, even in their imperfections, would be divinely appointed and regulated.[9] This is exemplified in the case of (implicit) murder. Though animal life could be taken for food, human blood could not be shed by another human being, for all persons, no matter how evil, representatively retained the dignity of the "image of God."[10] An act of premeditated homicide was therefore tantamount to deicide and must be punished by death at the hands of the collective community (government) for that reason (Gen. 9:6).

A final point to be made in the divinely intended function of the Noahic covenant is Noah's prophetic promise in the singling out of his son Shem as a vehicle of special interest in the plan of God for history (Gen. 9:26–27). The author develops this idea further by tracing Shem's line to Eber, the patronym of the Hebrew people, the first of whom was Abraham (Gen. 10:21; cf. 11:10–26).[11] The Hebrew people would thus be known as S(h)emites, the bearers of the ultimate fulfillment of God's historical plan of redemption and renewal.

The Abrahamic Covenant

Its Presentation and Purpose

The Noahic covenant signaled that creation renewal was already under way. Shem's offspring would include Eber, the "original" Hebrew, and would culminate in the Shem genealogy with Abram, the first man in the Bible to be called a Hebrew (Gen. 14:13). God's unconditional call of Abram was founded on grace alone, but with Abram's selection came the corollary of obedience if the promises of the covenant were to come to pass. Clearly, the dispensation introduced in Abraham coupled the creation mandate with regulations as to how it could be implemented through one man and his seed.

Almost certainly a pagan worshiper of the moon god Nanna/Sin, head of the pantheon at Ur, Abram was called by Yahweh into a covenant relationship through which the seed already hinted at in Genesis 3:15 would find penultimate expression in a nation (גּוֹי). That nation (or people) would function in two ways: (1) It would be the bearer of blessing to the nations of the earth that blessed it and (2) it would be the occasion of the cursing of nations that cursed it (Gen. 12:1–3).[12] The covenant here is called penultimate because it does not clearly focus on a single messianic deliverer as later texts do.[13]

Its Development in Genesis

The terms of the covenant with Abraham are restated in precisely the same terms to Isaac and Jacob, the son and grandson of Abraham. Each was chosen by God, as was Abraham, by an act of sheer grace. Isaac, not Ishmael, was elected (Gen. 21:12; 22:16–18) as was Jacob, not Esau (Gen. 27:29; 28:13–14; 35:9–13; 48:3–4).[14] Again, the essentials of the promise to Abraham recur in the declarations to both Isaac and Jacob: land, multiplied seed, the blessing of the nations that blessed Israel (Gen. 26:24), and the cursing of those that did not (Gen. 27:29; 28:3, 14).

Its Crystallization in a Nation

The dispensation of grace now comes to the fore, at least in germinal form, casting a beam of light toward a glorious future day when that principle would be more fully manifested. Two Hebrew words are used interchangeably in the Old Testament for both "people" and "nation," namely, עַם and גּוֹי, and both occur with reference to Israel. However, the political and structural differences between the two in modern conceptualization are important in tracing the development of the Old Testament promises concerning redemption and God's renewed plan for history in a fallen world. As we shall see, the plan unfolds in a funnel-like structure in which one man, Abraham, stands as head of a people/nation which then inversely narrows to one man again, this time the messianic figure of whom the later prophets speak.[15]

The Mosaic Covenant

Historically, the line of demarcation between Israel as a people rather than a nation was drawn at the time of the exodus, specifically at Sinai with the giving of the Mosaic covenant, which functioned as the constitution and bylaws of the nascent state.[16] There and then Israel as a body lost its loosely formed tribal affiliations and melded into at least a modicum of a nation among nations. A pivotal text recounts God's gracious offer to Israel that if it swore undivided allegiance to Him and to the covenant about to be disclosed, He would make of it "his own possession,"[17] a priestly kingdom and a holy nation (Exod. 19:5–6).[18] Israel's role is thus clear: It is to be a nation that intercedes between God and the nations of the world, that is, the "image" nation through which God will work out His plan for history. To speak of it in rather New Testament terms, Israel is called to undertake the "Great Commission" of proclamation of the good news to all nations (Isa. 43:8–10; 49:5–7).

When viewed from this perspective, Israel has no end in itself, as it were, but is ancillary to God's larger program of a new creation in which dwells righteousness. It is a servant nation called to bear witness to all other nations. The Mosaic covenant, whether in its Sinai or Deuteronomy rendition, is not therefore salvific in its form and function but one subsidiary to the Abrahamic covenant. Its purpose is to provide guidance to the nation Israel as to how it must conduct itself before a Holy God and carry out its evangelistic commission.

THE ROLE OF ISRAEL IN GOD'S PLAN FOR THE FUTURE

The Conquest and Judges Period

Taking Ownership of the Land

The major theme of the book of Joshua is related to the land to be acquired by the people Israel, now rightly to be called a nation in the more technical sense. A nation without territory is self-contradictory, so it must be acquired even if, as in Israel's case, by conquest. But Israel's conquest was not without historical and theological underpinnings. First, all land is God's land and is distributed to the nations as He sees fit. Second, the land was Israel's by descent from Abraham. God had commanded Abraham to go to a land that He would show him (Gen. 12:1) and when he arrived there he began to assert ownership by "crossing over" the land and establishing altars at certain strategic places that marked the presence of Yahweh. These included Shechem in the north (Gen. 12:6–7), Bethel in the middle (12:8), and, after some time, Hebron (13:18) and Beersheba (22:19) in the near and far south.

Not to be overlooked in all this is the use of the Hebrew verb הָלַךְ, especially in the *hithpael* stem of the verb (הִתְהַלֵּךְ) as in Genesis 13:17. In such uses of the verb there is an unmistakable assertion of dominion and ownership.[19] Abraham's sojourns from border to border laid claim to all of Canaan so Israel's conquest was nothing more or less than coming back home, albeit after a more than four-century delay. This had been promised by Yahweh to Abraham from the beginning: "Your offspring will be strangers in a foreign land and will serve them under strict bondage for four hundred years. . . . Afterward I will bring them back here again" (Gen. 15:13–16).[20]

A Time of Anarchy, a Desire for a King

The central theme of Judges is the strange juxtaposition of anarchy and kingship (or the lack thereof). If land is a *sine qua non* for nationhood, the need for government is every bit as essential. This was an element deeply embedded in the Noahic covenant and later, implicitly at least, an important ingredient in the Abrahamic covenant. The patriarch was promised that kings would issue from him (Gen. 17:6). Moreover, of Sarah it was said that she would be the mother of kings (17:16). Her name change from Sarai to Sarah ("princess") already hinted at the royalty that would be manifest in her descendants. The chaotic disorder of the three hundred and fifty years of the Judges era is presented climactically in the two narratives that close the book—the apostate priest of the tribe of Dan (Judg. 17–18) and the rape and murder of a Levite's concubine (Judg. 19–21). Strikingly, each of these has a connection with Bethlehem, the priest being a citizen of that small town in Judah and the Levite's concubine likewise hailing from there. To complicate the matter further, the aforementioned priest was none other than a grandson of Moses and the place of the savage treatment of the concubine was Gibeah of Benjamin.[21] As it turned out later, David, God's chosen king, was also a Bethlehemite, whereas Saul was from Gibeah. Clearly, the stage was being set already in the days of the judges for the struggle for kingship between Benjamin and Judah and their respective royal progenies, Saul and David.[22]

In fairness to those who demanded a king for Israel, one must acknowledge that the generations of anarchic spiritual and national life could easily lead to despair. The surrounding nations, after all, had their kings and seemed to enjoy relative peace and security. Was it unreasonable for Israel also to yearn for such a system? And hadn't Moses promised that kings would arise at some point in Israel's future? And might not their present time seem to be propitious for that to begin?

The United Monarchy Period

The prophet Samuel lived in the latter part of the Judges era (ca. 1120–1025 BC) and thus witnessed with his own eyes the abysmal conditions described in the book of Judges.[23] He could understand the people's longing for stability and their demand for a king who would secure a peaceful society. Despite (1) a failed attempt to induce Gideon to rule over them a century earlier, an invitation he declined with the reminder that Yahweh alone must be king (Judg. 8:22–23), and (2) a grab for power by Gideon's son Abimelech, which ended disastrously (Judg. 9:1–57), the plea made to Samuel for a king was as insistent as ever. "Establish for us a king," they pleaded with Samuel in his old age (1 Sam. 8:5). The Lord, of course, heard the appeal and authorized Samuel to grant the wishes of the people but to inform them that their unrelenting and premature begging would bring upon themselves the consequence of a king who would virtually reduce them to enslavement (vv. 11–18).

Despite this warning, the response of the people was as predictable as ever. Their rationale for a king was threefold: (1) to mimic all the other nations, (2) to have a central figure who would regulate internal affairs, and (3) to have a military leader who would save them from their enemies (v. 20).

God's Choice for King

At this point it will be helpful to recall that human kingship was not inimical to the plan of God; in fact, as we have argued, it was implicitly at the very heart of the creation mandate. Moreover, it had roots also in the dispensation of government following the great flood. But timing is everything in the overall purposes of God, and He was not ready yet for the promised royal seed to make his grand historical entrance. The reign of Saul was a concessionary move by the Lord designed to show two things: (1) The plan and program of God is always best and (2) human attempts to move it forward or to replace it with human endeavors are sure to fail. Saul turned out as Samuel had predicted, but not all was lost, for God all the time was seeking the "man after [his] own heart" (1 Sam. 13:14; cf. 16:1–3).[24]

The choice of David long preceded his own awareness of it, to say nothing of the understanding of anyone else. He was the youngest son of an apparently ordinary citizen of the small village of Bethlehem, so unlikely a candidate that when Samuel asked to see all of Jesse's sons, David was overlooked, having been relegated to the care of the family flocks. The verb "chosen" (בָּחַר) occurs three times in the scene of the parading of the sons of Jesse before Samuel (1 Sam. 16:8–10), all in a negative sense ("not chosen"), and "rejected" (מָאַס) in one case (v. 7). On the other hand, the chosen one is called the "anointed" (מָשִׁיחַ), the one set apart by the Lord to be king (vv. 6, 12, 13). The divine seal of approval was the removal of God's Spirit from Saul and His/its[25] resting upon David from that time forward (vv. 13–14). The anointing and empowering of the Spirit here has nothing to do with salvation but with equipping for a special service (see, e.g., Judg. 3:10; 6:34; 11:29; 13:25; 14:6, 19; and 15:14).

David eventually recognized the significance of his calling and the special role he must play in the plan of God for history. A few examples of this gradual unfolding must suffice. First, King Saul himself was forced early on to concede that Yahweh was with David in a unique manner (1 Sam. 18:12, 28) and eventually he verbalized it fully (1 Sam. 24:20). Saul's son Jonathan much more readily understood that his friend David would beyond doubt become Israel's king in the place of his own father (1 Sam. 20:14–15; 23:17). In fact, he went so far as to divest himself of his princely robes to place them on David as a symbol of the certainty of David's reign (1 Sam. 18:3–4). From a most unexpected quarter came the affirmation of the servants of the Philistine ruler Achish that David was the "king of the land" (1 Sam. 21:11). Finally, from the grave Samuel the prophet declared to Saul the unmistakable assertion that "Yahweh has torn the kingdom from your hand and has given it to your friend David" (1 Sam. 28:17).[26]

The Ongoing Davidic Dynasty

The Davidic line continued most immediately with his son Solomon, who was instructed as to its theological significance and who himself spoke of it with clear understanding. David in his final days strongly affirmed the covenantal nature of Solomon's kingship (1 Kings 1:30, 35; 2:1–4; 1 Chron. 28:5–7; 29:1), and Solomon commenced his reign in light of that commission. In his dedicatory prayer on the completion of the temple he refers to Yahweh's having chosen his father and then of his succession as one chosen as well (1 Kings 8:17–21; 2 Chron. 6:10). In a special revelation Yahweh repeated His commitment to the Davidic line through Solomon that it would be established forever (1 Kings 9:5; 2 Chron. 7:17). The caveats regarding the need for obedience to the covenant stipulations do not apply to the ongoing Davidic dynasty but to the people of Israel and the continuation of their place in the land (1 Kings 9:5–6; 2 Chron. 6:16; 7:17–18).[27] The dispensation of government was, as always, based on the sovereign grace of God.

The Divided Monarchy Period

Sadly, the demise of the Davidic kingdom as a united entity was not long in coming. The author of Kings assigns much of the blame for the rupture on Solomon; in fact, the record states that the Lord appeared to Solomon and informed him that because of his covenant disloyalty his successor would be left with only Judah. The remaining tribes would then be placed in the hands of another ruler (1 Kings 11:11–13). The retention of Judah was only for the sake of David, God's chosen servant (vv. 13, 32, 34, 36). The chronicler, however, omits the guilt of Solomon and places it on Rehoboam and his unwise decisions regarding forced labor, taxation, and the like (2 Chron. 10:12–15). The result was rebellion against Rehoboam by the northern tribes and their submission to the leadership of Jeroboam, their first king. The division between Judah and Israel remained, said the historian, "to this very day" (2 Chron. 10:18), that is, till about 400 BC.

The fact remained, however, that the Davidic promises and lineage survived intact. The plan of God for history would continue even through the five hundred years of national bifurcation and beyond. The following discussion will focus on the ebb and flow of events through the divided monarchy era up to the Babylonian conquest of Judah in 586 BC. Only those insights that contribute directly to the tracing of the plan of God for Israel can be included.

The first gleam of light is shone not on Rehoboam but, ironically, on wicked Jeroboam who was reminded by the prophet Ahijah that as powerful as he might become, he could not unseat the occupant of David's throne for that dynasty would shine forever as a lamp pointing to Yahweh (1 Kings 11:36). The same image is used with reference to Rehoboam's son Abijam who, though he was evil, still represented the light of the Davidic covenant (1 Kings 15:4; cf. 2 Kings 8:19; 2 Chron. 13:5) as did Jehoram later on (2 Chron. 21:7). Despite the defection of Jehoram of Judah, who emulated the wicked kings of Israel and married Athaliah, daughter of Ahab and Jezebel, Yahweh preserved Judah "for David his servant's sake" (2 Kings 8:19).

In the mid-ninth century, it seemed that the Davidic dynasty would die out because of the purges launched by Athaliah, but the boy-king Joash was hidden and reemerged under the tutelage of Jehoiada the priest, who declared of the child: "The king's son shall reign as Yahweh has spoken concerning the offspring of David" (2 Chron. 23:3). The proclamation was followed by a covenant ceremony that solidified Joash's legitimacy as a descendent of David who thus had a right to the throne (2 Kings 11:12, 17; 2 Chron. 23:3, 11, 16).

Little is explicitly said of David or the Davidic covenant, to say nothing of the ancient Abrahamic covenant, in the awful days of Israel's decline and exile in 722 BC. The same is true of even Judah's similar experience and for the same reasons in the Babylonian destruction of Jerusalem and its temple in 586 BC, followed by the massive deportation of much of its citizenry. The work of God in preserving His people as the channel of worldwide redemptive grace was anything but dead, however, as the prophets, poets, and sages of Israel and Judah make abundantly clear elsewhere.

The Exilic and Postexilic Periods

The Bible makes no attempt to trace the diaspora of the ten northern tribes except to list the major places of resettlement: Halah and "on the Habor, the river of Gozan" (both in Mesopotamia), and "in the cities of the Medes" (2 Kings 17:6).[28] Instead, the focus is entirely on the deportation of Judah to Babylonia in 586, which by then had supplanted Assyria as the dominant power of the Middle East. The scant information in the Old Testament historical books about conditions in the seventy-year exile is supplemented by both the prophets (especially Ezekiel and Daniel) and a number of Babylonian and Persian inscriptions.[29]

Key Events for Judea during Captivity and Release

The following data are especially relevant to the theme of God's plan for history:

1. The Judean captives consisted of King Jehoiachin, his wives, his mother, an entourage of his chief personnel, craftsmen, warriors, and all others but the "poorest people of the land" (2 Kings 24:10–17; 2 Chron. 36:9–10).
2. Kings ends, however, on a note of hope. Following Nebuchadnezzar's death in 562 BC, Evil-Merodach released Jehoiachin from house arrest, put him on a royal pension, and allowed him to live out his remaining days in peace, a harbinger of better times to come (2 Kings 25:27–30).
3. Chronicles, written at least 150 years after Kings (ca. 400 BC), concludes the exilic period with the release of Jews and all other captives to their homelands in 538 by the decree of Cyrus king of Persia (2 Chron. 36:22–23). This provided the Jews an opportunity to rebuild their nation and renew their hopes for a continuation of the Davidic dynasty with all that meant for God's plan in history.

The postexilic phase of Israel's existence is related primarily in the books of Esther and Ezra-Nehemiah. The ruling power was Medo-Persia under a succession of monarchs commencing with Cyrus II (550–530 BC) and continuing with Cambyses (530–522), Darius Hystaspes (522–486), Xerxes (Ahasuerus, 486–465), Artaxerxes I (464–424), and Darius II (423–404).[30] The narrative of Esther, set in the reign of King Ahasuerus (Xerxes), demonstrates the care and preservation by Yahweh of His covenant people no matter the circumstances

(Esther 8:11, 15–17; 9:26–10:3). When an edict was made by the king to exterminate the Jews of the kingdom, Esther interposed and succeeded in having the decree reversed so that the Jews could exact against their enemies what they had proposed to do to them. The plan of God to preserve His chosen is illustrated resoundingly in this instance.

Royal Favor Shown to Ezra and Nehemiah

Ezra and Nehemiah ministered in the reign of Artaxerxes I, who showed to both of them unusual favor, again an evidence of God's continuing outworking of His purposes for His elect nation. Ezra the scribal priest returned to Jerusalem from Persia in 458 BC. He recounts the decree of Cyrus, issued long before his own times (Ezra 1:1–4), and makes much of the return of the Jewish captives under the leadership of Zerubbabel, a descendant of David himself (1 Chron. 3:10:24; Ezra 2:2; 3:8; 5:2; Hag. 2:20–23), and of Jeshua, the chief priest, who traced his lineage to Aaron through Jehozadak and Zadok (1 Chron. 6:3–15; Ezra 3:8; 10:18; Zech. 6:11).

Nehemiah, a butler to Artaxerxes, led a group of exiles back to Yehud in 445 BC where he joined Ezra in attempting to reestablish a Jewish state. He served as a governor whereas Ezra filled the office of priest; thus, the two together made up a diarchy reminiscent of the Davidic monarchy in which David combined the two roles under his headship and was anticipatory of the Messiah who would also be priest and king.[31] As priest, Ezra was concerned primarily about the so-called second temple, finished under Zerubbabel by 516, but lacking in proper furnishing and in the orderly services demanded by the Mosaic law. He therefore saw as his mission a program of instruction and reformation that would bring the community into line with these expectations. His great prayer of confession before Yahweh is rife with repentance on behalf of the nascent Davidic state (Ezra 9:5–7), gratitude for God's blessings despite Israel's past transgressions (vv. 8–9), and fervent petition that the sins of the past will never again be repeated (vv. 10–15).

Nehemiah, though not unmindful of the needs of the temple, was mainly consumed with the burden of rebuilding the political and physical structures of Yehud, in particular Jerusalem. He was concerned with walls of protection against the enemies of the people of the Lord who were already displaying hostility of the most destructively insidious kind. But he also had to deal with social, economic, and organizational considerations necessary to the functioning of any state, even the state of a religious community.

The central events of the book of Nehemiah are (1) the public reading of "the book of the law of Moses" (Neh. 8:1–18; cf. 9:3; 2 Chron. 34:15)[32] and (2) the national confession of sin and plea to Yahweh for forgiveness and renewal that immediately followed (Neh. 9:1–38). Both great leaders coordinated a vast assembly "as one man" on the first day of Tishri, the seventh month. The timing was particularly apropos in that Tishri 1 marked (what was later called) *Rosh Hashanah*, Tishri 10 *Yom Kippur*, and Tishri 14–22 *Sukkoth*. This provided an occasion for a beginning again, an opportunity for the re-gathered nation to think long and hard about the past misdeeds that had brought them such misery and despair and now the open door of possibility for reinstatement as the people of God whose future was bright with the promises of an unfailing God. Now it might become possible that the role of Israel as a light to the nations would become a reality and that David *redivivus* might regain his messianic throne.

The Prophets

By "prophets" here is meant the so-called canonical prophets, that is, those whose writings are collected in the Old Testament canon as opposed to those mentioned in the historical narratives, whose messages have already been treated in passing. The vision of the prophets was bifocal: they looked to their own day and times and passed judgment on evil and covenant violation as necessary; and they looked to the eschatological age when a new covenant and new dispensation of grace would be instituted.

Isaiah

Common consent regards Isaiah as the "prince of the prophets" because of the beauty of his language and the strong and inspiring message he declared to Israel and the whole world concerning judgment, forgiveness, and messianic hope. Writing in ca. 680 in the wake of the Assyrian deportation of the northern kingdom of 722 BC, Isaiah saw in that tragedy a preview of what would happen to his own beloved nation of Judah. It is possible in Isaiah's experience and reflections to discover with great clarity the plan of God at work in both the time of the prophet himself and the unfolding ages to come. The abundance of references to this theme precludes a thorough and systematic review of the whole, so the present discussion must be limited to the major themes and texts that advance the central theological idea.

1. Zion is a favorite toponym of Isaiah (47 times) for the rebuilt Jerusalem, one especially connected to the historical reign of David (2 Sam. 5:7; 2 Chron. 5:2) and to the eschatological dominion of the messianic David (Isa. 2:3; 28:16; 33:17–24; 35:10; 59:20–21; 61:3; 62:10–12).
2. The return from Babylonian exile as both an historical and eschatological event is particularly at home in Isaiah. The prophet lived long before the return from Babylonia in 538 but he could see with the eye of faith that it would foreshadow a still greater return. In the latter case, the reference is to the redemption and regathering of the diaspora from all over the world in the end times as a sign of God's covenant faithfulness to His historical people (Isa. 10:21; 35:10; 43:1; 44:22, 26; 48:20; 49:6; 51:11; 52:9, 12; 61:4).
3. The identity and role of the Servant of Yahweh (עֶבֶד יְהוָה) is perhaps the most significant contribution of Isaiah to a full biblical theology of the Old Testament.[33] Though Israel as a corporate entity is usually identified as the servant (14 times), as is David one time (Isa. 37:35), the Servant *par excellence* is seen as an individual who transcends any limited human being in that through his suffering and death he will bring salvation (Isa. 42:1–4; 52:13; 53:11).
4. Akin to the previous point is the concept of messianism, the notion of an Anointed One (הַמָּשִׁיחַ) selected by God to bring about reconciliation between Himself and lost humanity. The verb form (מָשַׁח) occurs once in regard to a future Savior (Isa. 61:1) but the noun, also occurring only one time (Isa. 45:1), is a descriptor for Cyrus, the Persian liberator. Cyrus in this sense is a prototype of a great liberator who will free humankind from the shackles of sin and alienation (see Psa. 2:2; 20:6; 84:9; 89:51; 132:10).[34]
5. "Redeem" or "redemption" (פָּדָה or גָּאַל and their derivatives) is a major theme in Isaiah. It occurs only about a dozen times as a verb, but as the nominal "Redeemer" it is abundantly attested as a clearly messianic term linked to the descriptor "the Holy One of Israel." As such it is central to Isaiah's eschatological soteriology (41:14; 43:14; 44:6, 24; 47:4; 48:17; 49:7, 26; 54:5, 8; 59:20; 60:16; 63:16).

Jeremiah and Lamentations

A century after Isaiah, the Babylonian conquest he had predicted came to pass, one witnessed by another great prophet, Jeremiah, in its three stages (605, 598, and 586). His ministry commenced ca. 627 and extended at least until 562, the year of the release of Jehoiachin from Babylonian detention as recorded by the prophet (Jer. 52:31–34; cf. 2 Kings 25:27–30). This act of mercy portended to Jeremiah an eventual release of Israel from its historical captors as well as from its own self-inflicted separation from God.

In its essentials, the plan of God for history as recorded by Jeremiah is identical to that understood by Isaiah. He calls the ruined city of Jerusalem Zion in the context of the return of the diaspora (31:6, 12; 50:5, 28; 51:10) and makes much of the term "(re)-gather" (קָבַץ; HALOT, 1062–1063) as a way of describing Israel's reconciliation to her God (23:3; 29:14; 31:8, 10; 32:37; 40:15; 49:5, 14). More common is his use of "return" (שׁוּב) to say the same thing (16:15; 27:22; 30:17, 18; 31:8, 16, 17, 18, 21, 25; 32:44; 33:11, 26).[35] In the book of Lamentations, Jeremiah, though in deep despair over the utter ruin of Jerusalem and the temple, still sees cause for hope. He confesses that "God's compassions do not fail and his faithfulness is great" (Lam. 3:22–23). He will not cast Israel off forever (3:31) and the day will come when the Lord will no longer carry away His people (4:22).

Jeremiah employs the term "servant" much less frequently than Isaiah to refer to Israel (Jer. 30:10; 46:27, 28) and more commonly to refer to David explicitly (33:21, 22, 26). However, he never refers to the "anointed one" (מָשִׁיחַ) but doubtless has the same figure in mind under the image of a "branch" from Jesse (23:5; 33:15). Similarly, he refers to the future Redeemer only once (50:34). Like Isaiah, at the same time, he views a human ruler whom God raises up to accomplish His plan as God's servant, this time Nebuchadnezzar (25:9; 27:6; 43:10).

The concept of "covenant" (בְּרִית) is very much at home in the theology of Jeremiah (ca. 23x; in Isa. 8x). Almost always it refers to the new covenant that God will make with His redeemed people, one that is not written on stone but rather interiorized, written on the heart (31:31–33; 50:5; cf. Deut. 6:6; 11:18). It serves as a hallmark of the messianic dispensation in which the New Covenant would be cut by the Suffering Servant of whom Isaiah spoke (see Matt. 26:28; Mark 14:24; Luke 22:20).

Ezekiel

This priest/prophet ministered in the exilic period and primarily from his place of residence in Susa, the great Persian city in Southwest Iran. His vantage point was therefore quite different from that of Isaiah and Jeremiah, but his central theological concerns were very much the same. Again, the major themes relevant to God's plan for history in that context will provide the structure for the ensuing discussion.

Ezekiel, contrary to his earlier prophetic brothers, never describes Jerusalem as Zion, though others of the prophets did, as did exiles in hymnody (notably Psa. 137:1, 3). He does, however, resume the language of Israel's ongoing role as a servant people (Ezek. 28:25; 37:25) over whom will rule David as of old (34:23–24; 37:24–25), obviously presupposing a return from exile, if only eschatological. Unlike the others, however, Ezekiel says relatively little about a literal return to the land in his own time (see 11:17, 18); rather, he uses the term "return" to speak of spiritual renewal (16:55).

Ezekiel's major contribution is to the theology of the new covenant. The Lord, he says, will renew His covenant with Israel even though Israel had egregiously failed to keep its covenant commitments (16:60–63). The Promised Land will then be a place of *shalom* where none need fear (34:25; 37:26). In new covenant language the prophet speaks of a day when Israel will be reestablished in the land, its people will have hearts of flesh rather than stone, it will be energized by the Spirit of God to walk perfectly before Him, and it will become a light to the nations as it was created to be (36:22–31).

Daniel

Daniel was taken captive in Nebuchadnezzar's first deportation of Judah in 605, but he quickly rose to great prominence in the king's court because of God's favor upon him, enabling him to see and interpret visions and dreams. The central theme of his book is the sovereignty of his God and the exaltation of His kingdom over all human dignities and domains.[36] This motif is clearly in line with God's creation purposes and His plan for the nations and especially for restored Israel. The terms for king (מֶלֶךְ) and kingdom (מַלְכוּת) with reference to Yahweh occur with greater density in Daniel than any other book of the Bible, thus contributing to the concept of dominion in which Israel's God becomes the God of all the earth as was intended from creation.[37]

Most of the key concepts noted in the preceding prophets appear in Daniel as well, with the following exceptions. (1) Daniel never uses the term "servant" to describe either Israel or a coming messiah nor (2) does he ever speak of Israel's redemption, return, or restoration to the homeland. However, he does speak of the "most holy one" and "the prince," "the anointed one" who will bring in everlasting righteousness after being first "cut off" (Dan. 9:24–27). The messianic overtones here can hardly be disputed.

The Twelve

The twelve are the so-called Minor Prophets, designated thus because of the comparative brevity of their writings. Their books occur in generally chronological sequence and will be arranged in the centuries in which they undertook their ministries. One must bear in mind that precise dates within these categories cannot be achieved, but the variations are so minor as not to constitute any important exegetical and theological difficulty.

Jonah. Jonah's mission (ca. 765?) was not directly to his own nation but to the great city of Nineveh, the capital of the Assyrian Empire in this period. On the other hand, the more-subtle message was to Israel after all to remind God's chosen people of their failure to live up to the commission to which God had called them. The normal technical terms are not found in the book because it is narrative in form and only incidentally happens upon terms that have to this point characterized God's plan for history as worked out through Israel.

Jonah's call to Nineveh should not seem strange in light of the ancient Abrahamic promise that through his seed all nations would be blessed. Though the "Great Commission" of the Old Testament is generally understood to be centripetal in that Israel was to attract the nations to itself and, hence, to the Lord, the centrifugal is not altogether missing. This is seen most clearly in Jonah, but the various oracles to the nations in the longer prophetic writings also suggest God's interest in the wider world and the part Israel must play in demonstrating it.[38]

Jonah's disobedience to the commission epitomizes Israel's indifference to its mission as well. The prophet's bitter disappointment at God's failure to destroy Nineveh speaks volumes about Israel's stinginess in keeping the good news to itself. It is as though being chosen means to be hostile to the non-chosen, to wish them damnation simply because they are "not one of us." This is an attitude of which the prophets said that Israel must repent.

Amos. Amos was roughly contemporary with Hosea and likely a little later than Jonah (perhaps ca. 760 BC). Though he was from Judah his mission was to proclaim God's word to the northern kingdom. As a citizen of Judah, he refers to Jerusalem as Zion (1:2; 6:1), a term, as we have seen, that is common to Isaiah and Jeremiah—both of whom were from Jerusalem—as well as to Joel, Obadiah, Micah, Zephaniah, and Zechariah, all Judahites. Any reference to Israel as a servant or light to the nations is missing in Amos as is any reference to an anointed one. However, the prophet does predict the return of Israel from captivity and their being planted in the land forever (Amos 9:15). Among other things attendant to the return will be the reconstruction of the "hut" (סֻכָּה) of David (9:11), an oblique way of describing the temporary nature of the Davidic dynasty in Old Testament times. Its rebuilding (קוּם, lit. "raising up") will make it grander and more secure, enabling Israel to "possess" (יָרַשׁ)[39] the nations that Yahweh calls to Himself (v. 12). In this manner restored Israel will pick up the mantle of servanthood that she had lost in her covenant disobedience and will wear it again triumphantly.

Hosea. Against this background, one is not surprised to see the combination of such terms in the book as "return" (10x), "restore" (2x), "compassion" (3x), "forgive/ness" (2x), and particularly "love," especially in its sense of covenant relationship and renewal. This theologically rich covenantal term (חֶסֶד) occurs six times in the book, far more than in any other work of comparable size.[40] Hosea had demonstrated this kind of loyalty to his wife with whom he had entered the covenant of marriage and from that platform was able to draw attention most compellingly to the covenant loyalty of Yahweh to His adulterous people Israel. Rather than divorce them forever, He would bring them back to Himself as a loving husband (Hos. 1:11; 3:4–5; 8:8–10; 11:8–11; 13:14; 14:4–8).

Micah. Micah of Moresheh in Judah was the last of the "shorter" prophets of the eighth century, serving as he did in the last days of the northern kingdom or even a little after (Mic. 1:1). In any event, his audience was Judah alone even though the toponym Israel is frequently used (11x in 105 verses). In fact, the use of the term implies that though the northern kingdom has been carried off, Micah still holds in view a day of reunification of the nation (Mic. 2:12). Indeed, he goes so far as to announce that a king of Israel is to come in the future who will be born in the town of Bethlehem (5:2a). This unlikely circumstance, he says, had been predicted all along, from the distant past (v. 2b). Most certainly Micah has David in mind, the anointed one who came also from that obscure place.

The new ruler then will be Davidic, a scion of the messianic line.

Micah elaborates that this royal one will be the inaugurator of *shalom,* a shepherd over Israel who will both feed and protect the flock, one made up of both Israel and Judah. Though Assyria under mighty Nimrod should invade, the people of the Lord will prevail and, moreover, will be like dew, the coming of which and the pervasiveness of which is unstoppable (Mic. 5:6–9). All this will follow God's work of redemption and the performance of His ancient promises to Jacob and to Abraham (7:19–20).

Nahum. Nahum's major burden is a proclamation of the judgment of God upon Nineveh, the capital of the Assyrian Empire, which, having been the instrument of God's disciplining of His chosen people Israel, was now to be cast aside because of its overreaching hubris. The end came in a series of events brought about by the newly risen Babylonian kingdom under Nabopolassar (626–605 BC) and his illustrious son Nebuchadnezzar (605–562): (1) the destruction of Nineveh in 612, (2) the defeat of the Assyrian army at Haran in 609, and (3) the annihilation of what was left of its forces at Carchemish in 605.[41]

Its implications for the plan of God for history are quite evident. He is the ultimate sovereign over all principalities and powers, which therefore operate according to His designs (Nah. 1:2–7). Israel, the chosen people of God, can rest assured that He will bring to pass all that He planned for them as fulfillment of the Abrahamic covenant (2:13, 15).

Habakkuk. Habakkuk, who also lived in the chaotic days immediately prior to the Babylonian succession to the Assyrians, focuses on the presence of God in the midst of all Judah's anxiety and fears about its future. The prophet shares their concerns, going so far as to question the Lord about His ways (Hab. 1:2–4). He then confesses that the Chaldeans (Babylonians) are indeed a mighty power, but they, like the Assyrians, are but tools in God's hands who rise and fall at His bidding (Hab. 1:6). In conclusion, the prophet recounts the history of his people and the way God brought them to their current state of affairs (3:1–15). Then, despite all present appearances, he rejoices that the God of yesterday is the God of today and tomorrow and what He has done before He can and will do again (vv. 18–19).

Zephaniah. The last of the seventh-century prophets, Zephaniah no doubt witnessed the early stages of Judah's demise at the hands of Assyria and then Babylonia. In most extravagant and hyperbolic terms, he describes what God will do through these ruthless invaders. The setting merges from the contemporary into the eschatological with its universalistic scope (Zeph. 1:7–18). Not only the peoples of Israel's day and times—as well as Israel itself—will experience the wrath of a holy and offended God; the whole earth will be caught up in a cataclysmic judgment summarized by the repetitive phrase "the day of the Lord."[42]

The day of the Lord does not portend unmitigated disaster, however, for it is only preparatory for a brighter day when the Lord will call forth the remnant of His people, bring them back to the land from which they had been exiled, grant them security from the foes around them, make them to have a name and receive praise on the earth, and rule among them as their king (Zeph. 3:14–20).[43]

Joel. Joel and Obadiah are notoriously difficult to date. The decision to list them here is based on a number of considerations that need not be outlined here. Among them is the use of the term "day of the Lord" which, as seen in Zephaniah, is much at home in the later periods. Joel makes use of the theme nine times and Obadiah nine times, though less clearly eschatologically.[44]

Joel recounts the devastation of the land, including the city Zion, as a result of the Babylonian conquest (1:2–12). But this is nothing compared to the day when Yahweh will come with sword and spear to wreak havoc on Israel for its sin (1:15–20) and on the nations for their refusal to recognize Him as sovereign (2:1–11; 3:9–13). The plan of God for His people is not eradication, however, but vindication and restoration. The call for their repentance and renewal (1:13–14; 2:12–17) will efficaciously draw them back to the Lord and to previously unknown attendant blessing. They will no longer be despised by the nations (2:19); they will enjoy the bounties of the land (2:18, 23–26; 3:18–20); they will know in the fullest way that Yahweh is God and there is no other (2:27); they will be preserved from their enemies (3:16–17); and they will be recipients of the outpouring of God's Spirit that will radically change them from within (2:28–31).

Obadiah. The entire discourse in this brief writing has to do with Edom, a "brother nation" to Israel, and Edom's mistreatment of Isreal despite the relationship. A case can be made that Edom epitomizes all hostile nations or at least those close to Israel that are therefore all the more culpable. They must be punished by the Lord for this abuse of His people, in line with the Abrahamic curse (vv. 10, 12). The obverse is that Israel will be blessed by taking possession of the inheritance not only of Edom but other peoples as well (vv. 17–21).[45]

Haggai. Haggai's ministry took place in or about 520 BC, sixteen years after the return of the Jewish community to the homeland. Though the temple foundations had been laid in Jerusalem (cf. Ezra 3:8–10), little had been done afterward. Haggai's God-given task was to encourage the completion of the work and to reconstitute the religious and political structures of the state of Yehud. His message can be condensed to two main points: (1) Though the second temple was meager in the sight of those who had seen the glorious temple of Solomon, it would someday be so filled with the glory of God that it would outshine the first temple (Hag. 2:7–9); (2) The dynasty of David would continue as evidenced by the leadership of Zerubbabel, a direct descendant of David and thus the heir apparent to David's throne (Hag. 2:20–23; 1 Chron. 3:1, 19). The eschatological tone of the language suggests, of course, that a greater one than Zerubbabel is in view; in fact, one greater than David himself.[46]

Zechariah. A contemporary of Haggai, Zechariah was laden with the same concerns but he spelled out in much more detail God's plan for the infant state and its people. Over and over he envisions a day when Israel will return to the land in power and preeminence and as the light to the nations God intended it to be (Zech. 1:16–17; 2:10–12; 8:1–8, 18–23; 10:8–12; 14:16–21). More important, God Himself will be king (14:9), exercising His rule through a Davidic vice-gerent in precisely the manner that David ruled Israel in days of old and as God intended mankind as a whole to reign over all creation according to His first mandate (Gen. 1:28). The one to come in such regal splendor and authority is called by various epithets—servant (Zech. 3:8), branch (3:8; 6:12), priest (6:13), king (9:9; 14:9, 16), and shepherd (11:15–16; 13:7)—all messianic terms applicable to Jesus Christ (Matt. 20:28; John 10:11; 18:37; 1 Tim. 1:17; Heb. 4:14; 13:20; Rev. 17:14; 19:16).[47]

Malachi. The last of the canonical prophets composed his book in 475 BC or thereabouts. He addresses many concerns about the condition of the postexilic state, including abuse of the temple and its services by the priests (Mal. 1:7–9), religious syncretism (2:11), divorce (2:14–15), and failure to pay the tithe (3:7–10). Such behavior invites the displeasure of the Lord and disciplinary consequences (2:2–3, 12, 16; 3:5, 9). All the same, the Lord will send a messenger to announce the coming of the one whom they seek, the "messenger of the covenant" (3:1). He will come to judge (3:2–3) until righteousness is restored (3:3–6). The coming of this messianic figure will be preceded by the coming of Elijah, the one Jesus identified as John the Baptist. Thus, by inference Jesus announced that He was that messenger of the covenant whom Elijah, that is, John, would identify (Matt. 11:14; 17:10–12; Luke 1:17).[48]

Poetry and Wisdom

David's positive affirmations within the the Psalms[49] are particularly powerful, laden as they are with heavy theological content that transcends his own times and circumstances and that reaches forward to the Son of David *par excellence*. These are, of course, best found in the psalms attributed to him, the list of which, with abbreviated snippets, follows in Table 1.

Besides the Davidic self-references, other psalms also testify to David's own choice as God's servant and look forward to a larger eschatological dimension for him and his dynasty. See Table 2.

Table 1:
Davidic Royal Self-Allusions and Ascriptions

TEXT	AFFIRMATIONS
Psalm 2:6–7	God's messiah, king
Psalm 18:50	Deliverance to His King, covenant loyalty to His anointed
Psalm 20:6	The Lord saves His anointed
Psalm 21:7	The king trusts in the Lord and shall not be moved
Psalm 28:8	God is a fortress of salvation to His anointed
Psalm 63:11	The king will rejoice in God

Table 2: David as King Otherwise Attested to in the Psalter

TEXT	AFFIRMATIONS
Psalm 18:50	David and his descendants forever
Psalm 78:70	He chose David His servant
Psalm 78:72	David shepherded them with integrity
Psalm 89:3	I have sworn to David My servant
Psalm 89:20	I have found David My servant; I have anointed him
Psalm 89:35–36	I will not lie to David; his seed will continue forever
Psalm 89:49	In Your faithfulness You swore to David
Psalm 122:5	The thrones of the house of David
Psalm 132:1 Psalm 132:10	O Lord, remember David For the sake of David Your servant
Psalm 132:11 Psalm 132:17 Psalm 144:10	The Lord swore an oath to David I will make a horn grow for David The one who delivers David from the painful sword

(Author's translation)

CONCLUSION

A major thread of the Old Testament narrative is the fundamental purpose of God for His creation from its origination to its consummation. The strategy by which this is achieved might well be called, in ordinary parlance, God's plan, one to be viewed as a succession of dispensations that flow naturally from one to the other but which, at the same time, are different in their form and in their purposes. In line with the principle of progressive revelation, that plan was unfolded only gradually and only to the extent that each generation was equipped and ready to understand and advance it. Noah thus refined and added to what Adam and Eve had learned through revelation and experience, Abraham built on that foundation as did the succeeding patriarchs, and Moses even still more. It was he who was commissioned to canonize the history of the outworking of that plan from its inception to his own day, a work known as Torah ("instruction").

The purpose of Torah was to provide a legal and theological basis upon which the chosen nation Israel, as part of the divine plan, could fulfill its calling as a light to the nations. Israel's historians evaluated the progress of the nation against the prescriptions of Torah, commending or condemning it as was necessary.

The prophets composed their texts in the milieu of the historical situations in which they found themselves. They too judged Israel's behavior in terms of whether or not the nation was implementing God's great plan of redemption and renewal. They also shed light on what God had in view for the future and they increasingly came to understand that only a divine interposition of a messianic figure into history could rectify the human condition and bring God's plan to perfect resolution.

Finally, the writings both reveal the flawed nature of mankind and offer practical, theological, and eschatological hints and hope for life in the here and now in line with God's parameters of behavior. Beyond that, they provide glimpses of the future when God's heavenly kingdom will become an earthly reality and all things will consummate to His praise and glory and to the everlasting blessing of His creation.

Notes

1. The occurrences of the *waw* conjunctives (shown in italics) that follow the first verb in the series can be understood in this case as two sets of hendiadys: (1) "Be so fruitful that you fill the earth" and (2) "exercise complete sovereignty over it and all that is in it." For this understanding see Victor P. Hamilton, *The Book of Genesis 1–24,* New International Commentary on the Old Testament (Grand Rapids: Eerdmans, 1990), 131, n 2.

2. The usual translation "in the image of God" seems to miss the central point of the narrative, which is God's delegation to mankind the responsibility of being the caretaker of all else God has created. The preposition attests not only the common meaning "in" but also the so-called *beth essentiae* which serves as a term of equivalence. The terms for image and likeness (צֶלֶם and דְּמוּת) are virtually synonymous, the two functioning perhaps epexegetically, "image," i.e., "likeness," and in any case meaning representation. See the exhaustive discussion by Kenneth Mathews, *Genesis 1–11:26,* New American Commentary (Nashville: Broadman & Holman, 1996), 163–72. Cf. *Theological Dictionary of the Old Testament*, ed. G. Johannes Botterweck and Helmer Ringgren, vol. 3 (Grand Rapids: Eerdmans, 1978), 259.

3. The two verbs employed, עָבַד and שָׁמַר respectively, express throughout the Old Testament (1) an affirmation of submission to God as the Almighty Sovereign who rules over all things (worship) and (2) clarification of the role of humankind in light of that confession (service). Cf. Gen. 18:19; Lev. 19:37; Deut. 5:1, 32; 6:13, 25; 10:12–13, 20; 13:5; Josh. 1:7, 8; 24:15; 1 Sam. 12:10; 2 Kgs.17:37; 2 Chr. 33:8; Isa. 56:1; Jer. 30:9; Ezek. 18:9; Mal. 3:14.

4. See Eugene H. Merrill, *Everlasting Dominion: A Theology of the Old Testament* (Nashville: Broadman & Holman, 2006), 202–5.

5. The literary artistry of the author in the use of assonance is striking. Mankind had been commanded to multiply (רָבָה) and now the woman's pain in giving birth will be multiplied (הַרְבָּה אַרְבֶּה). The man was to work and care for the soil (see note 1), but in his fallen state he (אָדָם) will labor over cursed ground (הָאֲדָמָה) until he returns to it (הָאֲדָמָה) in death.

6. The verb translated "great" (רָבָה) is the same as that used with reference to God's first mandate to "multiply" (Gen. 1:28) and to the pain of childbirth as a consequence of the fall (3:16). The accumulated wickedness of the race now called for remedial judgment leavened with grace sufficient for a new beginning.

7. Unless otherwise noted, this and subsequent translations of the biblical texts are by the author.

8. Though Noah is described as "righteous" (צַדִּיק) and "upright" (תָּמִים), these traits were not the grounds of his deliverance from the flood. Nor is the fact that he "walked with God" (Gen. 6:9), though the latter is freighted with dominion overtones (see *New International Dictionary of Old Testament Theology and Exegesis*, ed. Willem A. VanGemeren, 1:1032–1035). Rather, as the author of the book of Hebrews makes clear, Noah was spared because of his faith, a faith that resulted in his righteousness before God (Heb. 11:7; cf. Abraham in Gen. 15:6).

9. The New Testament makes clear that all government is ordained by God, even those systems most barbaric and oppressive (Luke 22:25; Rom. 13:1–7; 1 Tim. 2:2–3; Titus 3:1; 1 Pet. 2:14).

10. That this is murder and not homicide in general is clear from (1) the immediate context, which authorizes the deliberate slaughter of animals for food; (2) the responsibility of government to exercise capital punishment, which is not considered murder and therefore different in kind from the act of the individual; and (3) the retributive nature of the penalty itself: government by premeditation takes a human life just as the perpetrator by plan and design had done to "his brother." Fallen man was still the image of God as is seen in the fact that Seth, the third son of sinful Adam and Eve, is said to be the "image and likeness" of Adam just as Adam was the image and likeness of God. See note 2 above.

11. The name Eber (עֵבֶר) in its gentilic form (עִבְרִי) may be rendered first as "Eberite," and then "Hebrew," just as "Israelite" derives from "Israel" via the gentilic "Israeli," the name for a citizen of modern Israel. Cf. Gary N. Knoppers, *I Chronicles 1–9.* Anchor Bible Commentaries AB 12 (New York: Doubleday, 2004), 276.

12. The technical term for covenant (בְּרִית) does not appear in connection with Abraham until Genesis 15:18, but then 14 times in Genesis 17.

13. Mathews prefers the term "proleptic" in that it anticipates an individual seed. Mathews, *Genesis 1–11:26*, 114–15.

14. Malachi states the choice of Jacob in what appear to be the harshest of tones: "I loved Jacob, but Esau I have hated" (Mal. 1:2–3). However, the love and hate language here occurs in secular texts to express choice and non-choice, not a visceral or emotional reaction.

15. Paul understood this plan and saw already in the Abrahamic covenant the ambiguity of the term "seed" (זֶרַע), which bears both a plural or collective sense ("seeds") and a singular one ("seed"). He argues the point that the singular form, though no doubt intended as plural by Moses, has the ultimate connotation of singularity, that is, in Jesus Christ (Gal. 3:16). Timothy George, *Galatians*. New American Commentary 30 (Nashville: B&H, 1994), 246–48.

16. This dispensation of law must not be misunderstood so as to see in it salvific overtones; rather, it has to do with how Israel must live as a servant nation within the covenant of grace.

17. "Possession" translates the Hebrew סְגֻלָּה, used elsewhere to refer to personal property (1 Chr. 27:25; 29:3; Eccl. 2:8; see *Hebrew and Aramaic Lexicon of the Old Testament* [Leiden: Brill, 1994–99], 742; cf. the cognate Akkadian *sikiltu*, CAD 15, p. 245, "treasured possession").

18. Thus Eugene H. Merrill, *Everlasting Dominion*, 269–73. Heb מַמְלֶכֶת כֹּהֲנִים וְגוֹי קָדוֹשׁ. The syntax here suggests that both "priests" and "holy" function as adjectives with their respective nouns. John N. Oswalt, *Exodus*. Cornerstone Bible Commentary 1 (Carol Stream, IL: Tyndale House, 2008), 432.

19. A few important examples suffice: (1) God's walking about in the garden (Gen. 3:8), (2) walking in the camp of Israel (Deut. 23:15), (3) walking among the people of Israel (2 Sam. 7:6, 7), and (4) walking in the heavens above (Job 22:14; Ps. 77:19); (5) the Lord's angelic emissaries (Zech. 1:10, 11; 6:7; 10:12); (6) the twelve spies of Israel scouting out the land (Josh. 18:4, 8); (7) kings parading their sovereignty (1 Sam. 12:2; 30:31; Ezek. 19:6); and (8) Satan exercising his temporary hegemony over the world (Job 1:7; 2:2; Ezek. 28:14). William A. VanGemeren, *New International Dictionary of Theology and Exegesis* (Grand Rapids: Zondervan, 1997), 1:1032–1035.

20. A corollary to this by extension is the claim by the modern state of Israel to the land it has settled, namely, the biblical promises beginning with Abraham and never rescinded.

21. The original Hebrew text clearly is to be read "Jonathan son of Gershom son of Moses" (מֹשֶׁה) as opposed to the *nun suspensum* reading מְנַשֶּׁה, the redactors of which obviously found the notion of a grandson of Moses reverting to idolatry too scandalous to be correct.

22. The author of the narratives most certainly lived after the events described therein. In fact, he must have been as late as the Davidic kingship since the stories, pro-David and anti-Saul, are clearly polemical. The place name "Bethlehem" occurs six times in the two narratives, in the first case associated with one who left the town to lapse into idolatry and in the second case with one who suffered unspeakable crime and with a rashness of response on the part of her husband. "Gibeah" occurs with the incredible density of 23 times in the span of 103 verses, or once in every 4.5 verses! The relative innocence of the one place as compared to the savage brutality of the other sets the stage for inter-tribal and interpersonal competition and warfare.

23. For the chronology of the period, see Eugene H. Merrill, *Kingdom of Priests: A History of Old Testament Israel*, 2nd ed. (Grand Rapids: Baker, 2008), 166–70.

24. The Hebrew reads literally, "Yahweh sought for himself a man according to his heart." "Heart" in Old Testament physiology and psychology more often than not (and certainly here) refers to the cognitive or rational rather than mere physical or even emotive makeup. Therefore, the sense here, both grammatical and intentional, is that God has sought a man according to His own predeterminative choice. Thus, the selection of David is in line with the previous selections of Abraham, Isaac, and Jacob, all of whom were chosen by divine grace alone. See Ronald F. Youngblood, *1, 2 Samuel*. The Expositor's Bible Commentary, vol. 3, ed. Tremper Longman III and David E. Garland (Grand Rapids: Zondervan, 2009), 137.

25. The nature of the "Spirit of God" cannot be addressed here at length except to say that New Testament revelation retrospectively supports the position that the reference here is to the Holy Spirit (as per NASB), the third person of the Godhead. This does not mean He was understood as such by the writers of the Old Testament texts or by their contemporaries. See Eugene H. Merrill, "The Samson Saga and Spiritual Leadership," *Presence, Power and Promise: The Role of the Spirit of God in the Old Testament,* ed. David G. Firth and Paul D. Wegner (Nottingham, UK: InterVarsity, 2011), 281–93.

26. For various interpretive options regarding the scene of Saul's resort to necromancy, see J. Robert Vannoy, *1–2 Samuel,* ed. Philip E. Comfort, Cornerstone Bible Commentary, vol. 4 (Carol Stream, IL: Tyndale, 2009), 242–44.

27. On this distinction see Merrill, *Everlasting Dominion,* 452–53.

28. For the location of these places and hypotheses as to the extent of the Assyrian diaspora, see *The Macmillan Bible Atlas,* 3rd ed., ed. Yohanan Aharoni and Michael Avi-Yonah (New York: Macmillan, 1993), maps 147, 150. The Habor (modern Khabur) is a major tributary of the Euphrates in what is now NE Syria. Gozan is identified with modern Guzana (Tell Halaf), 160 miles NE of Aleppo, Syria.

29. The so-called Murashu Inscriptions testify to the fact that in general the deportees were by no means internees in labor camps or that as a whole they suffered deprivation or oppression. In fact, these texts reveal that Jews owned property and businesses. For a full discussion, see Peter R. Ackroyd, *Israel under Babylon and Persia* (Oxford: The Oxford University Press, 1986); cf. M. D. Coogan, "Life in the Diaspora: Jews in Nippur in the Fifth Century B. C.," *Biblical Archeologist* 37 (1974): 6–12.

30. Most important in sketching the conditions of life for the Jewish diaspora is Edwin M. Yamauchi, *Persia and the Bible* (Grand Rapids: Baker, 1990).

31. Some second-temple Jewish traditions—notably the "Testaments of the Twelve Patriarchs"—envisaged two messiahs, one political (Davidic) and the other religious (Aaronic). See Lawrence H. Schiffman, *From Text to Tradition: A History of Second Temple & Rabbinic Judaism* (Hoboken, NJ: Ktav, 1991), 117, 173; Leonhard Rost, *Judaism outside the Hebrew Canon* (Nashville: Abingdon, 1976), 143.

32. The scripture in view here is clearly the book of Deuteronomy. It is described by this or equivalent nomenclature in Deut. itself (28:61; 29:21; 30:10; 31:24, 26) and elsewhere (2 Kgs. 22:8–16; 23:2, 3). For support of this contention, see Eugene H. Merrill, *Deuteronomy.* The New American Commentary 4 (Nashville: B&H, 1994), 32–37.

33. John Goldingay, *Israel's Faith,* Old Testament Theology, vol. 2 (Downers Grove, IL: InterVarsity, 2006), 221–28.

34. This conclusion is strengthened by the literary bridging between the end of Chronicles and the opening of Ezra which consists of a repetition of Cyrus' decree from the interpretive standpoint of the biblical historians. Sara Japhet, *I & II Chronicles* (Louisville: Westminster/John Knox, 1993), 1077. For a helpful discussion of Cyrus as the "anointed one," see Gary V. Smith, *Isaiah 40–66.* New American Commentary 15B (Nashville: B&H, 2009), 254–55.

35. W. L. Holladay, *The Root Šubh in the Old Testament* (Leiden: Brill, 1958).

36. Eugene H. Merrill, "Daniel as a Contribution to Kingdom Theology," *Essays in Honor of J. Dwight Pentecost,* ed. Stanley D. Toussaint and Charles H. Dyer (Chicago: Moody, 1986), 211–25.

37. These royal terms occur in all ca. 141 times in Daniel (once every .047 pages) and specifically to God at least 12 times in 30 pages of Hebrew text (once every 2.5 pages), 6 times in 106 pages of Isaiah (once every 17.6 pages), 7 times in 114 pages of Jeremiah (once every 16.3 pages), and never in 93 pages of Ezekiel.

38. See Isa. 10, 14–25, 34, 47; Jer. 48–51; Ezek. 25–32, 38–39; Joel 3; Amos 1–2; Obad. 1; Nah. 1–3; Hab. 2; Zeph. 2–3; Zech. 9, 14.

39. The verb here is best understood in context not as an aggressive invasion of nations but a receiving of them as an inheritance on behalf of the Lord. See *NIDOTTE,* ed. Willem A. VanGemeren, vol. 2 (Grand Rapids: Zondervan, 1997), 548.

40. For example, it is used six times in Isaiah, six times in Jeremiah, never in Ezekiel, and once in Daniel.

The book of Psalms is replete with its occurrences (ca. 120x), not surprising given the nature of its penitential and supplicatory prayers.

41. For details, see Merrill, *Kingdom of Priests,* 449–64, 487–90.
42. The phrase occurs 20 times in 53 verses, a density unparalleled elsewhere in the OT.
43. Cf. Yair Hoffman, "The Day of the Lord as a Concept and a Term in the Prophetic Literature," *Zeitschrift für die alttestamentliche Wissenschaft* 93 (1981): 37–50.
44. On the other hand, Hosea attests the term only six times, Amos twelve times, and Jonah and Nahum not once.
45. Esau and/or Edom occurs eight times in 21 verses and Israel by the name Jacob three times. "Israel" never occurs in the book.
46. Eugene H. Merrill, *Haggai, Zechariah, Malachi* (Chicago: Moody, 1994), 56–58.
47. Ibid., 141–42, 153–54, 197–99, 253–56, 271–73, 300–301, 338–40.
48. Ibid., 429–32.
49. The Wisdom books (Job, Proverbs, Qoheleth, and Song of Songs), because of their universalistic view of ethics and behavior, have little to contribute to the advancement of the concept of the plan of God for history, especially as it involves Israel. Therefore we will have only a brief look at the Psalms.

6

God's Plan for History:

THE FIRST COMING OF CHRIST

DARRELL L. BOCK

Dispensationalism is about stewardships, administrative arrangements across the program of God.[1] All Christians recognize such administrative elements in Scripture, as our two testaments point to such a reality; so does the fact Christians no longer are to circumcise their male children as a sign of covenant. Those differences, as a function of the progress of revelation, point to dispensations. What Christians end up discussing about the Bible is how many such arrangements there are and how complex they are.

A dispensation is different from salvation. Salvation is how one comes to be saved by God. That has always been by grace through faith.[2] Jesus' work is what always made salvation possible, even though it was through promise, anticipation, and hope during the Old Testament period. On the other hand, a dispensation is a way of managing that salvation program. The dispensations as a whole show how God is going about redeeming a creation that was flawed because of sin and rebellion. That program starts with the covenants. It involves a kingdom those covenants promised. Those covenants and the kingdom it promises come through Israel and her Christ to the world. As God delivered on promises made to Abraham, how He administered that program shifted, with new structures in place from time to time to manage the progress. The biggest factors in those changes involve Jesus' coming to inaugurate the plan's fulfillment as well as His return to complete that program.

So our essay takes a look at how the Gospels reveal the administration of God's kingdom program. Our survey focuses on the impact of Jesus' coming to earth. In sum, the kingdom and covenants are two of the key ways God reveals how He will execute His plan to restore creation to its intended goal for God's own glory. God's kingdom program is a reclamation project, taking humanity to where it was designed to be all along.

This essay also will look at how Israel relates to that program, since the covenants were originally made with her. The king who executes that program is Israel's Messiah. How Israel relates to God is an important part of grasping the structures God uses to administer His program. How the nations tie into that program is important as well. We begin with the kingdom, move to the covenants, and close with a look at Israel and the nations.

GOD'S KINGDOM IN THE GOSPELS

All students of Jesus' teaching in the Gospels agree that a central topic is the kingdom of God.[3] A check of the use of the term *kingdom* shows how widespread it is: Mark uses it thirteen times; Matthew and Luke share nine uses, while Matthew uses it twenty-seven more times and Luke twelve more times; and John uses it twice. Beyond this, though, all agreement stops. What is the kingdom Jesus has in mind? Is it a realm or a dynamic form of rule? Is it here or yet to come? Is it revealed in the Old Testament alone or does Jesus' teaching add to its definition? Each of these questions is important to understanding the kingdom as Jesus presents it.

The Kingdom Is the Arrival of a New Thing.

It is important to start with a definition. The kingdom Jesus preached is clearly a major structure through which God planned to administer salvation. The fact that both John the Baptist (Matt. 3:2) and Jesus (Matt. 4:17) announced it is near tells us much already. It tells us first of all that whatever kingdom tied to God that existed in the past is not what Jesus is discussing as coming. So the psalms that declare God's kingdom now extending over the earth is not what Jesus was presenting here. For what He announces has not yet existed. That is why the kingdom John and Jesus announce is said only to be near. There is a kingdom God rules over as creator that includes all His creation. That is what those Psalms texts are about, but there is a promised kingdom that brings redemption that John and Jesus announce.

So the first thing to recognize about the kingdom Jesus preaches is that it is a new administrative arrangement fulfilling expectations already announced but not yet realized. John the Baptist and Jesus announced the kingdom that brings deliverance and redemption.[4]

The Kingdom Is a Concept about Ultimate Deliverance.

Most people are surprised to learn that "the kingdom of God" is not a common expression in the Old Testament. In fact, the phrase does not appear at all there. But the concept of God ruling, the picture of God as King, or the hope of God ruling appears in numerous texts (as king: 1 Sam. 12:12; Ps. 24:10; ruling over Israel: Exod. 15:18; Num. 23:21; ruling over the earth or creation: 2 Kgs. 19:15; Ps. 29:10; Isa. 6:5; possessing a throne: Ps. 9:4; 45:6; 47:8; Isa. 6:1; ongoing rule: Ps. 10:16; 146:10; Isa. 24:23). The picture of God's rule shared through the vicegerent figure of Israel's king also appears in texts where the king's throne is said to be Yahweh's throne (1 Chr. 17:14; 28:5; 29:23; 2 Chr. 9:8; 13:8). So the one who took up David's mantle and hope takes up this rule and the hope for shalom that this rule was aiming to achieve. This Davidic rule was an extension of commitments God made to Israel and the world in the Abrahamic covenant, initially announced by God's promise in Genesis 12:1–3. These ideas of a shared rule tied to the covenants of hope serve as a backdrop for the coming rule Jesus announced.

This is why in Second Temple Judaism the kingdom often became linked to messianic hope and always pictured the vindication of the saints and judgment to come.[5] In OT pseudepigrapha, Psalms of Solomon 17–18 expressed this hope of a political messiah who purged Israel and defeated the nations; and the Ethiopic Book of Enoch 37–71 looked to a transcendent figure who shared rule and judgment with God. The echoes of such a comprehensive hope are in the background when Jesus spoke of the kingdom to come. The fact that Jesus does not define this term anywhere but only elaborates on it indicates He is working with a familiar general concept.

At its core the kingdom is about the rule of God, the deliverance and vindication of the righteous, and the judgment of God's enemies that brings peace. That this is where the kingdom of God is headed can be seen in Jesus' Olivet

Discourse (Matt. 24–25; Mark 13; Luke 21:5–37). There the return of the Son of Man pictures the vindication of the righteous, their ultimate deliverance, and the judgment of humanity.

The Kingdom Parables Develop the Meaning of the Kingdom.

Jesus' kingdom parables (Matt. 13:1–52; Mark 4:1–34; Luke 8:1–15; 13:18–20) are very important to this conversation. Through parables Jesus reveals mysteries about the kingdom. His teaching stories add to what we know about the kingdom to come. He complements what the Old Testament teaches with new disclosures. What Jesus reveals here is new; that is why it is called a mystery. However, that these teachings are a mystery and are new does not mean what He reveals cannot or does not connect to what had been revealed. This is precisely how revelation progresses. We get more revelation on a topic and those additions fill in gaps in the promise and deepen what we had understood about that promise.[6]

These parables teach us a variety of things.

The parable of the four soils teaches the different responses to the kingdom. There will be acceptance and rejection of the kingdom message contained in the Word of God. Satan, persecution, the cares of this world get in the way of an embrace of the kingdom hope.

The parable of the wheat and tares teaches the mixed character of the kingdom until the judgment at the end. It also tells us the field of the kingdom's presence is the world, not just the church. This is a crucial point as the kingdom makes a claim on all the earth. The kingdom's claim on the world represents a new level of God's accountability with the world as a whole. It indicates that judgment to sort good and evil out comes at the end and will involve every being made in God's image.

The parable of the mustard seed argues that the kingdom starts small but ends up being a dwelling place. This is a major disclosure, for many thought that when the promised kingdom came, it would conquer and be big from the start. It shows that God's kingdom program is not so much about a moment of arrival as a process of growth until it encompasses the world. This is one element that points to the mystery kingdom being connected and continuous with what is to follow, as the comprehensive kingdom is yet to come.

The parable of the leaven argues that the kingdom starts small, but ends up filling the whole. Do not be fooled by how small the new community is that gathers around Jesus. One day it will fill the earth.

The parable of the hidden treasure notes that the kingdom is worth selling all with joy, a point shared with the parable of the pearl of great price.

The parable of the dragnet teaches the kingdom's mixed character so that it is purged of evil at the end.

The parable of the kingdom scribe teaches things new and old, showing that what Jesus taught about the kingdom involved things that had been taught alongside new things. This is another parable arguing for a connection between what Jesus reveals here and what has been taught and what is still to come. With these parables in place, one can connect the dots and explain the kingdom program of God in more fullness.

Other parables outside the kingdom parable discourse also cover the kingdom. *The parable of the wedding feast* (Matt. 22:1–14; Luke 14:15–24) makes a very important point as it shows that those who were originally lined up to attend opted out of participation in the kingdom, while others made it in. This pictures Gentile inclusion and the rejection of many Jews, at least initially. It also makes another very important point. The kingdom comes when it is first announced; it is not postponed in terms of its arrival, something the inclusion of Gentiles also shows. The kingdom once announced comes as announced in the phases or administrative arrangements that have been outlined.

The parable of the ten minas, or ten talents (Matt. 25:14–30; Luke 19:11–27) also adds to our understanding. It shows the accountability that comes with associating with Jesus. It teaches that the kingdom is received by the Son not on His return, but on His departure before He returns. Only our full experience of it awaits His return.

All of these parables develop what Jesus meant by the kingdom, and they develop the definition of it coming out of the Old Testament. But one question they do not answer is, When does the kingdom come—is it with Jesus' first coming or at the end? The answer to that question comes in other texts.

The Kingdom Is Already and Not Yet.

It is sometimes suggested that dispensationalists only hold to a futurist view of the kingdom. That is true for some dispensationalists, but not for all. How they handle gospel texts about the kingdom's arrival shows the difference. All dispensationalists agree that the bulk of kingdom texts point to the kingdom in the future, a kingdom that has a phase of operation on this present earth involving Israel. But a few key texts are topics for discussion about whether there is an already element to this kingdom or are parts of distinct kingdom programs.[7] Here are those key texts.

The first text is Matthew 12:28 (Luke 11:20). Jesus has just healed a man who could not speak. His opponents have accused Him of healing by the power of Beelzebul. He responds to that conclusion and rejects it by noting that if true, then Satan is working against himself. So if He casts out demons "by the Spirit of God" (Matthew)/ "finger of God" (Luke), then the kingdom of God has come upon them. Two points are important here. First, the deliverance work of Jesus pictures the deliverance work of the kingdom. These exorcisms stand as evidence of the arrival of the kingdom authority that saves. Second, this is not merely an anticipatory picture of coming kingdom authority; it pictures the defeat of Satan that makes deliverance possible. These acts are the presupposition for being able to save and rule (Eph. 1:15–23). So miracles are evidence that the kingdom has come and Satan is in the process of meeting his ultimate defeat.

The second text is Matthew 11:12 (Luke 16:16). Here the kingdom of God is said to suffer violence since the time of John the Baptist. That period is marked out in its Lucan version as distinct from the period of the Law and Prophets that preceded it. This marks the kingdom as arriving with Jesus.

A third text is Matthew 13:16–17 (Luke 10:23–24). Here Jesus tells the disciples they are blessed to see what they are seeing. The Matthean context is important, for the remark comes with the parables of the kingdom in its mystery form, after the note that the nation of Israel has rejected the Messiah. There is no indication of the kingdom being postponed by the remark made here. The text instead says that the prophets and righteous (Matthew)/prophets and kings (Luke) longed to see and did not see it. This describes the arrival of the long-awaited promise of God in His program. It points to continuity and connection between what Jesus teaches here about the kingdom and what had been hoped for before His arrival. It is another way to say the kingdom has come. Had the prophets, righteous people, and kings of the past been alive now they would have been thrilled to see what Jesus is now doing to bring the kingdom.

A fourth text is Luke 17:21. Here Jesus says that the Pharisees do not need to look for the kingdom here and there, for it is in their grasp. In other words, in Him it is right before them.

Already noted is the parable of the wedding feast where the kingdom is not delayed by rejection but others simply are invited to participate (Luke 14:15–24; Matt. 22:1–10).

When John the Baptist asks if Jesus is the one to come, Jesus does not answer with a yes but notes the activity that He engages in points to who He is. He names the time as one of eschatological fulfillment (Matt. 11:2–6; Luke 7:18–23). As the blind see, the lame walk, lepers are cleansed, the deaf hear, and the gospel is preached, Jesus points to texts that Isaiah had said would be markers of the arrival of the new era of promise (Isa. 35:5–6; 26:19; 29:18–19; 61:1—all texts about the era of promise). By pointing to what He does, Jesus affirms the nature of the new time He brings and the new rule it represents. He also says He is the one to come who brings what was promised.

Another vitally important text is found in Luke 3:16, where John the Baptist declares that the way one can know the Christ has come. The new era John announces has arrived when the Messiah baptizes with the Spirit of God. This is a point Peter also makes in Acts 2. Peter tells Israel she can know God has made Jesus Lord and Christ by what has just taken place in the crucifixion, resurrection, and ascension, and the distribution of the indwelling Spirit. Jesus is the one to be called on to save because the Spirit has been poured out on God's people just as Joel promised would happen in the last days. So Jesus is executing salvation benefits in exercise of His messianic role. He is not passive at God's side after His resurrection, but active in rule, in forgiving and saving.

These series of texts show that although there is still much to come, some of what was promised about the kingdom and coming promise are currently in place or being accomplished. What is left to do comes when the Son of Man returns and executes judgment as Matthew 13 and 24 also affirm. Just as our salvation is already/not yet as we await glorification to complete all God does in saving us as individuals, so the kingdom is already/not yet in coming in stages of fulfillment. The very fact that forgiveness comes, which is rooted in the new covenant, and that Jesus' death also inaugurates the new covenant as His words at the Last Supper indicate (Luke 22:20; 1 Cor. 11:25), shows the kingdom has been inaugurated. The church celebrates these current realities every time her members worship in celebration of the Lord's Table. However, the kingdom is not yet consummated, as its coming is part of a process over time, coming in stages that parallel the comings of the Christ. This process of small to comprehensive is what the parables of the mustard seed and leaven show.

The Kingdom Is about Rule and Realm.

The kingdom is about a saving rule that forms a people delivered out of sin. Those people are given the Spirit because they have been cleansed and forgiven. The arrival of a functioning Messiah is a new administrative arrangement, as now the long-awaited promise is inaugurated with a Messiah who has suffered and opened the door to forgiveness, the Spirit, and life. Yet the program also looks forward to a consummation when full peace (shalom) will come to the earth and all the promises will be completely realized on this earth and in this history of reclamation.

So the past era of the Law and Prophets was an arrangement made with the hope of a Messiah. Israel was called as a bearer of hope. Now we have the kingdom inaugurated. The promised Messiah has come and done the core work that allows for salvation. Forgiveness of sin and the enablement of the indwelling Spirit are at the core of the gospel and kingdom presence. The church bears the message today because Israel's house is desolate *until* she says, "Blessed is the one who comes in the Lord's name" (cf. Matt. 23:37–39; Luke 13:34–35).[8] A vindicated Messiah has inaugurated kingdom blessing and rules from God's right hand granting forgiveness, the Spirit, and life (Col. 1:14; 3:1–4; Eph. 1:15–2:10). That arrangement differs from the past when Messiah was only promised and anticipated. It also differs from the arrangement of the future when He will be directly present on earth and ruling in a context of full shalom.

So another arrangement is yet to come. Then Messiah will be present on earth in a way distinct from His presence now. These arrangements are also called dispensations. They are distinct structures forming the structural parts on which God's program proceeds and progresses. Through them God administers His unified salvation program. So kingdom is one frame in which these dispensations can be seen. The biblical covenants also disclose dispensational change in God's plan of salvation.

THE COVENANTS OF PROMISE

The Abrahamic Covenant

The gospel does not begin with the coming of Jesus as told in the Gospels. It begins with a covenant promise made to Abram in Genesis 12:1–3 (cf. Gal.

3:8). At that time God promised to create a special people: a nation. God promised to make Abram's name great. He promised to bless the people of the world through Abraham (so renamed by God; Gen. 17:5). God promised a seed; the story of Genesis and Exodus shows He had specific individuals in mind, such as Isaac and Jacob (not Eliezer, Ishmael, or Esau). That seed also involved a nation that would be as numerous as the sands of the sea (Gen. 13:13–17) or the stars in the sky (Gen. 22:17). This would be a people with a land (Gen. 13:14–17).

That nation God honored as special when He delivered them and made a covenant with them through Moses. The covenant of Moses was not a covenant of promise, but one of national organization of blessing and cursing (Exod. 19:3–6; Deut. 28–32; Gal. 3). The Mosaic covenant was another means by which God administered His program, not through a covenant of promise as with Abraham. The Mosaic covenant was a covenant brought alongside to help until the promise was realized (Gal. 3:1–4:6). By contrast, the Abrahamic covenant was a national covenant that also promised blessing on the world. The covenant to Abraham is the backdrop for other key covenants of promise.

The Davidic Covenant

In 2 Samuel 7:8–16, in response to Israel's request for a king and after the failure of Saul, God promised a dynastic house for Israel to the family of David. This king would be a Son to Him and He would be a Father to the king (2 Sam. 7:14; Psa. 2:7). The king would shepherd God's people and eventually bring peace. This is the promise that looks to a kingdom of peace, as well as for a king who fulfills the ideals expressed in the dynastic line. When Jesus is called the Christ or is tied to David, as He is in Matthew's and Luke's genealogies, it is this covenant promise that is invoked. It is this kingship with its kingdom of peace that is appealed to as being present with Jesus.

There are a host of images that tie into this promise that the Gospels refer to as realized in Jesus. One can think first of all of the picture of Jesus as a shepherd (Matt. 9:36; John 10), imagery rooted directly in the covenant (2 Sam. 7:8).[9] The idea also extends to God's promise in Ezekiel 34:20–24 that a nation with bad shepherds will one day receive a good one from God. Ezekiel refers to David, but it is likely a reference to his line. The promise is of a covenant of peace in the land (Ezek. 34:25–30). These promises show God's commitment to Israel as a people in the midst of the nations. This is part of how God will shepherd

His sheep (Ezek. 34:31). However God has committed to bless the world, as He promised to Abraham, here He also makes commitments to one in the Davidic line to complete promises to Israel.

This throne is one that is both David's and God's. First Chronicles 29:23 describes the throne on which Solomon sat as the Lord's throne. Solomon sat there as David's dynastic successor. The king served as God's vicegerent and is ideally described as Son. He sits with authority shared with God as Psalm 2:7 and Psalm 110:1 declare for the one who realizes all the promise of the line. Even the geography of ancient Jerusalem made this point. The city of David was on the right side of God's presence as one looks in the direction the Shekinah faces as it looks toward the Mount of Olives. The entryway to the Holy of Holies, the way into that most sacred space, was on the Olivet side (on the east). If the Shekinah faces outward from the Holy of Holies toward the east, then the home of the king in the city of David would be to the right (on the south). This pictured the close relationship the dynasty was called to have with God, a relationship the Messiah would fully realize.

New Covenant

Israel's failure did not cause God to give up on the nation. God did not abandon Israel, because He is gracious and faithful to His promises. So He issued the promise of a new covenant in Jeremiah 31:31–34. This covenant is explicitly described as different from the covenant made on the mountain, an allusion to the Mosaic covenant. It is a different administrative arrangement. The new covenant was another covenant of promise, whereas the Mosaic was not. According to the new covenant promise God will place His law within them. They will all know Him. He will forgive their sins. Other texts in the prophets speak of being sprinkled clean and having God's Spirit (Ezek. 36:24–27). Ezekiel's remarks are part of the development of the promise of a new shepherd for the people from Ezekiel 34. The same work of restoration is in view in Ezekiel 36. God will no longer administrate His salvation merely with outside stipulations; He promises to enter into the community from within the hearts of the people who reside in it. The result is that people will know Him.

Sometimes it is claimed that this new covenant has provided access to forgiveness through Jesus' death just as He taught at the Last Supper, but that its other provisions await realization in the future. This ignores clear New Testament language and teaching in the Gospels. For example, John 6:45 refers to the language of the new covenant, saying, "They all will be taught by God" (NIV), as Jesus positively refers to those who are responding in faith to Him. Jesus is saying the new covenant is in evidence in this response. John 17:3 speaks of eternal life as knowing the Father and the Son in language that echoes the new covenant idea that those who participate in the covenant know God. Note how eternal life in mentioned in John 6:47, just as it is noted in John 17:3. So we see a new structure realized in the new covenant's promise of the Spirit indwelling people as the means for new life.

This new arrangement explains why the disciples are told to wait to be clothed with power from the promise of the Father in Luke 24:49. They have to be equipped and empowered for the mission Jesus gives them to do. Acts 2:30–36 describes this equipping as the evidence Israel should recognize as showing that Jesus is the promised Lord and Christ. Peter is appealing not to things merely promised, set up, or anticipated here, but to accomplished events that show realization of those promises. So Israel can know that God has shown Jesus to be Lord and Christ.

We see here how the Davidic and new covenant hopes come together. We also see how a new arrangement, a new dispensation, is inaugurated when Jesus, having died to provide for the forgiveness of sins, is vindicated by God and brought to God's right hand to mediate the giving of the Spirit that places God's law on the heart. This shows the giving of life so that those who have the Spirit can know the Father and cry out "Abba, Father" (Rom. 8:15). Jesus rules over His people and mediates the blessing of the kingdom as a functioning Messiah who is confessed as Lord and Christ. In this, we see the uniting of kingdom and covenants in a new arrangement that will remain in place until Jesus returns and exercises His rule even more directly after He returns. That return completes what He has inaugurated in kingdom blessing here. It is when the kingdom's comprehensive presence comes in line with all the Old Testament had promised (Acts 3:18–22).

This overview of the covenants also shows how Trinitarian this program is. The Father mediates kingdom and covenant blessing through the Son, who gives the Spirit as the means of connecting God's people individually and corporately to Him.

ISRAEL AND THE NATIONS

One of the distinctive emphases in dispensationalism is its belief about a future for ethnic Israel. This grows out of the conviction that the Scriptures teach that God has made a covenantal commitment to them. His grace and faithfulness means God will not abandon Israel. In the face of Israeli rejection of Jesus as Messiah, God will graciously persevere and draw the nation back to Himself.

Israel *and* the Gentile Nations

Many of the texts cited above show this commitment. In saying this, one does not deny how the nations have been included in the promise, plan, and people of God. Their place for blessing also has roots in the Abrahamic covenant in the idea of the blessing of the nations coming through Abraham. The idea that Gentiles can be sons of Abraham is something Paul explicitly affirms (Gal. 3:28–29). However, to include Gentiles does not mean hope for Israel is excluded. To suggest that Gentile inclusion means Israel's exclusion is to commit a logical *non sequitur*. One can add recipients without excluding those who had earlier received the promise.

It is one thing to say this in principle and another to show that it is explicitly taught. So it is important to see that several Gospel texts and a few texts tied to Jesus' ministry in Acts show that the New Testament makes this point.

It is often asserted that Jesus has become the new temple and has replaced a need for Israel as a nation in the program of God by being Israel in Himself.[10] That Jesus occupies such a representative position is not to be doubted, but that it requires a loss of hope for Israel ignores what Jesus Himself taught.

In Luke 13:34–35 and Matthew 23:37–39, Jesus declares Israel's house desolate in judgment for her rejection of her Messiah. The language comes from Jeremiah 12:7. For some, this judgment and rejection is permanent. The appeal is to the picture of the destruction of the temple in Matthew 24, Mark 13, and Luke 21 or the picture of new leaders replacing Israel in the parable of the wicked tenants. But this ignores the very passage in which the desolate house is set forth. For that very text goes on to say, "until you say, 'Blessed in he who comes in the name of the Lord' " (Luke 13:35 NIV)—language clearly from Psalm 118:26. It looks forward to a time when Israel will respond with a majority embrace, just as en masse the people have not responded to Jesus in His first coming. At the least, such a door is left open. It also ignores the fact that it is the Twelve who replaced Israel's leaders in the program of Jesus. Notably, all were Jewish! So the leadership at the core of the new community Jesus formed never left Israel. The foundation of that redeemed people is still the apostles.

Other "until" texts make similar points. In a passage unique to Luke's gospel, Luke 21:20–24 looks to the destruction of the temple in his version of the Olivet Discourse. In the midst of describing destruction to come, Jesus speaks of Jerusalem's desolation and its being trampled down by the nations. This is a description of the defeat of the city in AD 70 by the Romans. The remark answers the question the disciples raised when Jesus said there would not be one stone left upon another at the temple (21:6). Jesus says it this way: "Jerusalem will be trampled on by the Gentiles until the times of the Gentiles are fulfilled" (v. 24). Now this looks like a limited delineation of time in which the Gentiles have control of Jerusalem. One does not delimit such a time unless there is another time coming to follow that is no longer the time of the Gentiles. The contrast in Scripture with Gentiles is Israel. So this text strongly implies that there is a time to come for Israel, a time when Messiah comes to His city, as other Old Testament texts declare (Zech. 14; Isa. 2:1–4).

This deduction is confirmed in Jesus' last dialogue with the disciples in Acts 1:6–11. Here the disciples have spent forty days with Jesus. He has discussed how He fulfills the promises of the Old Testament in His death, resurrection, and preaching of repentance to the nations (Luke 24:43–47). After that time and instruction, the disciples ask in Acts 1:6 if this is the time Jesus will restore the kingdom to Israel. Despite many commentary claims to the contrary, nothing in Jesus' reply rejects the premise of that question. He simply says that act is the Father's business.[11] In the meantime, they have a mission to perform. The angel notes as Jesus departs that the ascended one will return just as He has departed. This appears to suggest that the rest of the program awaits His return.

Peter confirms that this resumption of the divine program is the case when he issues a commentary on Jesus' heavenly session in Acts 3:18–22. Here Peter calls on Israel to repent so that her sin can "be wiped out that times of refreshing [might] come from the Lord" (v. 19). In particular the national sin of rejecting her Messiah has been noted (Acts 3:17). Then Jesus goes on to note that the Messiah Jesus will be sent for them one day. Heaven receives Jesus "*until* the time comes for God to restore everything, as God promised long ago through his holy prophets" (v. 21, emphasis added). Note the use again of the crucial term "until." God has a planned program and even though Messiah is in heaven now ruling, He will rule one day in a return to earth. In that return He will do all that the prophets promised for the nation. The context of Peter's speech is making that specific point.

Yet to Come

This is the restoration the apostles asked Jesus about in Acts 1. It is what the Old Testament describes as what is yet to come. Nothing Peter says here implies that things have been reconfigured from what the Old Testament described and promised. Yes, Acts shows how the nations are now included to the glorious praise of God. This inclusion also has taken place under His direct direction. Yes, that means the configuration of God's people now spans all nations. Yet nothing in that shows that Israel has permanently been excluded from hope. These texts with their "until" sequence point to the fact that God is keeping His covenant commitments to Israel even as He realizes those commitments in Jesus Christ, even as the promise now includes the nations en masse. The presence of one does not exclude the other. In fact, the presence of fulfillment in Christ includes His maintaining commitments already made.

The result is that kingdom and covenant commitments show periods of differing administrative arrangements. These are dispensations planned and directed by God. They deliver both the kingdom and salvation in line with covenant promises made by a faithful and gracious God. The God of promise keeps His commitments to the original recipients.

CONCLUSION

The administrative arrangements tied to kingdom and the covenants of promise in Scripture look to three periods. There is a period of promise, when the hope of covenant realization is set forth beginning from the seed of Abraham, Israel. God makes commitments to her on behalf of the world. That promise focuses on a dynastic house, the line of David. It culminates in a messianic hope of one who brings deliverance and shalom. To make that deliverance effective, sin must be forgiven, people must be empowered from within, and they must come to know God from the heart. That is the promise of the New Covenant. It all aims at a rule that the New Testament at its start declares as near.

John the Baptist says the promise is arriving, coming near. He says one can know it has come when the one to come baptizes with the Spirit and fire, a baptism that purges humanity and draws some to Him (Luke 3:15–17).

From the era of promise, we come to the time of inaugurated realization. Here forgiveness of sins is provided for through Jesus' death on the cross and His resurrection from the dead. Here the empowerment comes through Messiah's baptizing with the Spirit, the very sign the forerunner said would indicate the arrival of the promised new era. With Jesus' coming, the promised kingdom arrives. It does so in arranged stages. First, His rule comes from God's side as He directs and leads His people through the provision of the Spirit. He makes a claim on every soul because His kingdom work of deliverance extends to authority over every soul, whether good or evil. This comprehensive claim on humanity is what the kingdom parables show. This is an era where Gentiles dominate. It looks toward a day when a full restoration will come.

The third period is a time of consummated realization. Here all the promises meet their final amen. Jesus will return to preside even more directly over His people. It is a time when Israel will say "blessed is the one who comes in the name of the Lord." Jew and Gentile will share in a fullness of blessing on this earth that also prepares for a new heaven and new earth. This history meets its completion as promise now is completely realized, even as eternity is prepared for.

These are themes and administrative structures the Gospels teach. The Gospels reflect the ordering of dispensations as ways to enact kingdom and covenants for all nations, Israel included. The story of the dispensations is our story. It is the story of the reclamation of humanity so people can live life in the way God designed it to be lived. In God's dispensational arrangement He shows His grace and faithfulness to His promise, all for the glory of God.

NOTES

1. Charles C. Ryrie, *Dispensationalism Today* (Chicago: Moody, 1965), 24–33; cf. Charles C. Ryrie, *Dispensationalism*, rev. ed. (Chicago: Moody, 2007), 29–36.
2. Romans 4 shows this clearly. Abraham and David are the examples. One belongs to the pre-Mosaic period, one to the period after.
3. I have detailed the kingdom in the gospels in Darrell L. Bock, *Jesus According to Scripture* (Grand Rapids: Baker, 2002), 565–93.
4. Charles C. Ryrie, *Dispensationalism* (Chicago: Moody Press, 1995), 156, discusses three forms of the kingdom: a universal kingdom through which God rules the world (Ps. 145:13), a Davidic/messianic kingdom which the Lord will rule in a present earth millennium to come, and a mystery form of the kingdom, announced and revealed in Matthew 13. Dispensationalists discuss the relationship of the

latter two kingdom arrangements, which are both part of what Jesus presented. Classic and revised dispensationalists maintain a distinction between those two kingdoms (mystery then Davidic) and have them separated from each other. Progressive dispensationalists see them as two related phases of one kingdom promise with elements of realized Davidic messianic activity present in both phases.

5. Herbert Bateman, Gordon Johnston, and Darrell L. Bock, *Jesus the Messiah* (Grand Rapids: Kregel, 2012), traces the hermeneutics and development of the messianic hope including how the second-temple period contributes to what we see in the New Testament.

6. What dispensationalists discuss among themselves is whether that mystery represents a distinct program tied only to the church period (as classic and revised dispensationalists conclude) or whether that mystery introduces a continuity and connection to the promise made to Israel before and tied to the earthly millennial kingdom to follow (so progressive dispensationalists). What all dispensational groups share is the idea that an earthly kingdom involving this earth and Israel is to follow the current administrative period or dispensation. For treatments of these themes tied to kingdom and covenants in side-by-side discussion and dialogue, see Herbert W. Bateman IV, ed., *Three Central Issues in Contemporary Dispensationalism: A Comparison of Traditional and Progressive Views* (Grand Rapids: Kregel, 1999).

7. See notes 4 and 6 above for an overview of that discussion.

8. This "until" is important. It shows that a period of reinvolvement for Israel follows. This is a point often left undiscussed in covenantal or historic premillennial treatments of kingdom promise. Two recent such efforts are Peter J. Gentry and Scott J. Wellum, *Kingdom through Covenant* (Wheaton: Crossway, 2012), and Gary Burge, *Jesus and the Land: The New Testament Challenge to Holy Land Theology* (Grand Rapids: Baker, 2010). Neither of these works cover, this text or other "until" texts. Luke-Acts is especially ignored. See Darrell Bock, "The Restoration of Israel in Luke-Acts," in *Introduction to Messianic Judaism*, ed. David Rudolph and Joel Willits (Grand Rapids: Zondervan, 2013), 168–77. See the Israel and the Nations section of this essay below.

9. In fact the New Testament invokes twenty images tied to messianic promise for Jesus' current activity. For this full list, see Darrell Bock, "Covenants of Progressive Dispensationalism," in Bateman, *Three Central Issues*, 195–203. This entire chapter (169–203) covers the covenants theme in much more detail than there is space for here.

10. For example, Burge, *Jesus and the Land*. This is but one key and important biblical theme not developed in Gentry and Wellum, *Kingdom through Covenant*. It is significant that neither of these key works discusses the texts presented in this section. The result is an imbalance in their presentations that slights Israel.

11. The remarks by John Stott, *The Message of Acts* (Downers Grove, IL: InterVarsity, 1990), 41, come most to mind here. He sees the question as full of errors and presumptions Jesus rejects. However, nothing Jesus has said to them over His forty days with them after His resurrection nor anything said to them here shows their question was flawed.

7

God's Plan for History:

FROM THE ASCENSION TO THE SECOND COMING OF CHRIST

STANLEY D. TOUSSAINT

What happened, what is happening, and what will happen from the ascension of Christ to the conclusion of the thousand-year reign of the Lord Jesus? The events during this period are extremely important to dispensational theology.

Generally, there is agreement among dispensationalists on the main historical points of prophecy, namely the church age, a seven-year period of tribulation, the millennial reign of Christ, and eternity. However, there is a minority who hold to different interpretations of the time of the rapture—when those in the church are "snatched away." The pretribulation view will be presented and defended here.

We will proceed in the historical order as recorded in Acts and then in the prophesied order from the rapture through the tribulation as we consider God's plan.

PRAYER AND THE CHOOSING OF THE TWELFTH APOSTLE

After the Lord's ascension, the first item of business for the apostles was prayer (Acts 1:14). The Greek text states they were devoting themselves continually to *the* prayer. This could be the generic use of the article, but more probably it is referring to a specific prayer. What was their request? Undoubtedly they were praying for the coming of the Holy Spirit as Christ implied they should in Luke 11:12–13. Their request was granted on the day of Pentecost, so believers today do not pray for the Holy Spirit to indwell them (cf. Rom. 8:9; 1 Cor. 12:13). The apostles, and the others with them especially, would have been encouraged to pray for the Holy Spirit by Christ's words in Acts 1:4–5 (cf. Luke 24:49; John 7:37–39; 14:16–18, 26; 16:7–15).

In a very real sense they were praying for the coming of the kingdom because they assumed the descent of the Holy Spirit would inaugurate the kingdom (cf. Ezek. 36:26–32; 37:14; 39:28–29; Joel 2:28–29; 3:1; Zech. 12:10–13:1, etc.). After all, the disciples in the Sermon on the Mount were told to pray for the coming of the kingdom (Matt. 6:9–10).[1] So they "with one mind" were continually devoting themselves to prayer for the coming of the Holy Spirit. They assumed He would cause Israel to repent; this national conversion of Israel to Christ would bring the kingdom (cf. Zech. 12:10ff; Matt. 23:39).

The second item of business carried out in the period between the Lord's ascension and the day of Pentecost was the selection of the twelfth apostle to take the place of Judas (Acts 1:12–26).[2] It appears the apostles, headed up by Peter, remembered the promise of the Lord Jesus in Luke 22:30 and Matthew 19:28. If the coming of the earthly kingdom was imminent, they certainly would not want that twelfth throne vacant! One does not gain the impression the apostles acted too hastily or wrongly in selecting Matthias. There is no hint of censure in Luke's account in Acts.

After this the apostles are not referred to as the eleven, but the twelve (Acts 6:2). These twelve, then, are not only future leaders of Israel in the coming kingdom but they also became the leaders of the fledgling church in Jerusalem.

THE DAY OF PENTECOST

The Significance of the Day of Pentecost

The day of Pentecost is first and foremost a Jewish holiday; therefore it, like the Passover, must first be interpreted from the perspective of an Israelite. The question then is, what was the original Jewish significance of the day of Pentecost? It must have been very important because it was one of the three main annual feasts—Passover, Pentecost (Feast of Weeks, Feast of the Harvest), and Booths (Tabernacles, Feast of the Ingathering; cf. Exod. 23:4–17; 34:24; Deut. 16:16). The term "Pentecost" is a Greek word meaning "fiftieth," based on its being observed seven weeks following the day after the Feast of Firstfruits (Lev. 23:15). Pentecost as a name for the feast occurs only in the New Testament. Because the feast was based on the wheat harvest following the barley harvest, it was a thanksgiving celebration for the Lord's provision of grains. It was probably observed during the forty years of wandering in anticipation of Israel harvesting crops in the land. The provision of manna ceased when the children of Israel entered the land (Josh. 5:12).

Therefore, the day of Pentecost was a celebration of God's provision for Israel in the *land of promise.* It thus became a picture of God's future abundant supply of the promised Holy Spirit for the coming of the prophesied kingdom (cf. Ezek. 36:22–32; 37:14; 39:28–29; Joel 2:26–32; Zech. 12:10–13:1). This is the Jewish significance of the Feast of Pentecost.[3]

For the church, Pentecost marked its birthday, as will be seen in the discussion of Acts 11:15 and 1 Cor. 12:13 below.[4] Dispensationalists agree that the church began on the day of Pentecost, even though the church was totally Jewish for a time.[5] The day of Pentecost was introduced with two signs of God's presence—wind (*pnoe;* only here and Acts 17:25 in the New Testament) and fire. Both of these displayed God's presence in the Old Testament; e.g., wind (1 Kgs. 19:11–13; Job 38:1) and fire (Exod. 3:2–6).[6]

The Phenomenon of Speaking in Tongues

The outstanding sign was the disciples' ability to speak in tongues.[7] This gift was the supernatural ability to speak a foreign language without having learned it or understanding it. It can be said dogmatically that the gift was not gibberish or "ecstatic utterances" because each tongue is called a language (*dialektos)* in

Acts 2:6, 8. Some believe the gift of tongues in 1 Corinthians 12–14 is a different kind of tongues, namely "ecstatic sounds" and not languages. However, a careful study of 1 Corinthians 12–14 will not support this. In 1 Corinthians 12:10; 14:5, 13, 26 the tongues can be translated.[8] The crowning proof that "tongues" refers to languages is 1 Corinthians 14:21, where Paul quoted from Isaiah 28:11–12. This passage is a prediction of the deportation of the northern kingdom of Israel to foreign countries. There, Jews would hear foreign "tongues," an evidence of God's judgment. Paul equates the languages of Isaiah 28 with the gift of tongues spoken in the Corinthian church. The meaning of "tongue" in Acts 2, 10, 19 is presumably the same as the spiritual gift of tongues in 1 Corinthians.

The question asked by dispensationalists is what is the purpose of this sign gift? Because it occurred on the day of Pentecost, some hold it is a mark of Spirit baptism (cf. Acts 1:5; 2:4). However, this cannot be so because all believers in Corinth were baptized by the Holy Spirit (1 Cor. 12:13) but not all spoke in tongues (1 Cor. 12:30).

Others assert the purpose was to preach the gospel to those assembled at Pentecost or in the local church. The problem is this is never stated; it is only an inference from Acts 2:11. It seems, as Paul states in 1 Corinthians 14:14, 16–17, that tongues were used for prayer and praise. This fits with Acts 2:11 but may not explain the purpose of tongues.

The one passage that designates the purpose of tongues is 1 Corinthians 14:22, an evidence of God's judgment. Tongues are not meant to be a sign for believers but for unbelievers. In Isaiah, tongues were a sign of judgment on Israel; so in the early church tongues were a warning to Israel of a coming cataclysm (the destruction of Jerusalem in AD 70). This fits perfectly with the theme of judgment in Peter's sermon, which immediately follows (cf. Acts 2:40). Tongues are mentioned three times in Acts and each may imply judgment on Israel. In Acts 10, the second reference to tongues, Gentiles (as in Isa. 28) speak in tongues to indicate God's blessing on Gentiles at the expense of Israel (cf. Matt. 21:43). Because the nation of Israel was in the process of rejecting Jesus as their Messiah (cf. Acts 12:1–3), the gospel was going to become primarily the possession of Gentiles. The whole book of Acts involves the theme of Israel rejecting Jesus Christ and God turning to Gentiles.[9]

The third time tongues are mentioned in Acts is in chapter 19. A remnant of twelve Jews believe and speak in tongues to imply a remnant of Israel will believe but judgment will be the part of the majority (cf. Rom. 9:27; 10:1–4; 11:1–5, 25).

This helps to explain the temporary nature of this gift (cf. 1 Cor. 13:8). With the destruction of Jerusalem in AD 70 the need for this gift would cease. God's judgment had fallen.

The dispensational implications of tongues when seen in this light are huge. Tongues are a precursor to God's judgment of Israel and of His moving to Gentiles to become heirs of His kingdom (Rom. 11:11–24). Ultimately Israel as a people will be saved (Rom. 11:25–27).

The Sermon by Peter

After explaining that it was not rational to say the people were speaking in tongues because they were drunk, Peter applied Joel 2:28–32 to the situation. When the apostle said, "This is what was spoken," he evidently was stating this speaking in tongues was the *beginning* of the fulfillment of the prophecy, as implied by his assertion that the prophecy was for "the last days"—an addition made by Peter but not in the original prophecy. To the apostle the last days had been initiated at Pentecost and would finally culminate with the judgment of the day of the Lord at the end of the tribulation. If Israel repented the signs would continue to the fulfillment of Acts 2:19–20 with its heavenly signs. In other words, the coming of the judgment of Joel 2 was contingent upon Israel's acceptance of Jesus as the Messiah.[10]

Because Israel rejected Jesus as the Christ, the kingdom did not come and the prophecy of Joel 2 was only partially fulfilled. When Israel repents, as it certainly will (cf. Zech. 12:10–14), the prophecy will be fulfilled totally.[11]

THE RE-OFFER OF JESUS AS MESSIAH TO ISRAEL IN ACTS

The Theme of the Message in Acts 2

Israel—as well as the Gentiles—were responsible for crucifying Jesus, who was the Christ, but God had resurrected Him and exalted Him to the right hand of the Father (Acts 2:22–36). Judgment was about to fall on that generation of Jews except for those who repented (Acts 2:40–41).

The major issue in Acts is not the substitutionary atonement of the Lord Jesus; it is only mentioned briefly and in passing in Acts 20:28 where Paul reminded the Ephesian elders that the church was acquired, or purchased, by God's own blood. The death of Christ is referred to often but not in the sense of a vicarious payment for sin. The large issue in Acts is the messiahship of Jesus, as proven by His resurrection and ascension. The great sin of Israel was their rejection of Jesus as Messiah.

The Theme of the Message in Acts 3

Few passages show the conditionality of the coming of the kingdom more clearly than this one in Acts 3:12–26. Verses 19–20 indicate *personal* and *individual* forgiveness of sins when a person repents. This is seen in the first purpose clause, "that your sins may be wiped away." A second purpose clause discloses "that times of refreshing may come from the presence of the Lord; and that He may send Jesus, the Christ." The word "that" occurs two times in this translation. The second "that" is not in the Greek text, indicating it is one extended purpose clause. The "times of refreshing" cannot be separated from the "sending of Jesus"; they occur at the same time. This second purpose clause is meant for the nation of Israel; when they repent as a people the Messiah will come.[12] This refers to national salvation (cf. Zech. 12:10–13:1; Matt. 23:39; Rom. 11:25–27).

The subject of the return of the Messiah prompted Peter to describe Jesus as the new Moses predicted in Deuteronomy 18:15, a prominent subject in the New Testament (cf. John 1:21, 25; 6:14). When the Lord Jesus returns as the new Moses, He will judge Israel (Acts 3:23).

THE JEW-GENTILE CHURCH

Dispensationalists believe the church began on the day of Pentecost. Christ predicted in Acts 1 the apostles would be baptized with the Holy Spirit, and this took place on the day of Pentecost (Acts 11:15–16). Spirit baptism is the means by which the church (the body of Christ) is formed (1 Cor. 12:13). This brings one to the conclusion that the church began at Pentecost. Clearly, the church at first was totally Jewish; in time however the church became more and more Gentile. Today it is almost completely Gentile with a Jewish remnant (Rom. 11:5).

The Church Is a Result of Israel's Rejection of Jesus as Messiah.

A key element in dispensational theology is the rejection by Israel of Jesus as Messiah, the turning by God to the Gentiles and the formation of the church. The Gospels, Acts, and the Epistles record and refer to the steadfast rejection of Jesus as Messiah by Israel. Paul in his missionary journeys always preached the gospel to Jews first, and when they did not believe he would turn to the Gentiles (cf. Acts 13:44–49; 18:6; 19:8–10; 28:25–28). As a result Israel now is living in judicial blindness, a hardening of its heart.

Luke sometimes would record a historical event as a cameo of what will happen in the future. An illustration is found in Acts 13:6–11, the account of the blinding of Bar Jesus (or Elymas), the Jewish soothsayer. Because he attempted to stop Sergius Paulus, a Gentile proconsul, from believing, he was temporarily blinded. This is a picture of what will happen in the remainder of Acts and of Paul's statement in Romans 11:25. When the full number of the Gentile elect is saved, God will remove the judicial hardening of Israel, and the vast majority of Jews will be converted (cf. Zech. 12:10–14; Matt. 23:39; Rom. 11:26–27).

The Church as a Mystery

All theologies recognize the phenomenon of history that because Israel rejected Jesus as Messiah, the gospel message is now going to Gentiles.[13] What is distinctive to dispensationalism is the idea that the church is not predicted in the Old Testament. It is a mystery revealed only in the New Testament.[14] The Lord Jesus anticipated the church in John 10:16, where He referred to "other sheep, which are not of this fold" and "they will become one flock." It seems Matthew 19:30–20:16 teaches the same truth. In this parable of the laborers in the vineyard, the ones with the contract represent Jews who have Israel's covenants; Gentiles are seen in the workers who work without a contract. In the end they are paid equally (20:12; 19:30; 20:16). This seems to be an illustration of the equality of Jews and Gentiles in the church (Eph. 3:6).

Significantly, Gentile salvation is prophesied in the Old Testament (Isa. 2:2–4; 9:23–25; Amos 9:12, etc.). It needs to be noted that although Gentile salvation is predicted, the Jews are seen as being in a superior position (Isa. 11:10; 56:7; Zech. 8:22–23). One of the great New Testament "mysteries" (Rom. 16:25; Eph.

3:3–9; 5:32; 6:19; Col. 1:26–27; 4:3) is the new revelation that in the New Testament church Gentiles are equal with Jews.

The Church and Jewish Blessings

As a result of this equality, Gentiles will participate in future Jewish blessings. In Ephesians 2:11–12, Paul declares that Gentiles were excluded from Jewish privileges, even the covenants of promise, but now they are brought near (2:13–19). In Hebrews 11:39–40 the Old Testament saints are said to have died without receiving what was promised, but the church will participate with them in their fulfillment.

In Matthew 19:28, Jesus Christ promised the twelve apostles they would sit on twelve thrones judging the twelve tribes of Israel. Of course, this will be fulfilled for all twelve except Judas (cf. Acts 1:15–26). Significantly, these same apostles form the foundation of the church (Eph. 2:20). This can only mean the church will rule with the Lord Christ in the coming kingdom. This concept helps to explain passages in the epistle where Paul describes the members of the body of Christ as "kings" (1 Cor. 4:8) and that saints will judge the world (1 Cor. 6:2).

The fact the church has Israel's blessings extended to it does not mean the church is Israel. The New Testament sees three groups of people—Jews, Gentiles, and Christ's believers, that is, the church (cf. 1 Cor. 10:33). Notice that in Romans 11 the wild olive branches—Gentile believers—are grafted into Jewish blessings (vv. 16, 18). It is assumed that the root is comprised of the patriarchs of Israel to whom the promises were given. Nevertheless Paul carefully makes a distinction between the natural and the wild branches, even after the wild branches have been grafted in. In other words, the church is not the new Israel.[15] The new man described in Ephesians 2:15 is the church made up of Jews and Gentiles, and this is the mystery not previously revealed (Eph. 3:2–6).

The Church and the Law of Moses

All Bible students say Christians are not under the Mosaic law; however, not all evangelicals agree on what is meant by "the law." Most theologians divide the law of Moses into three parts—the ceremonial law, the civil law, and the moral law. The majority of nondispensational theologians agree that New Testament believers are not under the ceremonial and civil laws of Israel. It is contended by some, however, that Christians are still under the moral law, especially the Ten

Commandments. Most dispensationalists disagree. They say, "We are not under any part of the law of Moses." First, the Mosaic law is a unified whole and cannot be separated into parts (cf. Gal. 5:3; James 2:10). Second, Paul says Christians died to the Ten Commandments. In Romans 7:4 believers died to the law and in verse 7 Paul refers to the tenth commandment as the law. The same argument is seen in 2 Corinthians 3:7, where Paul describes the law as being the ministry of death, engraved on stones. Exodus 34:28 specifically states that it was the Ten Commandments that were written on the tablets of stone. Further, 2 Corinthians 3:11 says the ministry of those commandments was a temporary one.

Some would accuse dispensationalists of being antinomian because of this teaching. On the contrary, dispensationalists recognize nine of the Ten Commandments are reiterated in the New Testament.[16] This does not mean the law of Moses is the rule of the believer's life. Similarly it does not prove identity. The laws of Minnesota prohibit murder, stealing, and perjury; so do the laws of Texas. However, those states' laws represent two different systems. The same is true of the Old Testament law of Moses and the injunctions of the New Testament. They are similar but different. Under the Old Testament law there was no enablement; in the New Testament there is the enabling work of the Holy Spirit (Rom. 8:3–4). In the Mosaic system penalties were affixed for disobedience; in the New Testament there is discipline, but no prescribed penalties. There is a difference between penalty and correction.

The Church and Three Old Testament Covenants

Of great interest and importance to dispensationalists are three covenants in the Old Testament—the Abrahamic, the Davidic, and the new.

God announced many promises to Abraham (cf. Gen. 12:1–3; 13:14–17; 15:7–21; 17:1–21; 22:16–18). These promises were confirmed by a covenant (Gen. 15:18) and an oath (Gen. 22:15–18). They could be summarized as sevenfold: (1) Abraham's name would become great (Gen. 12:2); (2) a nation would come from him (Gen. 12:2; 13:16; 15:5; 22:17; (3) in him all nations would be blessed (Gen. 12:3); (4) the land of Canaan would be given to him and his seed as a permanent possession (Gen. 13:15; 15:7–18; (5) those who blessed him would be blessed and he who cursed him would be cursed (Gen. 12:3); (6) he would be the father of many nations (Gen. 17:4, 6, 16); and (7) in his seed all the world would be blessed (Gen. 22:18).

The primary promises for the church are the third and seventh. Abraham has himself become a blessing because he is the model of how a person is justified (cf. Gal. 3:6; Rom. 4:9–12, 17). Gentiles are called "sons of Abraham" (Gal. 3:7) because they walk in faith like Abraham did. To be a "son of" means to be like (cf. "sons of thunder," Mark 33:17; "son of the devil," Acts 13:10; "son of encouragement," Acts 4:36; "sons of your Father," Matt. 5:44–45). Therefore, it must be concluded that the justification of humans is by the same method in all ages and dispensations—by grace through faith in God's Word. Abraham believed God's promise that he would have a son by Sarah even though both were far advanced in age. Of course, this justification was accomplished through Abraham's seed, Jesus Christ (Gal. 3:16; Rom. 4:24–25).

This leads to the seventh blessing given to Abraham, "In his seed all the world would be blessed." Galatians 3:8 says, "And the Scriptures, foreseeing that God would justify the Gentiles by faith, preached the gospel beforehand to Abraham, saying, 'All the nations will be blessed in you.' " The verb translated "preached the gospel beforehand" could be taken "preached good news beforehand." Abraham was not given the New Testament gospel (1 Cor. 15:1–4); he was told Gentiles would be blessed in him and his seed.

It is important to notice the fourth of the promises listed above—the land of Canaan would become the possession not only of Abraham's seed, but also of Abraham himself. God said, "to give you this land to possess it" (Gen. 15:7; cf. Gen. 13:15, 17). This promise is given also to Isaac (Gen. 26:3) and to Jacob (Gen. 28:13). The fact is that neither Abraham, Isaac, nor Jacob received the promised land while they were alive. That is why they must be resurrected to fulfill God's promise! (cf. Matt. 22:31–32; Mark 12:26; Luke 20:37–38). Abraham, Isaac, and Jacob are now alive in the presence of the Lord and they are waiting for the resurrection to inherit the land!

The second important Old Testament covenant for dispensationalists is the Davidic covenant. This is first given in the form of a promise to David (2 Sam. 7:12–16). These promises are later called a covenant (Psa. 89:3–4, 34–37; 2 Sam. 23:5).

In 2 Samuel 7 David is promised a house, a throne, and a kingdom forever. The "house" cannot refer to a building, as it does in verses 57 and 13, but a royal line of dynasty. The "throne" refers to an eternal reign and the "kingdom" to an eternal realm of rule. It is clear from Psalm 110:1—where David calls his offspring "Master"—that David looked ahead to the One who would fulfill this promise. Psalm 72 anticipates the reign of this future righteous King in His future kingdom.

For dispensationalists, these promises are very significant. Gabriel in Luke 1:32–33 applied these exact promises to Jesus who was to be born of the Virgin Mary. The promises are to be fulfilled literally. This is how David would have taken them. When John the Baptist, the Lord Jesus, and the disciples announced the nearness of the kingdom of heaven/God (Matt. 3:2; 4:17; 10:7), the audiences were thinking of an earthly kingdom of David. Never does the Lord teach anything different from their expectations. In Acts 1:6 the disciples asked about the restoration of the kingdom to Israel. Again Christ did not say they had a wrong view of the kingdom. Christ Himself looked ahead to a time when the disciples would be reigning with Him over Israel (Matt. 19:28).

The Messiah of Israel is not now seated on the throne of David in heaven. He is at the right hand of the Father, but He is waiting to return when His enemies become a footstool for His feet (Heb. 10:12–13; cf. Acts 3:20–21). The reference to the rebuilding of the "tabernacle of David" in Acts 15:16 is a quotation of Amos 9:11 which looks ahead to the future kingdom when Christ, the son of David, will reign as King of Kings and Lord of Lords.

As with the Abrahamic covenant, so with the Davidic covenant, most of the promises await future fulfillment.

The third major covenant is the new covenant, primarily found in Jeremiah 31:31–34. Actually the remainder of Jeremiah 31 contains a guarantee the covenant will be kept (vv. 35–37) and a description of the conditions of Jerusalem in the kingdom age (vv. 38–40).

While Jeremiah 31 is the primary reference for the new covenant (cf. Heb. 8:8–12), other references are made to it in the Old Testament prophets. It is given various names—"everlasting covenant" (Isa. 61:8; Jer. 32:40; Ezek. 16:60; 37:26); "covenant of peace" (Ezek. 34:25; 37:26); and "my covenant" (Isa. 59:21; Ezek. 16:60).

Once again it must be stated that most of the promises of this covenant are still unfulfilled—"they shall all know me" (Jer. 31:34); "I will restore their fortunes" (Jer. 32:44); Israel will not be threatened by other nations (Ezek. 34:28); and God's sanctuary will be in Israel forever (Ezek. 37:28). The new covenant will be with Israel and it is yet unfulfilled (cf. Jer. 31:31, 33).

A problem that has troubled some dispensationalists is the church's relationship to the new covenant. In 2 Corinthians 3:6, Paul calls himself the minister of a new covenant. When the church drinks the fruit of the vine at the Lord's Table they are reminded of the Lord's words, "This cup is the new covenant in my blood" (1 Cor. 11:25). The new covenant quoted in Hebrews 8:8–12 is related to New

Testament believers. It is difficult to deny there is some connection between the church and Israel's new covenant. First, the basis for the new covenant is in the shed blood of Christ on the cross. Second, the new covenant will be fulfilled with Israel in the future in the kingdom age (Isa. 61:4–9; Jer. 31:27–40; 32:36–44; Ezek. 34:22–32; 37:24–28). In each of the preceding lists of references the new covenant and the kingdom are joined together. Third, in the meantime, God in His grace is extending many blessings of the new covenant to the church. It is very similar to the wild olive branches participating in the blessings of the root of the natural olive tree in Romans 11.

The basis of the new covenant has been established in the death of Christ. Israel will receive the full benefits of the new covenant in the future. In the meantime the church is benefitting from the blessings of the new covenant.

THE RAPTURE OF THE CHURCH

The term "rapture" does not occur in Scripture but it has come to be used so extensively that dispensationalists have a common understanding of what it means. The term *Trinity* carries a very theological concept even though it, too, is not in the Bible. When the Lord Jesus returns for His own He will resurrect the dead in Christ and transform living Christians into their new bodies. This is what is meant by "the rapture." In 1 Thessalonians 4:17 the term is "caught up" (Greek *harpazo*). The Greek word means "to seize" or "to snatch." At the rapture, living Christians will be snatched or seized by Christ and removed from this world.

The Sequence of Events at the Rapture

In 1 Thessalonians 4:13–18, the apostle Paul gives the clearest description of what will happen to dead and living Christians when the Lord returns. Only New Testament believers will be resurrected, not the saints of all ages.[17] This is derived from the term "the dead in Christ" (1 Thess. 4:16); only the church is said to be "in Christ." Jesus Christ will return with the souls and spirits of deceased Christians. When the spirits of the dead Christians will be reunited with their bodies simultaneously they will be given their resurrected bodies. What a miracle this will be! Bodies that have been consumed by animals or cannibals, bodies reduced to ashes by fire, bodies in the depths of the sea somehow will be miraculously reconstituted as heavenly bodies. The living Christians will be "caught up" or "raptured" with transformed bodies. In 1 Corinthians 15:51 the apostle informed the Corinthian believers that some Christians will not sleep (die) but all will be changed. This will take a split second of time.

Together the resurrected dead and the transformed living will be taken in the clouds of heaven to meet the Lord in the air. From that point on we will be forever with the Lord. This wonderful doctrine brings comfort to Christians (2 Thess. 4:18) and causes thanksgiving and praise to God (1 Cor. 15:57); it also should motivate believers to be stable and immovable in their faith (1 Cor. 15:58) and encourage them to abound in godly service (1 Cor. 15:58).

The Time of the Rapture

By no means is there unanimity among dispensationalists as to when the rapture will occur. Some of the views are pretribulation rapture, midtribulation rapture, posttribulation rapture, prewrath rapture, and partial rapture. The majority of dispensationalists hold to the pretribulation rapture and that is the view that will be defended here. This teaching says the rapture will take place before the beginning of the tribulation.

Several arguments are used to defend a pretribulational rapture. One is the doctrine of imminency. If the apostles taught there was no other event to precede the rapture, then the rapture must occur before the tribulation. It is very clear the early church was taught they should expect the rapture before anything else happened. In 2 Corinthians 5 Paul expresses a desire to be clothed with his heavenly body before dying physically (2 Cor. 5:2–4). He desires this mortal body to be swallowed up by his immortal body. This will occur at the rapture. This same truth is underscored in Philippians 3:11. Paul desired to live a Christ-exalting life until (the verb is "attain," *katantao*) the rapture (the out-resurrection, *exanastasis*). The verb *katantao* means to reach, to arrive. Paul's hope was to live until "the resurrection from the dead," that is, the rapture event. It is difficult if not impossible to deny that believers in the apostolic age expected the next prophetic event to be the resurrection of the church and the rapture of the living saints.

A second reason the pretribulation rapture view is held is because of the statement that Jesus "rescues us from the wrath to come" (1 Thess. 1:10). This statement is fortified by Paul's later declaration, "For God has not destined us for wrath" (5:9). This verse explains the "hope of salvation" mentioned in 5:8.

The tribulation is definitely a time when God's wrath is poured out on planet Earth. In Revelation 6:17, after the sixth seal is broken in the middle of the tribulation, humans cry out to be hidden from the wrath of the Father and the Lamb and they say, "The great day of their wrath has come." Because the tribulation is one expression of God's wrath and believers have not been appointed to wrath, the conclusion is that the rapture will take place before the tribulation begins.

Still a third reason to hold to the pretribulation rapture is Revelation 3:10: "Because you have kept the word of My perseverance, I also will keep you from the hour of testing, that hour which is about to come upon the whole world, to test those who dwell on the earth." Clearly this verse is a prophecy of the coming tribulation. The promise is not to preserve or watch out for the church at Philadelphia during or through the tribulation, but to keep it from the *hour*, or the time, of the tribulation. The saints will not be on earth in the tribulation period. It should be noted the seven churches of Revelation 2–3 represent seven kinds of churches that have been in existence during the entire church age. The words addressed to one are for all the churches (Rev. 2:7, 11, 17, 29; 3:6, 13, 22). These warnings and promises are for churches in this dispensation.

A fourth line of defense lies in the necessity of a span of time between the rapture and the end of the tribulation. (This argument is primarily in opposition to the posttribulation view of the rapture.) The Scriptures teach that when the Lord Jesus returns to reign there will be a judgment of all the people who are alive at the end of the tribulation. The judgment of Jews is described in Ezekiel 20:33–44, and that of Gentiles in Matthew 25:31–46. Only saved, living people will go into the kingdom. They will reproduce and live normal lives. Isaiah refers to boys, a nursing child, and a weaned child in the coming age (11:6–8). People will die after living long lives (Isa. 65:20). They will build houses, plant crops, and bear children (Isa. 65:21–23). Many of the children born to those who live in the kingdom will finally rebel against the Lord (Rev. 20:7–9). If the rapture of the saved will take place at the end of the tribulation this will be impossible. In the posttribulation view everyone would have resurrected and heavenly bodies. They would not be able to reproduce! (Cf. Matt. 22:30; Mark 12:25; Luke 20:34–36.) If the rapture occurs before the tribulation, then people will be converted during the tribulation and if they live through that terrible time they will go into the kingdom with their natural bodies. They will cohabit and have children. Then the Old Testament prophecies of life on earth will be fulfilled.

THE JUDGMENT SEAT OF CHRIST

After the resurrection and rapture of the church, Christians will be judged at the Judgment Seat of Christ. Several passages indicate it will be after the Lord Jesus comes for His church (Luke 14:14; 1 Cor. 4:5; Rev. 22:12). Because all judgment has been assigned to the Son (John 5:22), the Lord Christ will be the judge. This is confirmed by 2 Corinthians 5:10 which refers to the "judgment seat [*bema*] of Christ." The ones to appear ("be manifested") before Christ are Christians (cf. 1 Cor. 3:15).

The purpose of this judgment is to reward believers for their good deeds done with the right motive. It must be emphasized that no sins of a Christian will be brought before the Judgment Seat of Christ.[18] A Christian's sins are all forgiven and gone (Heb. 8:12; 10:17)! Why, then, are the wood, hay, and straw mentioned in 1 Corinthians 3:12? They are good deeds performed with wrong motives (cf. Matt. 6:1). A Christian can do a good deed for self-centered reasons; that good deed is not rewardable; in fact it will go up in flames at this judgment seat. However, there are rewards for good deeds done to please the Lord (2 Cor. 5:9).

What are the rewards? First, praise from God (1 Cor. 4:5). Can anyone imagine a simple believer being praised by God? Second, this person will be given greater responsibility in the coming kingdom (Matt. 19:28; Luke 19:17, 19; 1 Cor. 6:2). Third, the reward is a crown or crowns. The word for crown is not diadem (*diadema)*, a royal crown, but *stephanos*, a victor's crown. Usually this was a wreath woven from plants (cf. 1 Cor. 9:25); however, the New Testament refers to *stephanos*/crowns made of gold (Rev. 4:4; 9:7; 14:14). These crowns were rewards for athletic victors. So likewise, spiritual victors will be given crowns at the Judgment Seat of Christ.

Five of these crowns are referred to in the New Testament—(1) a crown of rejoicing (1 Thess. 2:19); (2) an incorruptible crown (1 Cor. 9:25); (3) a crown of life (James 1:12); (4) a crown of righteousness (2 Tim. 4:8); and (5) a crown of glory (1 Pet. 5:4). There is some dispute as to what these crowns are. It is very possible they are actual victors' wreaths, which believers will cast at the feet of Jesus in worship (cf. Rev. 4:10).

Others say they are genitives of apposition; that is, the crown of life will be a greater appreciation of eternal life. According to this view, all of the crowns are explained in this way. This is possible, but not as probable as the former position.

THE TRIBULATION

Terms for the Tribulation

The Scriptures refer to a future time of tribulation as the "tribulation" (Matt. 24:21); "the day of the Lord" (1 Thess. 5:2); "that day" (Jer. 30:7); "Jacob's distress" (Jer. 30:7); "a day of wrath . . . of trouble and distress . . . destruction and desolation . . . of darkness and gloom . . . of clouds and thick darkness . . . of trumpet and battle cry . . ." (Zeph. 1:15–16). Other terms of judgment and destruction are used.

The term *day of the Lord* refers to any time God specially manifests Himself, especially in times of judgment. There are past Days of the Lord as in God's past destruction of Babylon (Isa. 13:1–22, called "the Day of the Lord" in v. 6).

The Nature of the Tribulation

The tribulation will be a time of judgment on both Jews and Gentiles. That the judgment will be on Jews who refuse to believe in Jesus as Messiah is seen in the term "Jacob's distress" (Jer. 30:7). Ultimately this time of tribulation will result in the national repentance of Israel (Zech. 12:10–14; Matt. 23:39; Rom. 11:26). The tribulation will conclude for Israel in individual judgment for Jews (Ezek. 20:35–38).

Judgment is also in store for Gentiles during the tribulation period. Revelation 3:10 refers to "the hour of testing which is about to . . . test those who dwell on the earth" (cf. Rev. 6:15–17). As there is a personal judgment for Jews at the end of the tribulation, so will there be for Gentiles (Matt. 25:32–46).

While the emphasis of the tribulation is on judgment, some will be saved by God's grace (Ezek. 20:37–38; Matt. 25:34–40).

The Beginning of the Tribulation

Students of prophecy have sometimes left the impression the tribulation will begin just after the resurrection and rapture of the church. This is not precisely accurate. The actual *terminus a quo* is the signing of the covenant between the Man of Sin and the nation of Israel (Dan. 9:27).

The prophecy known as Daniel's prophecy of "seventy weeks" (Dan. 9:24–27) is critical to a study of the chronology of the tribulation. Daniel 9 begins with Daniel's realization that Jeremiah's prophecy of a seventy-year captivity

(Jer. 25:11–12; 29:10) was at its end; so Daniel confesses sin and prays on behalf of Israel. Gabriel responded by giving a prophecy concerning Israel that involved seventy sevens ("weeks").[19] Many scholars take this to be sevens of years; that is, 490 years.[20] The beginning of this 490-year period is stated in Daniel 9:25, the "decree to restore and rebuild Jerusalem." It was Artaxerxes who issued this decree in 444 BC (cf. Neh. 2:1–8). Then Daniel refers to two periods of time in sequence—49 years and 434 years—totaling 483 years (Dan. 9:25). That is from 444 BC to the time the Messiah "will be cut off and have nothing," which would be 483 years of 360 days length. This has been computed to be AD 33.[21]

The final seven years are separated from the first 483 years and are still waiting fulfillment. It should be noticed that the cutting off of the Messiah and the destruction of Jerusalem with the temple is predicted to take place *after* the 483 years have been completed. The destruction of the temple and Jerusalem took place in AD 70. The gap between the sixty-ninth and seventieth weeks is necessary because the events prophesied in Daniel 9:24 have not yet taken place! A second reason a gap must be inserted is found in the Lord's words in Matthew 24:15 where the Lord Jesus warned of coming abomination of desolation predicted by Daniel (cf. 9:27; 12:11). This did not happen until AD 70.

Finally, gaps in prophetic chronology are not unusual. For instance Zechariah 9:9 describes the Messiah as riding on the colt of a donkey; this was fulfilled in the so-called triumphal entry of Christ in Jerusalem (cf. Matt. 21:5). The next verse in Zechariah's prophecy describes Jesus reigning over the world. Obviously this has not yet been fulfilled. Other gaps are seen in Isaiah 9:6, where the birth of the Messiah is predicted followed immediately with the clause, "And the government will rest on His shoulders."

The beginning of the seventieth week or the seven-year tribulation period is introduced by the signing of a covenant between "the prince who is to come" (Dan. 9:26) and Israel. This prince will be from the people who will destroy Jerusalem and its sanctuary. This was done by Rome in AD 70.[22]

The Ten Kings

Prophecy consistently refers to a coalition of ten kings and kingdoms that will arise out of the Roman Empire (Dan. 7:7, 20, 24; Rev. 12:3; 13:1; 17:3, 12, 16). These will be contemporaries who will reign together with the Man of Sin for "one hour" (Rev. 17:12).

These kings are part of the seventh mountain (these seven mountains are sequential, Rev. 17:10) and evidently represent seven world powers that have controlled or will oppress Israel: (1) Egypt, (2) Assyria, (3) Babylon, (4) Persia, (5) Greece, (6) Rome, and (7) the ten kings.

The Man of Sin in his pursuit of power will subdue three of the ten kings (cf. Dan. 7:8, 24). The remaining seven kings give their kingdoms to the Man of Sin because of their hatred of a harlot that is controlling these ten kings (Rev. 17:16–17). It may be assumed she is in control because she sits on the beast with the seven heads and the ten horns (Rev. 17:3). In Scripture, false religion is often described in terms of harlotry and prostitution. This implies some aberrant religion will influence, even control, the ten kings. In hatred of this religion the kings will give their power to the Man of Sin to destroy this "harlot." He will accomplish his goal, but alas, he will set himself up as God. This action by the Man of Sin will take place in the middle of the tribulation when he will break his seven-year covenant with Israel.

The Covenant with Israel

The Man of Sin, also commonly called the Antichrist, as the head of the seven-king coalition will make a seven-year covenant with Israel (Dan. 9:27). The construction of the language could be translated, "to strengthen a covenant." This is unusual because normally in the Old Testament a covenant is "cut." This may imply the covenant is forced on Israel.

This covenant will be made with Israel after they have returned to the land. Much of the land of Israel that had been desolate will be inhabited by Jews (Ezek. 38:12). It will be a time of relative prosperity (Ezek. 38:12).

Some provisions of this covenant may be assumed. For instance, it seems Israel will be guaranteed security if it gives up its own armaments. During the tribulation period after the signing of the treaty Israel will be a place where villages have no walls and people dwell securely in cities without gates or bars (Ezek. 38:11). It is difficult today to imagine Israel without military forces!

Evidently Israel will be given a measure of religious freedom to practice their religion. This will be short-lived because this liberty will be forcibly taken away.

The Restraining Ministry of the Holy Spirit

Because 2 Thessalonians 2:7 says, "only he who now restrains will do so until he is taken out of the way," some believe the Holy Spirit will not minister on planet Earth during the tribulation.[23] But this cannot be the case since the Holy Spirit will not be removed. People will be converted during the tribulation (Rev. 7:4–17; 11:13; 12:17; 13:10; 14:13; 15:2–4). Revelation 7 is an interlude between the sixth and seventh seals; certainly this is in the time of the tribulation. The passage refers to 144,000 Jews who are sealed for ministry in the tribulation and an innumerable number of Gentiles come from "the great tribulation" (v. 14). No one is converted without the work of the Holy Spirit, so it must be concluded His ministry is not removed from the earth.

What then does 2 Thessalonians 2:7 mean? It simply indicates His work of restraining the appearance of the Man of Sin will be removed.[24]

Israel During the Tribulation

When the tribulation begins, a large proportion of Israel will be regathered to the land. It would not be possible for them to make a treaty with the Man of Sin (Dan. 9:27) if they were not a body politic. Several passages predict the regathering of Israel from the nations of the world (cf. Isa. 43:5–6; Ezek. 34:13; 36:24; 37:21). Evidently the coming together of Israel in the land will be in a time of unbelief (cf. Isa. 43:8).

As there always has been a remnant of Jews that was saved (cf. Rom. 11:1–3), so it will be in the tribulation. A special group within this remnant will be the 144,000 described in Revelation 7:4–8. It seems they are sealed as special messengers and servants of the Lord. They will preach to the world (Rev. 7:9–10; Matt. 24:14). Of course Israel also will be an object of their evangelism. In addition, Israel will know the ministry of the two witnesses (Rev. 11:3–6). Gripped by terror because of the miracles accompanying their resurrection and ascension and also the ensuing massive earthquake, many will "give glory to God" (Rev. 11:13).

During the terrible time of "Jacob's Troubles" (Jer. 30:7), especially the last half of the seven-year period, Satan will focus his efforts on annihilating the Jews. God will intervene to save them and a special place will be provided as a refuge (Rev. 12:6, 13–17; cf. Matt. 24:9–22; Mark 13:9–23; Luke 21:20–22).[25]

Evidently, near the end of the tribulation Israel will repent and know the cleansing of their hearts by God (Rev. 12:12; Ezek. 36:25; Zech. 12:10–14). Malachi prophesied a prophet in the spirit of Elijah will come and be a strong force in bringing about national repentance by Israel (cf. Mal. 4:5–6; Matt. 17:10–11;

Mark 9:11–12). The 144,000 and the two witnesses will be instruments in this movement.

Then "all Israel" will be saved (Rom. 11:26–27). Ultimately this national conversion will be the work of God the Holy Spirit (Ezek. 36:26–27; Zech. 12:10). "All Israel" does not mean every Israelite will be saved, but those who are alive and elect will be saved.

The tribulation will conclude with judgment, specifically a judgment for Jews and Gentiles. (These judgments will be discussed later.)

Gentiles in the Tribulation

The "times of the Gentiles" (Luke 21:24) will be brought to a conclusion by the return of Christ at the end of the tribulation. Two visions interpreted by Daniel portrayed the dominion of Gentiles from his time to the end. A statue constructed of various substances is used in Daniel 2. The nations in sequence are Babylon, Medo-Persia, Greece, and Rome. In Daniel 7 the same four kingdoms are portrayed as animals, God's perspective on these kingdoms. The fearsome fourth creature described in Daniel 7:7 emphasizes ten horns, the final form of this Gentile power. In both of the chapters, the kingdoms are brought to an end by God's kingdom, beginning with the millennium but extending into eternity. Prominent in Daniel's dream in Daniel 7 is the Man of Sin, or the Antichrist. His reign and power are discussed later.

It seems the "times of the Gentiles" represent the time when Gentiles hold sway over Jerusalem and particularly the temple site. Some may say the times of the Gentiles are now over because Israel regained old Jerusalem and the temple mount in 1967. However, the times of the Gentiles are not completed until the Lord takes over permanently. In the second and first centuries BC there was a time when the Maccabees controlled the temple area, but alas it was only temporary.

It will be during the tribulation that the gospel will finally reach all nations (Matt. 24:14). Israel was to be a light to the nations (Isa. 42:6) and the 144,000 Jews will be God's instruments to accomplish this (Rev. 7:4–10).

The Man of Sin—The Antichrist

Commonly called the Antichrist because of 1 John 2:18, the Man of Sin is a major subject of prophecy. Not a few passages anticipate his coming, his nefarious work, and his destiny (Dan. 7:8, 24–26; 8:9–14, 23–26; 9:26–27; 11:36–39; Matt. 24:15; Mark 13:14; 2 Thess. 2:3–4, 8–11; 1 John 2:18; Rev. 13:1–10; 17:8–17; 19:19–20). A number of titles are given to him which also describe his character and actions—"little horn" (Dan. 7:8; 8:9); "a king" (Dan. 8:23; 11:36); "the prince who is to come" (Dan. 9:26); "the man of lawlessness" (2 Thess. 2:3, 8); "Antichrist" (1 John 2:18); and "beast" (Rev. 13:1–4).

He probably will be a Gentile; in Daniel 9:26 he is referred to in the phrase, "the people of the prince who is to come." Furthermore, his appearance originates in the "sea" (Rev. 13:1), which represents Gentiles (cf. Rev. 17:15).

The Antichrist/Man of Sin will be the culmination of seven world powers who opposed Israel (Rev. 17:10), the final four being Rome, Greece, Persia, and Babylon (Rev. 13:2)—listed in reverse chronological order in Revelation 13 because John is looking back historically. In the images of Revelation 13 and 17 the seven heads represent seven kingdoms in sequence (Rev. 17:10); the ten horns will be in existence contemporaneously (Dan. 7:7, 20, 24; Rev. 13:1; 17:12). In his rise to power the Antichrist will conquer three of the ten kings (Dan. 7:8, 24).

He will attest his greatness by miracles. One that is debated is the meaning of the healing of "his fatal wound" (Rev. 13:3). The Greek text says the head "had been slaughtered unto death" and "the wound of his death was healed." The same verb and construction translated "as slain" is used of Christ in Revelation 5:6. It seems this person will die and be resurrected to life! This fits with Matthew 24:24, which predicts miracles so outstanding that if it were possible they would deceive even the elect. This Man of Sin will perform a number of miracles (cf. 2 Thess. 2:9). It should be noted the same three words used of the Antichrist's miracles are used of Christ's (Acts 2:22)!

Finally, in the middle of the seven-year covenant this Antichrist will break his covenant with Israel and set himself up as God in the temple of God (2 Thess. 2:4; Dan. 9:27; Rev. 13:4–5, 8). This means a temple to God will be rebuilt in Jerusalem. Much speculation abounds as to the precise location of this temple and how it will be built. The Antichrist will be characterized by blasphemous propaganda. This is associated with him (cf. Dan. 7:20; 2 Thess. 2:10; Rev. 13:5–6). Not only will the whole world worship this imposter, but he will bring the entire world in subjection to him (Rev. 13:7–8; 17:8).

A primary promoter of this Man of Sin will be a false prophet who will be able to perform fantastic miracles (Rev. 13:12–15). He will even duplicate the miracle of Elijah recorded in 1 Kings 18. The issue in 1 Kings 18 was, "Who is the true God, Baal or Yahweh?" The false prophet will essentially say, "How did Elijah prove who the true God is? I will do the same." Besides this, he somehow will give life to an image of the first beast of Revelation 13 and force people to worship it. Commerce will be controlled so no one will be able to buy or sell without the mark of the beast—his name or number.

Even though the Antichrist will ultimately rule the world (Rev. 13:7), he will meet some opposition from other nations. Described in Ezekiel 38 as a coalition of nations, Persia, Ethiopia (Cush), Put, Gomer, and Beth-togarmah—headed by the prince of Rosh, Meshech, and Tubal—will plan an offensive against Israel with its unwalled cities. God will supernaturally intervene and destroy these armies (Ezek. 38:18–23; 39:2–6). These powers will come from "the remote parts of the north" (Ezek. 38:6, 15; 39:2) and make this invasion in the "latter years" (38:8) and "the last days" (v. 16). So great will be the devastation that it will take seven years to burn the rubble of battle as firewood (39:9) and seven months to bury the dead (v. 12). Evidently this supernatural destruction of Israel's enemies will be a factor in Israel's conversion (Ezek. 7, 22).

Most students of prophecy place this battle sometime during or after the tribulation. It seems best to locate it in the middle of the tribulation. The fact that Israel is dwelling securely in unwalled cities indicates the battle must be after the signing of the seven-year treaty between Israel and the Antichrist. When this powerful group of nations is defeated, it will make it possible for the Antichrist to break his treaty with Israel and rule unhindered.

In the middle of the seven-year tribulation a war will take place in heaven between Michael and his angels and Satan and his angels (Rev. 12:7–10; cf. 12:6, 14). Satan will be defeated and will be filled with wrath, which he will vent against Israel and the nations (Rev. 12:3–6, 12, 13–15).[26] He will attempt to destroy Israel so that God's promises to them cannot be kept.

At the end of the tribulation the campaign of Armageddon will take place. It appears a large army from the East will approach Israel in rebellion against the Antichrist. Revelation 9:13–16 refers to a massive army; this is not the final campaign but is simply the preparation for it. The Euphrates River will dry up in preparation for the march of this massive army to the west. The sixth bowl in the series of judgments to fall on the earth involves Satan, the Antichrist, and his false prophet. They will supernaturally inspire the world to come together in Israel. It is possible the kings of the East and other armies will ally to combat the Man of Sin.

THE CONCLUSION TO THE TRIBULATION: CHRIST'S RETURN AND JUDGMENT

The Return of Christ

The Lord Jesus promised that "a sign of the Son of Man" will appear in the sky (Matt. 24:30) just before He Himself returns. It can only be speculated what that sign will be; an educated guess would say the Shekinah glory. Thus, the sign of the coming of the Son of Man is the Son of Man Himself.

This will lead to Israel's repentance (Zech. 12:10b; Matt. 23:39; 24:30); the nation as a whole will turn to Christ (Rom. 11:26–27). Evidently, at the same time the armies on earth will combine forces and turn against Christ to make war (Rev. 19). This battle will be short-lived, for the leaders of the human armies and the Antichrist will be brought to an end "by the appearance of His coming" (2 Thess. 2:8; cf. Rev. 19:15). The armies will be slain by "the sword which came from the mouth of Him who sat upon the horse" (Rev. 19:21; cf. 19:15).

The Judgments at the End of the Tribulation

The Judgment of the Antichrist and His Prophet

Evidently the first judgment will be of the two beasts described in Revelation 13. They will be thrown alive into the "lake of fire which burns with fire and brimstone" (Rev. 19:20).

The lake of fire was prepared for the devil and his angels (Matt. 25:41), but the first two inhabitants will be the Antichrist and his false prophet.

The Judgment of Satan

Surprisingly, Satan is not assigned to the lake of fire like the Antichrist and the false prophet. Instead he is bound and cast into the abyss for a thousand years. After a short release and final defeat he will join the beast and the false prophet in the lake of fire (Rev. 20:10).

The Judgment of Israel

At the end of the tribulation, in spite of the terrible decimation of human lives, there will be humans who survive. These will be judged to determine if they are qualified to enter the kingdom age, also called the millennium.

The judgment of Jews precedes the judgment of Gentiles (Rom. 2:9). At the end of the tribulation God will bring the Jews who have been scattered by persecution to the border of Israel and will hold a judgment there (Ezek. 20:33–38). Several facts are noteworthy. This regathering will take place "with wrath poured out," an evident reference to the tribulation. Furthermore, it will be a judgment of individuals, as seen in the expression "pass under the rod" (v. 37). There is some discussion as to the meaning of "the bond of the covenant" (v. 37). This must refer to the Abrahamic covenant, which promised the land to the patriarchs—Abraham, Isaac, and Jacob—and their descendants. Finally, those who pass the judgment will serve the Lord "in the land" (Ezek. 20:40, 42). Ezekiel 36:22–38 discusses the regathering and cleansing of Israel to place them in the land as well.

The Judgment of the Gentiles

The judgment of the Gentiles, like the judgment of Jews, is of people who survive the tribulation. It is described in Matthew 25:31–46. Interestingly, it involves three groups of people—"the sheep," "the goats," and those referred to as "my brethren." This becomes a touchstone in this judgment. It is evident that the people's faith will be seen in their deeds, specifically in how they treat the Lord's brethren. The "brethren" would be Jews who are Christian believers and are persecuted for their faith. During the tribulation it will be very risky to show mercy toward those Jews. In a sense it will be like helping Jews in Nazi Germany during the Second World War. As in the judgment of Israel, the judgment will be of each individual, like a shepherd separating sheep from goats. The lost will be consigned to the lake of fire forever (Matt. 25:41, 46).

THE MILLENNIAL RULE OF CHRIST

Finally, Christ's return to the earth will bring judgment on His enemies and the establishment of an earthly reign, in fulfillment of biblical prophecy (Isa. 66:17–24; Zech. 14). He will establish a kingdom, one thousand years in length (Rev. 20:1–7), during which He will reign over the earth from His throne in Jerusalem. During this period, Satan will be bound (Rev. 20:1–3). This millennial kingdom of righteousness, peace, and prosperity under the reign of the Davidic king is not the culmination of the plan of God; it is an intermediate phase, the front porch to eternity. The millennium ends with apostasy, as Satan is released from prison to deceive the nations (Rev. 20:7). One final judgment, fire from heaven, will destroy him and the armies of the nations (Rev. 21:9).

Then a new heaven and new earth will be created (Rev. 21:1–5). Finally, "the earth will be filled with the knowledge of the glory of the Lord, as the waters cover the sea" (Hab. 2:14).

Notes

1. The Sermon on the Mount was given to the disciples as an ethic for them in the interval between the announcement of the nearness of the kingdom and its arrival.
2. Judas vacated the position of Apostle by apostasy, not death. When James was executed in Acts 12 no one was chosen to replace him as an apostle.
3. It is sometimes stated Pentecost celebrated the giving of the Law because of the time interval between the original Passover and the arrival of Israel at Mt. Sinai (cf. Ex. 19:1; 12:6, 51). However, this tradition is not found in the Old Testament and is much later, the second century BC.
4. Charles Caldwell Ryrie, *Dispensationalism Today* (Chicago: Moody, 1965), 136, 199, 203; cf. *Dispensationalism* (Chicago: Moody, 2007), 126, 202.
5. Ultra-dispensationalists have different views on the beginning of the church—Acts 8, 13, and 28. For a discussion of ultra-dispensationalism see Ryrie, *Dispensationalism Today*, 192–205.
6. Although the Old Testament has few occurrences of God manifesting Himself as wind (cf. Ezek. 37:9–14), many times God and fire are associated with Him (Ex. 13:21–22; 19:18–19; Judg. 6:21–22; etc.).
7. For an alternative view, see Tony Richie, "Is Pentecostalism Dispensationalist: An Honest Answer to a Hard Question," www.christianzionism.org/Article/RichieT01.pdf. Geir Lee observes that there has been little extensive research on the interrelatedness of the Holiness Movement and dispensationalism, which is surprising since Darby's views "permeated most segments within the Holiness movement" ("E. W. Kenyon and Dispensationalism," www.pctii.org/cyberj/cyberj17/Lie.pdf, 1).
8. Walter Bauer, *A Greek-English Lexicon of the New Testament and Other Early Christian Literature*, rev. ed. Frederick W. Danker, 3rd ed. (Chicago: University of Chicago Press, 2000), 193, gives the primary meaning of *diermeneuo* as "translate," although it can also mean "interpret," as in the NASB.
9. A key word to use in interpreting Acts is "transition." Cf. the figure of the olive branches in Romans 11.
10. For a fuller discussion of the conditionality or the contingency of the coming of the promised kingdom see Alva J. McClain, *The Greatness of the Kingdom* (Grand Rapids: Zondervan, 1959), 319–20; George N. H. Peters, *The Theocratic Kingdom*, 3 vols. (1884; repr., Grand Rapids: Kregel, 1972), 1:176–80; Charles Caldwell Ryrie, *Dispensationalism* (Chicago: Moody, 2007), 64–68, 151–53]; Stanley D. Toussaint, "The Contingency of the Coming of the Kingdom," ed. Charles H. Dyer and Roy B. Zuck, *Integrity of Heart, Skillfulness of Hands* (Grand Rapids: Baker Books, 1994), 222–37; and Stanley D. Toussaint and Jay A. Quine, "No, Not Yet: The Contingency of God's Promised Kingdom," *Bibliotheca Sacra* 164 (2007): 131–47.
11. Some believe Peter here is using a *pesher* method of hermeneutics. The word *pesher* is a Hebrew term meaning "explanation." This method is a way of applying an OT passage to a contemporary situation. This system is commonly used in the Qumran Community and is illustrated by Acts 4:25–26 where Psalm 2 is applied to the opposition the early church was experiencing. Psalm 2 will yet be fulfilled in the future. If Peter is using the *pesher* method in the prophecy of Psalm 2 it must yet be fulfilled. Peter would then be saying, "This is like what will yet be fulfilled in the future." The result of the *pesher* idea

would still say the prophecy of Joel 2 was unfulfilled in Acts 2.

12. Colin Brown takes the "times of refreshing" to be "the age of salvation, which is promised to the nation of Israel if it repents." (Colin Brown, *New International Dictionary of New Testament Theology* [Grand Rapids: Zondervan, 1971], 3:686.) Cf. *anapsuksis,* Eduard Schweizer, *Theological Dictionary of the New Testament*, ed. Gerhard Friedrich, trans. Geoffrey W. Bromiley (Grand Rapids: Eerdmans Publishing, 1974), 9:664–65; Peter J. Gloag, *A Critical and Exegetical Commentary on the Acts of the Apostles* (T. & T. Clark, 1870; repr., Minneapolis: Klock & Klock Christian Publishers, n. d.), 1:132–35; Stanley D. Toussaint, "Acts," *Bible Knowledge Commentary: New Testament,* ed. John F. Walvoord and Roy B. Zuck (Wheaton: Victor Books, 1983), 361.
13. But it should be noted that not all Christian traditions understand the implications the same way many dispensationalists do. And, even within dispensationalism, not all emphasize the "offer" of the kingdom in the same way.
14. A "mystery" is a previously unrevealed truth. It is not difficult to understand once it is taught. Several mysteries are found in the NT—the postponement of the coming of judgment and of the kingdom with an unprophesied age preceding the kingdom (Matt. 13:11), the rapture of those in Christ (1 Cor. 15:51–52), and equality of Jew and Gentile in the church.
15. For a defense of the view that the church is not the new Israel in Gal. 6:16 see S. Lewis Johnson, Jr., "Paul and 'the Israel of God': An Exegetical and Eschatological Case-Study," *Essays in Honor of J. Dwight Pentecost,* ed. Stanley D. Toussaint and Charles H. Dyer (Chicago: Moody, 1986), 181–96.
16. The fourth commandment dealing with observing the Sabbath day is not repeated.
17. Other dispensationalists believe that the saints of all ages will be raised at the rapture.
18. Concerning the phrase "deeds . . . whether good or bad," the word commonly translated "bad" in 2 Cor. 5:10 is not *kakos* (bad, wicked), *athesmos* (lawless), *hamartia* (sin, missing the mark), or *poneros* (evil). The adjective used here is *phaulos,* which basically means "worthless," although it may refer to "sin" as it seems to mean in Rom. 9:11. Here it clearly means "worthless" (cf. Philip E. Hughes, *Commentary on the Second Epistle to the Corinthians* [Grand Rapids: Eerdmans, 1962], 181–83).
19. The Hebrew word translated "weeks" is *shabue,* which means "seven."
20. The years are taken to be 360-day years (cf. Rev. 11:2–3).
21. Cf. Harold W. Hoehner, "Daniel's Seventy Weeks and New Testament Chronology," *Bibliotheca Sacra* 132 (1975): 47–65.
22. For a more complete discussion of Daniel's seventy weeks prophecy see Alva J. McClain, *Daniel's Prophecy of the Seventy Weeks* (Grand Rapids: Zondervan, 1969); J. Dwight Pentecost, *Things to Come* (Findlay, OH: Dunham Publishing, 1958), 239–50; John F. Walvoord, *Daniel* (repr., Chicago: Moody, 2012), 266–96; John C. Whitcomb, *Daniel* (Winona Lake, IN: BMH Books, 1985), 128–35.
23. That the Holy Spirit is who is being considered here fits with the change from the neuter in verse 6 to the masculine in verse 7. The word "spirit" in Greek is neuter and the Holy Spirit is a person. Furthermore, the One who restrains the Man of Sin and Satan must be greater than he. Some take the restrainer to be human government, but the government of the Man of Sin will be ultra strong. It cannot be said government will be restrained in the tribulation.
24. Cf. Pentecost, *Things to Come*, 263–74.
25. The woman of Rev. 12:1 represents Israel. The twelve stars are the twelve tribes of Israel (cf. Gen. 37:9).
26. Some may contend Satan was cast out of heaven during Christ's earthly ministry (cf. Luke 10:17–18). However, in Luke 10 the Lord is seeing in the disciples' conquering of demons a foretaste of the future when Satan will be cast out of heaven.

8

God's Plan for History:

THE CONSUMMATION

CRAIG A. BLAISING

Consummation, quite simply, is said to occur after the return of Christ and the final judgment of all humanity ushers each person into an eternal state in either heaven or hell. Dispensationalism was formulated at a time when this Christian view of the consummation had been well established through the centuries of late patristic, medieval, and early modern thought.

This view of consummation is not to say that the conceptions of either heaven or hell were simple in themselves or that all theologians were unanimous in their descriptions of them. Nevertheless, in both popular conception and in formal theology, a basic twofold view of the consummation remained fixed—eternal existence either in heaven or in hell.

HEAVEN IN NT TEXTS AND CHRISTIAN THOUGHT

The biblical basis for the traditional Christian conception of heaven was found in New Testament texts speaking of Christ's present exaltation in heaven, His current activity of preparing a place for us in His Father's house, and His future return to take us to be with Him where He is.[1] The New Testament explicitly teaches that at death, Christian souls go to be with Christ in heaven. This was seen to support the view of heaven as the ultimate destiny of the saved. Further support was found in Christ's promise of paradise to the thief on the cross together with Paul's subsequent vision of paradise in "the third heaven" and with John's use of paradise imagery to describe the Jerusalem that comes down from heaven in Revelation 21:9–22:5. Furthermore, Paul spoke of the heavenly Jerusalem as our "mother" (Gal. 4:26) and the location of our true "citizenship" (Phil. 3:20). Hebrews also states that "here [taken to mean on earth] we have no lasting city, but we are seeking the city that is to come" (Heb. 13:14), that is, the city in heaven.

The location of heaven is always "up," in Christian thought, which means it is away from the earth. This correlates with biblical descriptions of God's throne in or above the heavens (seen throughout the Psalms) and by the very real fact of Christ's ascension up into the clouds and subsequent declaration to be seated at the right hand of God in heaven. It was to Jesus in heaven that Stephen, the first martyr of the church, commended his spirit when he died. And, Paul explicitly speaks of being "caught *up* to the third heaven" in 2 Corinthians 12:2–3.

The vertical separation of heaven from earth in late antique and medieval cosmology was coordinate with conceptions of a graded vertical hierarchy of goodness and worth. Physics and ethics joined with theology to conceptualize a comprehensive worldview in which the hope of blessedness lay in an ascension into heaven (or as high into the heavens as one could possibly go) to be present with Christ and God, beholding the divine glory in an unending ecstatic joy. The state of the damned was, by contrast, the lowest point in this cosmology—most often located at the center of the earth.

In spite of the near uniformity and traditional bearing of this Christian conception of a heavenly consummation, much in biblical eschatology is not so obviously reconcilable with it. Admittedly, the Old Testament evidences a progressively revealed and developing eschatology. However, it would be more accurate to say that the developing hope in the Old Testament is one of long-lasting or unending life on an earth blessed by God in fruitfulness and peace. Even the few Old Testament references to resurrection seem to fit with this. And there are elements in the New Testament that would seem to support this as well. Furthermore, such hopes are tied to divine promises given to Israel corporately and nationally and often set in a context of multiple nations of peoples on the earth.

The challenge for theology has always been how to understand this earthly-oriented biblical eschatology focused on Israel in relation to God's plan and purpose revealed for the church. Traditional Christian theology read the Old Testament earthly eschatology spiritually, anagogically, or typologically as a metaphor for the heavenly hope that Christian traditionalists believed was promised to the church. In this way of thinking, earth in the biblical narrative comes to be replaced by heaven, and Israel is replaced by the church.[2]

However, at the time that dispensationalism came to be formulated theologically, over two centuries had passed of Puritan, Anglican, and British nonconformist theological reconsideration of the plan and purpose of God for the Jews.[3] The impetus for this was Paul's expressed expectation of the future salvation of all Israel in Romans 11:26. Paul himself connected this expectation to Old Testament promise and prophecy. Puritan and Anglican eschatological revisionists saw this Pauline hope as a doorway through which some accommodation could be made for the earthly features of Old Testament eschatology in the things to come. The immediate result was the rehabilitation of millennialism in Christian thought, with the millennium as a future period on earth in which the future national promises to the Jews would be realized along with the peace and fruitfulness that characterize the Old Testament hope of an earthly consummation.[4]

A REAPPRAISAL OF THE IDENTITIES AND FUNCTION OF ISRAEL AND THE CHURCH

How to fit these "heavenly" and "earthly" eschatologies together was not immediately apparent. Can one simply add an earthly, politically structured millennium to an otherwise traditional Christian heavenly eschatology? Is further theological adjustment required? Dispensationalists believed what was required was a radical reappraisal of the identities and functions of Israel and the church in Christian theology.

Dispensationalists saw the positive role afforded to Israel eschatologically as an opportunity to clarify, and in their minds to purify, a theological understanding of the church as a *new reality* in history, having been brought into existence through the death, resurrection, and ascension of Jesus Christ. It was a new reality that did not replace, cancel, or "spiritually" fulfill the plan and purpose of God for Israel. Dispensationalists were able to highlight the language and narrative themes of newness in the New Testament in relation to the formation of the church. This included a new coming of the Holy Spirit historically at Pentecost, and the historically new baptism of the Holy Spirit, forming a relationship between believers with the newly resurrected and ascended Lord in heaven. They emphasized the multiethnic character of the church as a body wholly related to Christ in heaven as a new reality in biblical history.

This newness of the church was interpreted by dispensationalists as a newly added feature to the previously revealed plan of God—not a resignification or new interpretation of that plan. With respect to eschatology, this would allow a fully positive theological appreciation of the covenant promises and prophecies regarding Israel and the nations, the earth, and the various lands that comprise it, especially that land promised by God to Israel without any need to redirect those elements toward a heavenly fulfillment. In short, it would allow the development of an "earthly" eschatology much more robust and more consistent with canonical Scripture than what had developed in millennialism up to that point. As for the church, early dispensationalists would employ a modified version of the traditional heavenly eschatology to interpret the new eschatological features revealed in the New Testament as signaling a second eschatological program in the plan of God.

Consequently, dispensational views of the eschatological consummation must be understood as attempts to give full theological justification to the hopes of Israel and the hopes of the church as distinctively, progressively, and historically revealed and affirmed in Scripture.

In the remainder of this chapter, we will summarize the impact of dispensational concerns for a distinction between Israel and the church upon the dispensational conception of eschatological consummation, noting dispensational views on (1) personal eschatology, (2) the doctrine of hell, and (3) the consummation of salvation.

PERSONAL ESCHATOLOGY: DEATH AND RESURRECTION

Death

"Personal eschatology" is the traditional label given to doctrines and beliefs about what happens to individuals after death. Dispensationalists are in agreement that death is a separation of body and soul and that at death a Christian goes to be with Christ and is conscious and secure in the presence of his/her Lord (Luke 23:43; Phil. 1:23; 2 Cor. 5:8; Rev. 6:9–11) until the day when he or she is brought with Jesus in the rapture to be raised from the dead (1 Thess. 4:14–17) and glorified with Christ (Col. 3:4). However, the experience of unbelievers in death is one of conscious suffering in hades until their resurrection at the end of the millennium to face the final judgment (Luke 16:22–26; 2 Pet. 2:9; Rev. 20:12–15).

Dispensationalists were quite concerned to distinguish their views from all doctrines of soul sleep. Article 13 of the 1878 Niagara Bible Conference doctrinal statement adopted to oppose millennial dawnists (and later incorporated into the Dallas Theological Seminary doctrinal statement) expressed the view commonly held by dispensationalists:

> We believe that the souls of those who have trusted in the Lord Jesus Christ for salvation do at death immediately pass into His presence, and there remain in conscious bliss until the resurrection of the body at His coming, when soul and body reunited shall be associated with Him forever in the glory; but the souls of unbelievers remain after death in conscious misery until the final judgment of the great white throne at the close of the millennium, when soul and body reunited shall be cast into the lake of fire, not to be annihilated, but to be punished with everlasting destruction from the presence of the Lord, and from the glory of His power: Luke 16:19–26; 23:43; 2 Cor. 5:8; Phil. 1:23; 2 Thess. 1:7–9; Jude 6:7; Rev. 20:11–15.[5]

John Darby dismissed soul sleep as "an invention."[6] Lewis Chafer stated definitively, "No ground is found in the Word of God for the supposed sleep of the soul. On the other hand, by terms which cannot be mistaken it is declared that those who die go on in consciousness, and in the case of believers, into the immediate presence of the Lord."[7]

While universally affirming that church-age believers ascend to be with Christ in heaven until their resurrection, dispensationalists did not all agree as to the state of the righteous dead prior to Christ. Many taught that Christ Himself brought about a change in the destiny of the righteous dead at the time of His own death, resurrection, and ascension. According to this view, prior to Christ's resurrection, the righteous dead descended to the upper compartment of hades, where they were conscious and comforted, awaiting their resurrection. This would seem to be consistent with the Lord's description of the experience of Lazarus in Luke 16:22–25. However, it was believed that their location and experience was changed by Christ. He closed the upper chamber of hades and removed the righteous dead to heaven (Eph. 4:8). Other dispensationalists demurred, believing that Scripture was not explicit on this point. One can compare differences in dispensational views of this matter by consulting the note on Luke 16:23 in the 1917 and 1967 editions of *The Scofield Study Bible*.[8] The former supports the view noted here, the latter declines to be specific on it. One can also compare the contrasting views of Herman Hoyt, who supports the view, and Charles Ryrie, who rejects it, the latter stating his belief that all the righteous at all times went to heaven upon death.[9]

Dispensationalists have also differed on whether the dead are embodied in the intermediate state between death and resurrection. Chafer argued for intermediate bodies on the basis of 2 Corinthians 5:1–5 as did Hoyt, who noted various descriptions of the dead in Scripture portray them as embodied.[10] Darby, however, understood the intermediate state as disembodied.[11] Others simply did not address this issue.

Resurrection

Dispensationalists agree that all the dead will be raised, some to everlasting life and some to everlasting condemnation. Their contribution, however, is on the identification of stages in the resurrection of the righteous.[12] This primarily involves the distinction of the resurrection of the church at the rapture from the resurrection of tribulation martyrs at the beginning of the millennium. Dispensationalists differ on whether the Old Testament righteous dead will be raised at the rapture or at the beginning of the millennium. Some have also considered the resurrection of mortals who may die during the millennium to occur most likely at the end of the millennium. Except for this last possibility, the righteous are all resurrected "out from the dead" (Phil. 3:11) to participate in Christ's millennial glory. The resurrection is a precious truth by which the believer enters into eternal life and the fullness of Christ's glory.

THE DOCTRINE OF HELL

One of the key differences between the present condition of creation and the consummation is future absence of sin and evil. Sin must be removed in order for the transition from old to new to take place. This, of course, happens in the lives of the redeemed through the application of Christ's death and resurrection to their lives. Although the new creation begins in mortal conditions with their union with Christ by faith, it is completed by their resurrection or transformation with glorification in immortality. This is the only way into the kingdom. It cannot be simply inherited by flesh and blood, nor can one force one's way into it. Anyone who is not redeemed through Christ is removed at the final judgment into everlasting hell.

Dispensationalism has consistently taught the reality of hell as the state of final, everlasting punishment for unredeemed humanity. The point of final separation is at the last judgment described in Revelation 20:11–15 and predicted frequently in earlier texts of Scripture, particularly in the teachings of Jesus (e.g., Matt. 18:8–9; 25:41–46). It is there that the resurrection of all humanity is completed and the final judgment takes place. Those whose names are not in the Book of Life are cast into the lake of fire forever. They, by virtue of the life that characterized them, have no place in the new creation.

To be sure, the state of the unredeemed between death and resurrection for final judgment is described in Scripture as existence in hades, or sheol. Of the many references to hades/sheol, Luke 16:19–31 has been determinative for Christian theology, dispensationalism included. One's future course is already set at death, and hades, for the unredeemed, is a place of torment anticipating the judgment to come. But at the final judgment, hades is emptied by resurrection, and both hades and its former inhabitants are cast into the lake of fire (Rev. 20:13–14).

A typical dispensational view on hell is given by Lewis Chafer in his classic *Systematic Theology*. There he is concerned to establish first the fact that hell is a real place of misery, evidenced by the various location descriptions ascribed to it by Scripture: gehenna (Matt. 5:22, 29–30; 10:28; James 3:6), lake of fire (Rev. 21:8), bottomless pit (Rev. 20:1), furnace of fire (Matt. 13:42), outer darkness (Matt. 8:12), and [a place] where their worm does not die (Mark 9:44). These same texts speak of the misery experienced in that place—a place of weeping and gnashing of teeth (Matt. 8:12), of everlasting or unquenchable fire (Matt. 25:41; Luke 3:17), a place in which there is torment with no rest day and night (Rev. 14:11).[13]

Second, Chafer notes that Scripture speaks of the eternality of this condition, stressing the fact that "forever" is used of hell in the same way that it is used of the eternal life for the redeemed. The key text for him is Matthew 25:46, where the Lord, at the judgment, separates the righteous and the unrighteous into parallel destinies: "These will go away into eternal punishment, but the righteous into eternal life." Other texts speaking of the eternal nature of the punishment include Revelation 14:11 and Daniel 12:2.[14]

One can compare this treatment on hell to that given by Herman Hoyt in *The End Times*. Hoyt divides his treatment into four parts: the place of punishment, the duration of the punishment, the nature of the punishment, and the severity of the punishment. The last topic treats the matter of degrees of punishment in hell, which is traditional in Christian thought.[15] John Walvoord defended a "literal view" of hell in the popular, *Four Views on Hell*, edited by William Crockett. There he traces hell as a theme in Scripture with special focus on the teaching of Jesus. He concludes that hell is a place of everlasting punishment in a literal fire.[16]

THE CONSUMMATION OF SALVATION

The basic agreement that dispensationalists share on hell is a set feature of traditional Christian theology. However, dispensationalists were on new ground when it came to articulating a view of the consummation of redemption that accounted for the differing divine purposes for Israel and the church. Their concern was to affirm the integrity and surety of the earthly eschatology revealed in Scripture, particularly as that has to do with the divine promises given to Israel and the revealed eschatological order by which they would be fulfilled. In addition, dispensationalists wished to set forth the consummation of the new reality of the church in a manner that affirmed the integrity of the church, without compromising the "earthly" eschatology in which the particular identity of Israel is secure.

Taking these concerns into account, dispensationists have envisioned the consummation in basically three ways. They correspond to three forms of dispensational thought that I have classified elsewhere as classical, revised, and progressive.[17]

CLASSICAL DISPENSATIONALISM: A HEAVENLY AND EARTHLY DUALISM

Use of the designations *earthly* and *heavenly* to refer to Israel and to the church, respectively, had long been traditional in Christian theological discourse. Equally traditional was the view that the latter replaced the former in the divine plan, the earthly being but a temporal image of an eternal heavenly reality. But early dispensationalists affirmed both the earthly and the heavenly as two parallel dimensions of redemption that would be consummated in two corresponding dimensions of the millennial and eternal orders. Some found confirmation of this in the biblical language of eschatological cosmology, "a new heaven and a new earth" (Rev. 21:1). The consummation of God's purpose and plan for the church—His heavenly people—would take place in a renewed heaven, while the fulfillment of God's plan and purpose for Israel—His earthly people—would be on a renewed earth. The consummation for each would be eternal or everlasting in keeping with the Word of divine promise.[18]

The classic statement of this view was given by Chafer: "Every covenant, promise, and provision for Israel is earthly, and they continue as a nation with the earth when it is created new. Every covenant or promise for the church is for a heavenly reality, and she continues in heavenly citizenship when the heavens are recreated."[19]

The Heavenly Consummation

As has been noted, a heavenly consummation for the church is traditional for Christian theology. But in traditional theology, heaven was the one and only consummation for the entire plan of redemption, which meant that the Bible's language of earthly consummation had to be reinterpreted and thereby refitted to the heavenly fulfillment. By postulating a dual consummation in heavenly and earthly spheres, dispensationalists not only sought to preserve the integrity of the former without hermeneutical resignification, but also found thereby an opportunity to purify the conception of heaven to correlate with what they believed was an equally purified theology of the nature and purpose of the church.

The heavenly consummation can be described in terms of its location, mode, and quality of life. Certainly, as its label suggests, its *location* is in heaven. More precisely, it is in the heavenly city, the heavenly Jerusalem, the Father's house, whose accommodations Christ is even now preparing for us (Gal. 4:26; Phil. 3:20; John 14:2–3; Rev. 21:9–22:5). The *mode* of the heavenly consummation is resurrection from the dead or, for some, translation to the resurrection mode directly from mortal life. The *quality* of the life is a direct and personal relationship with Christ. The latter is the chief characteristic of heavenly life. In this sense, heaven is not so much a place as it is a Person.[20]

The heavenly people are first and foremost the church that even now is the body and bride of Christ. The church is already "in Christ." It is already "raised with Him" and its life is "hidden with Christ in God." When Christ appears, the church will appear with Him in glory. Heaven, then, for the church is the consummation of its identity and reality as a people united personally to Christ in glory. The quality of personal union with Christ in glory is the chief defining characteristic of heaven for the church.[21] But the heavenly people includes more than the church. In keeping with its mode, "heavenly people" encompasses all the redeemed who are raised from the dead or translated from mortality.

The heavenly consummation begins with the rapture of the church. Christ descends to take the church to be with Him by resurrection or translation, where the church, or bride, is forever with the Lord. Most dispensationalists placed the resurrection of Old Testament saints at the rapture as well, but they were distinguished as a different group of heavenly people from the church. At the beginning of the millennium, martyrs from the tribulation will be raised (Rev. 20:4) to join the other heavenly people, and if millennial believers were to die, they would be raised (most likely at the end of the millennium) to join the heavenly people and heavenly experience as well. Resurrection life is heavenly life, identical for all the heavenly people in mode and in location. But not all the resurrected have the same quality of life. Classical dispensationalists reserved the highest quality of heavenly life for the church, which unlike other redeemed peoples has had an identity in Christ from its inception and is alone to be designated the bride of Christ. The others originally had earthly hopes but lost them through death. They will subsequently be made perfect with the church (Heb. 11:39–40). They will be glorified and dwell in the heavenly city, but remain distinct from the church in accordance with the descriptive list found in Hebrews 12:22–24.

The heavenly consummation begins for all heavenly people at the time of their resurrection and continues forever, extending through the millennium and into the eternal state. They share in Christ's rule and reign, not just during the millennium but forever. However, ruling and reigning should not be seen a distraction from their consummative experience of union with Christ. It is probably best to understand it as an aspect of Christ's Person with which they experience union.

The Earthly Consummation

The earthly dimension of the eschatological dualism is ushered into its consummation by the second coming of Christ to earth. It consists of the blessed organization and living activity of peoples on earth—peoples whom Christ finds on earth at His return and who are allowed to enter His kingdom. This takes place through the judgment of the nations recorded in Matthew 25:31–46.

The millennium is the first stage of this eschatological kingdom, and in it we see the beginning of the fulfillment of the covenant promises of Israel: promises of an explicit national existence, in its particular land, under its ruling messianic king, with individual and national, physical and spiritual blessings. Since all of these blessings are declared to be everlasting in Scripture, classical dispensationalists saw a necessary connection between the millennial kingdom and the eternal state as two stages of the consummation. At the end of the millennial kingdom, as Chafer notes, it is the destiny of "the earthly citizens . . . to go on into eternity as the dwellers on the earth" just as it is the destiny of "the heavenly citizens . . . to occupy the new heavens."[22]

However, the linkage of the two stages of consummation was so close that classical dispensationalists could speak of the millennium itself as being "the final form" of kingdom promise.[23] Accordingly, dispensationalists typically used the label *premillennialism* to refer to the entire earthly eschatological program.[24]

Nevertheless, the millennium remained a distinct stage in the consummation due to "the presence of imperfections" that would be absent from the eternal state, Chafer noted, adding, "In his entire millennial reign Christ will be putting down enemies (cf. 1 Cor. 15:24–25)."[25] The presence of evil will climax in the release of Satan and the rebellion he will instigate. The crushing of the rebellion, the punishment of Satan, and the final judgment are necessary to bring in the perfect state. Yet Chafer also noted, "The presence of imperfections in the final form of the kingdom of heaven [the millennium] should not be allowed to obscure the glorious truth that, due to the enthroning of Christ and the binding of Satan, righteousness and peace shall then cover the earth as the waters cover the deep."[26] At the end of the age, the "tares" (Matt. 13:30) that are present in the kingdom will be removed. Only those truly born again will abide in the everlasting kingdom (John 3:5).

Elsewhere, Chafer describes the millennial kingdom this way: "Life will be tranquil (cf. Isa 11:6–9; 65:18–25; Jer 31:31–33). The King shall reign in righteousness (cf. Isa 11:1–5; Ps 72:1–19; Mt 5:1–7:29). Creation, too, shall be restored to Edenic blessedness (Rom 8:18–23)."[27] In light of the national organization of earthly peoples, "it will be the time of Israel's glory, and with Israel, some of the Gentiles will be blessed (cf. Isa 11:10; Matt 25:34). . . ." This will come about because "the Spirit will have been poured out on all flesh."[28] The common gift of the Spirit does not erase the distinction between peoples; it just brings about a peaceful harmony in their interrelations. For classical dispensationalists, these distinctions were not just ethnic but also class distinctions. Chafer notes, "Gentiles must serve Israel (Isa. 14:1–2; 60:12; 61:5)" in the millennial order.[29] Class distinctions apply, in their minds, even to the heavenly peoples in which the church is set in higher status than other classes of resurrected humanity (OT saints and tribulation martyrs).

As blessed as earthly life will be in the millennium, it is even more so in the eternal state of the new earth to come. The continuity between the two stages of consummation is guaranteed by the everlasting nature of Israel's national and territorial promises. "There must be an everlasting new earth because God has given Israel the promise of an everlasting possession of the land (Deut 30:1–10)."[30] But the blessedness of that new earth is seen in the promise of Revelation 21:4, when God "will wipe away every tear from their eyes; and there will no longer be any death . . . mourning, or crying, or pain." As Chafer explains,

> Sorrow, crying, and pain have never belonged to heaven; therefore the reference is to earth and to a new earth. [Verse 3 of] the same passage declares that God will make His tabernacle with men. This is not new concerning heaven because He has always had His habitation in heaven. The new earth will be as suitable for His abiding presence as heaven ever has been.[31]

REVISED DISPENSATIONALISM: DIFFERENCES ON THE ETERNAL CONSUMMATION

By the middle of the twentieth century, dispensational writers introduced some careful modifications to dispensational thought. They were just as insistent on the distinct identities of redeemed peoples as had been their theological forebearers. All were also vigorous defenders of premillennialism against (1) an aggressive amillennialism—whose denial of a future millennium went hand in hand with their supersessionistic dismissal of the national and territorial eschatological promises of Israel—and (2) a nondispensational premillennialism which, although it affirmed a future millennial kingdom on the basis of Revelation 20, nevertheless isolated that promise from the earthly eschatology of the rest of the canon.[32]

Against these views, dispensationalists of the second half of the twentieth century argued strongly for the millennial kingdom as the consummation of the plan for and promises of God to Israel.[33] Many maintained the traditional *heavenly* and *earthly* distinction to describe the consummative experience of the redeemed in the millennial period, but they were reticent to extend that distinction clearly into the eternal state. Charles Ryrie limited Lewis Chafer's distinction of the heavenly and earthly peoples and programs strictly to the millennial kingdom. He wrote, "The earthly purpose of Israel of which dispensationalists speak concerns the national promise which will be fulfilled by Jews *during the millennium* [emphasis mine] as they live on earth in *un*resurrected [emphasis his] bodies."[34] The heavenly purpose would be fulfilled for the resurrected or translated church together with resurrected Old Testament and tribulation saints in the heavenly city of that millennial kingdom, the "heavenly Jerusalem" described in the writings of Paul, the epistle to the Hebrews, and the vision of John in Revelation 21:9–22:5.

Consistent with earlier dispensationalists, these later dispensationalists spoke of resurrection from the dead as the transition into heavenly eternal life. It was also the transition into glory. The heavenly experience of the resurrected was alike one of glory and was altogether distinguished from earthly millennial life not only in bodily distinction and degree of glory, but by its relation to Christ. The heavenly people are coheirs and co-rulers with Christ rather than subjects of His kingdom. The church shall remain distinct from the rest of the glorified saints in the intimacy of its relation to Christ. It alone would be the "queen" of the kingdom.[35] Other heavenly peoples would simply be members of His court.

Understanding the New Heaven and New Earth

Revised dispensationalists differed on whether the heavenly city of the millennium was located in heaven, on earth, or somewhere in between. Wherever it is, it would be the locus of the heavenly experience to which the church looks forward and the rest of the resurrected are privileged to share. The millennial earth, on the other hand, is the location where the "earthly" eschatology would be consummated. Similar to their predecessors, revised dispensationalists described the millennial earth as a peaceful, prosperous, and socially just state of affairs. They did not deny the presence of spiritual blessings but saw the whole as a temple-centered religious system, which they believed was required by the eschatological vision of Ezekiel 40–48. The sacrifices predicted to take place there were understood "as a means of memorializing the death of Christ."[36]

While basically in agreement on the millennium, revised dispensationalists differed in their views of how the eternal state consummated God's dual purposes. This appears to be somewhat related to how they understood Revelation 21:1: "Then I saw a new heaven and a new earth, for the first heaven and the first earth [had] passed away." Walvoord took the view that the old creation would be annihilated, utterly destroyed, and a new heaven and new earth would be created ex nihilo.[37] In his various writings, he has very little to say about the new earth per se, choosing to focus exclusively on the New Jerusalem of Revelation 21:9–22:5 as the locus of eternal life. Significantly he places Israel's eternal future in that "heavenly" city along with the church.[38] Ryrie is reticent to say anything about the eternal state in his writings, except that he does see the eternal state of all the redeemed *in heaven*.[39] There is, in his view, no earthly sphere of redemption in the eternal state. The eternal consummation appears to be entirely "heavenly" in its quality and mode.

Consequently, there is an emphasis in the writings of Ryrie and Walvoord on the millennium as itself the final consummation of the territorial national promises of Israel, in fact the entire earthly eschatology.[40]

Walvoord, Pentecost, and Hoyt

J. Dwight Pentecost, while agreeing with Walvoord on the annihilation of the present heaven and earth and the creation ex nihilo of a new heaven and earth, nevertheless sees the new earth as sufficiently similar to the present earth as to function for the eternal fulfillment of the earthly eschatology. He wrote,

> Israel's covenants guarantee [to] that people the land, a national existence, a kingdom, a King, and spiritual blessings in perpetuity. Therefore there must be an eternal earth in which these blessings can be fulfilled. By a translation out of the old earth Israel will be brought into the new earth, there to enjoy

> forever all that God has promised to them. Then it shall be eternally true, "Behold, the tabernacle of God is with men, and he will dwell with them, and they shall be his people and God himself shall be with them, and be their God" (Rev. 21:3). The creation of the new heavens and new earth is the final preparatory act anticipating the eternal kingdom of God. It is now true that God has a kingdom "wherein dwelleth righteousness" (2 Pet. 3:13).[41]

This conception of the new earth as the locale for the earthly eschatological consummation is more strongly emphasized by Hoyt, who disagrees with Walvoord's annihilationist interpretation of Rev. 21:1. Hoyt rightly points out the problems of an annihilationist view for maintaining any continuity at all between the old and new creations including the continuing identities of both redeemed and lost peoples.[42]

Rather than annihilation, Hoyt notes that it is more consistent to understand the language of Revelation 21:1 as referring to "a change or rearrangement of order."[43] This is what is more generally understood as the *renovation* view of the new creation, a view that is more consistent with Paul's language of the redemption of creation in Romans 8:18–23.[44] Hoyt spends several pages describing the various changes that will characterize the eternal state—geological changes that make the planet more inhabitable and hospitable to life; functional changes that accompany the lifting of the curse—increased fertility and productiveness; organizational changes with the various classes of the redeemed from inhabitants of the New Jerusalem to the peoples who populate the whole of the new earth. Clearly for Hoyt, the New Jerusalem is a city on the new earth—part of the new earthly order instead of a symbol for heaven, or a heavenly experience apart from the earth. In Hoyt's view the city, the New Jerusalem of Revelation 21:9–22:5, is the central source of glory radiating out through the entire new creation and the focal point of universal worship, containing as it does the throne of God Incarnate, Jesus Christ.[45]

PROGRESSIVE DISPENSATIONALISM

Progressive dispensationalists are just as concerned as previous dispensationalists to affirm God's distinctive purposes for Israel and for the church. But to do this, one does not need to postulate dual dimensions of eschatological consummation in either the millennium or the eternal state. Progressive dispensationalism sees only one eschatology in the Bible—one in which the so-called earthly eschatology is affirmed without re-signification and also in which the newness of the church, with its present heavenly orientation to Christ, fits coherently without resorting to a separate eschatological program. That one eschatological program is best described as new-creation eschatology, similar to that found in Hoyt, but with a more pronounced emphasis on the holistic unity of its various features.[46]

A Holistic Consummation

As in Hoyt, the consummation is viewed as a redemption and renewal of the present creation rather than its annihilation and replacement by a completely different, heavenly reality. This means that there is an ontological continuity between the present created order in which the plan and promises of God have been revealed (and in which the history of redemption has unfolded) and the consummation in which it will be fulfilled. That continuity extends not only into the millennial order but into the eternal state as well, constituting it as a fit and proper consummation of the entire plan and purpose of God.[47]

The holistic consummation of progressive dispensationalism can be described as a worldwide multinational kingdom order of redeemed peoples on a renewed earth.[48] The nations constituting this multinational order are Israel and various Gentile nations. Israel is a key irreducible and indissolvable feature of this kingdom order whose national and territorial identity is guaranteed by divine promise. Gentile nations are also explicit elements of this prophesied pattern. This multinational structure of the kingdom consummation is a consistent expectation of biblical eschatology from Genesis to Revelation.[49] It is specifically covenanted to the house of David, and it became an explicit feature of messianic prophecy. It informs Jesus' proclamation of the eschatological kingdom and is the basis for the mission He gave to the church.

What is not revealed in the Old Testament is how this worldwide order would cohere in an enduring, peaceful unity. That revelation comes with the formation of the church, when salvific and pneumatological blessings promised to Israel in the Old Testament are inaugurated after Christ's ascension—not only with Jewish believers in Jesus but with Gentile believers as well.[50] The church, which came into being for the first time on the day of Pentecost (Acts 2), reveals the key relational structure that unites the peoples of the eschatological kingdom to Christ and to each other. That structure is the indwelling Holy Spirit. The indwelling Spirit unites all believers directly to Jesus Christ for the blessings of salvation that come through His cross and resurrection. That same Spirit also unites them to each other (whether Jews or Gentiles) in the bond of peace.

Thus the whole kingdom order is rendered a holy communion fit to be the dwelling place of God. It is this reality that stabilizes, pacifies, and sanctifies the whole multinational, worldwide messianic kingdom that is consistently revealed in Scripture to be the consummation of the divine plan.[51]

Jewish and Gentile Believers Share the Blessings

The fact that the salvific and pneumatological blessings promised to Israel for the kingdom would also be given to Gentiles was a mystery revealed for the first time in the reality of the church. The church is neither Israel nor a Gentile nation—though Jewish and Gentile believers are part of the church, for they share a relational reality in Jesus. The church has come into existence as the body of Christ during the time of His ascension into heaven. In the church, Jewish and Gentile believers share an inaugurated form of the salvific and pneumatological blessings that will, in their fullness, characterize the kingdom.[52] In that sense the church itself is an inaugural form of the kingdom, which precedes its full political, governmental establishment.[53]

The full establishment of the kingdom awaits the return of Christ, as does also glorification and the completion of the salvific and pneumatological blessings that are presently experienced in inaugural form. In the final consummation, the resurrected or translated church of this dispensation (composed of Jews and Gentiles) will be joined by resurrected Old Testament saints (Jews and Gentiles) and by translated or resurrected millennial saints (Jews and Gentiles) so as altogether to be the redeemed peoples (Jews and Gentiles) that constitute Israel and the Gentile nations of the final multinational worldwide kingdom order. All the peoples—Jews and Gentiles—of that kingdom will be united to Christ with the same blessings of salvation and sanctification that are now enjoyed in inaugural form by Jewish and Gentile believers who comprise the church.

The inaugural kingdom reality, which is the church, thus finds its fulfillment in the spiritual union of all redeemed peoples with Christ and with one another.

These are the same peoples who in their ethnic, national, territorial, and political identities and assignments constitute Israel and the Gentile nations of that multinational, worldwide kingdom.[54] The purposes of God for Israel and for the church thereby find their distinctive fulfillments in one unified eschatological consummation.

Without Class Divisions

Quite clearly, the church is not a distinct people group in the consummation set within a hierarchical class system. Progressive dispensationalism does not see the redeemed separated by class. There are personal, ethnic, and national identity features among the redeemed but not differences of class. There are also individual assignments and degrees of reward among the redeemed, but not social divisions by class. In that final order, some may have their primary location in the city, whereas others may be located elsewhere in the new creation. But this is not seen as a difference in the quality of salvific experience. Rather, the church's purpose in this dispensation is to reveal that identity, and assignments will *not* be the occasion for class subordination. All the redeemed will be directly united to Christ and, in Christ, to each other, so that the standing of each in Christ and the quality of consummate salvation given to each one is the same for all. That reality will unite peoples of varying personal, ethnic, and national identities and of varying assignments for service in the kingdom. Consequently, the church does not and cannot exist as a separate people group in the order of the redeemed.[55]

Like some earlier dispensationalists, progressive dispensationalists see the millennial kingdom as the first stage of the consummation. It is the kingdom that Christ establishes on earth at His second coming. The righteous dead are raised to share in this kingdom, some at the pretribulational rapture (Old Testament saints and the church of this dispensation) and some after His return (tribulation martyrs). By resurrection or translation (for living believers at the rapture) these citizens of the kingdom enter into the glory of Christ, which will continue for them into eternity. However, mortal believers living on earth at the time of Christ's return are invited by Him to inhabit and populate the millennial kingdom. Consequently, even though it has a large number of glorified constituents, the kingdom is established on earth under mortal conditions in accordance with biblical prophecy (Isa. 65:17–25).

The millennial kingdom period will be a time of abundant fruitfulness and productiveness for life on earth. The nations will experience peace and justice under the rule of Christ. The glorified will share in His reign; the mortals will flourish under His blessing. Israel will enjoy her national and territorial blessings according to covenant promise and the nations will likewise be blessed in their lands, which together with Israel constitute the entirety of the millennial earth. The capital of Christ's worldwide kingdom rule will be a restored, enlarged, and glorified Jerusalem in accordance with prophetic prediction (Isa. 60–65). To it the nations have access and from it will come the guiding rule of the Lord Christ that unifies the world order in peace and righteousness. Nations will turn their swords into plowshares and their spears into pruning hooks; they will learn war no more (Isa. 2:2–4; Mic. 4:1–4).

Nevertheless, the condition of fallenness remains for unglorified mortals in the millennial kingdom, which seems to account for harsh descriptions of coercive rule in some prophecies (Isa. 11:4; Zech. 14:17–19) as well as the rebellion predicted in Revelation 20:7–9. Although Satan will be bound for a thousand years, Revelation 20:7–9 tells us that he is released at the end only to incite a rebellion by many peoples who presumably are a later generation born in the kingdom. The crushing of the rebellion, the judgment of eternal punishment for Satan, and the final resurrection, judgment, and everlasting punishment of the unredeemed humanity at the end of the millennium mark the end of sin and evil and make way for the renovation of all creation and consummation of the eternal order.[56]

A Unified Consummation

Like classical dispensationalists, but contrary to some revised dispensationalists, progressive dispensationalists do not see the millennium as the terminal fulfillment of the national and territorial promises given to Israel or of the "earthly" eschatology in which they are contextualized. Like many other dispensationalists, they believe that the promise of an "everlasting" fulfillment of the covenanted blessings requires an accommodating eternal state.

However, like revised dispensationalists, but contrary to classical dispensationalists, progressive dispensationalists expect a unified consummation. For them, the church reveals the mystery of the eternal stability of that prophesied kingdom order. It is therefore the eternal order that fully reveals the plan and purpose of God in creation and redemption. That eternal order is a holistic new creation, which can be described as follows:

> When Christ has subjected all things to Himself and has destroyed sin and death, the eschatological kingdom of God in all its fullness will be manifest eternal and immortal on a renewed earth. This kingdom is the goal of redemption, the culmination of all previous revelations of God's kingdom. It is the rule of God the Father, God the Son incarnate as Messiah, Son of David, Son of Man, and God the Holy Spirit over the earth with all its inhabitants and over the heavens and all contained therein forever. This kingdom is *earthly*. The curse which came through sin will be replaced with the blessing of life and fruitfulness over the earth. Death, disease, and demonism will be eliminated and the City of God will be established on the earth. The kingdom is also *spiritual*, as redemption is extended in full in both individual and social aspects of human existence. It will be characterized by life eternal and immortal, by righteousness and justice. Wickedness will have been judged and removed. Grace, mercy, compassion, and forgiveness of sins will abide forever. . . . The kingdom is also *national* and *political* in that it involves the establishment and administration of Israel and all nations through the Messiah of Israel, Jesus, Son of David. God will reign over the nations in glory, power, and majesty, blessed, honored and worshiped by all forever.[57]

Notes

1. For a history of Christian thought on heaven, see Jeffrey Burton Russell, *A History of Heaven: The Singing Silence* (Princeton: University Press, 1997); Alister E. McGrath, *A Brief History of Heaven* (Oxford: Blackwell, 2003).
2. See the discussion in Russell, *History of Heaven*, 6–9. The spiritual interpretation of the Jewish elements of the Bible's "earthly" eschatology can be seen even in early Chiliasm after the suppression of the Bar Kochba rebellion. Tertullian writes, "As for the restoration of Judea, which the Jews, misguided by the names of towns and territories, hope for exactly as described, it would be tedious to explain how the allegorical interpretation of it is spiritually applicable to Christ and the church and to the possession and enjoyment of it"; *Adversus Marcionem* 3.24, trans. Ernest Evans, in *Tertullian Adversus Marcionem* (Oxford: Clarendon, 1972). Allegorical or spiritual interpretation soon expands to exclude Chiliasm itself as can be seen in the work of Origen.
3. Puritan interest in a future for the Jews has been noted in many works. See H. Iain Murray, *The Puritan Hope: Revival and the Interpretation of Prophecy* (Edinburgh: Banner of Truth, 1971); Peter Toon, ed., *Puritans, The Millennium and the Future of Israel: Puritan Eschatology 1600 to 1660* (Cambridge: James Clarke, 1970); Crawford Gribben, *The Puritan Millennium: Literature and Theology, 1550–1682*, rev. ed., (Milton Keynes: Paternoster, 2008). For its development in the late eighteenth and early nineteenth centuries, see Donald Lewis, *The Origins of Christian Zionism: Lord Shaftsbury and Evangelical Support for a Jewish Homeland* (Cambridge: University Press, 2010).
4. For an overview of the development of millennialism and of the scholarly literature on the topic, see

Evangelical Millennialism in the Trans-Atlantic World, 1500–2000, ed. Crawford Gribben, (London: Palgrave Macmillan, 2011).

5. *The 1878 Niagara Creed*, article 13, in Ernest R. Sandeen, *The Roots of Fundamentalism: British and American Millenarianism, 1800–1930*, Appendix A (Chicago: University of Chicago Press, 1970), 276.
6. J. N. Darby, *The Collected Works of J. N. Darby*, ed. William Kelly, 34 vols. (repr., Sunbury, PA: Believers Bookshelf, 1971), 31:182, 183.
7. Lewis Sperry Chafer, *Systematic Theology*, 8 vols. (Dallas: Dallas Seminary Press, 1948), 4:414.
8. C. I. Scofield, ed., *The Scofield Study Bible* (New York: Oxford Univ. Press, 1917), 1098–99; idem, *New Scofield Reference Bible* (New York: Oxford Univ. Press, 1967), 1106.
9. Herman A. Hoyt, *The End Times* (Chicago: Moody, 1969), 45–46; Charles C. Ryrie, *Basic Theology* (Wheaton: Victor Books, 1986), 519–20. Ryrie writes, "I believe the Old Testament saint at death went immediately to the presence of the Lord. . . . Are we to understand that this conversation [at the Transfiguration] between Christ, Moses, and Elijah took place in the upper compartment of hades where Moses at least would have been until after the death of Christ? Are we to understand then that the transfiguration of Christ took place in paradise-hades? Are we to understand that Elijah was taken at his translation to sheol/hades and not heaven? I think not; rather the Old Testament saint went immediately to heaven to wait for the resurrection of his body at the second coming of Christ."
10. Chafer, *Systematic Theology*, 4:414–15; Hoyt, *End Times*, 46–47.
11. "There is an immense difference between my condition in this body and that in which I shall be stripped of it after this life, as there is likewise between the latter state and that in which the redemption of this body shall be completed in the resurrection. . . . We at least in dying lay aside a burden, a spotted garment, that we may at once enjoy the presence of the Lord, without hindrance; and so that the pure air and genial warmth of His presence may penetrate our souls, now liberated from my distraction." Again he writes, "I am merely stripped of a body, which had not partaken of redemption, to be introduced to the presence of Jesus before my heavenly Father, waiting for what remains, to wit, that I should be clothed with a glorious body, fashioned like unto the glorious body of Jesus Christ." Darby, "The Doctrine of the Wesleyans on Perfection," in *Collected Works*, 3:173–74. See also in vol. 31, "The State of the Soul after Death," 178–86. There he writes, "The intermediate state is not glory (for that we must wait for the body. It is raised in glory. He shall change our vile bodies to be like His glorious body); but it is blessedness where no unholy evil is. It is being with Christ Himself, the source of joy ineffable," 185.
12. See Lewis Sperry Chafer, *Major Bible Themes*, rev. John F. Walvoord (Grand Rapids: Zondervan, 1974), 340–42; J. Dwight Pentecost, *Things to Come: A Study in Biblical Eschatology* (Grand Rapids: Zondervan, 1958), 411; Ryrie, *Basic Theology*, 518; John F. Walvoord, "End Times," in *Understanding Christian Theology*, ed. Charles R. Swindoll and Roy B. Zuck (Nashville: Thomas Nelson, 2003), 1331–38.
13. Chafer, *Systematic Theology*, 4:427–33; esp. 430.
14. Ibid., 431–32.
15. Hoyt, *End Times*, 238–40.
16. John F. Walvoord, "The Literal View," in *Four Views on Hell*, ed. William Crockett (Grand Rapids: Zondervan, 1992), 11–31. Note also Walvoord's response to other views on pp. 77–81; 119–21; 167–70. See also Walvoord, "End Times," 1346–49. An interesting speculation on the literal nature of hell is found in Pentecost, *Things to Come*, 559–61, where he quotes extensively from an article by C. T. Schwarze, "The Bible and Science on the Everlasting Fire," *Bibliotheca Sacra* 95 (1938): 105–12, suggesting stars as the lakes of fire in which eternal punishment would take place.
17. This classification is found in my chapter, "The Extent and Varieties of Dispensationalism," in Craig A. Blaising and Darrell L. Bock, *Progressive Dispensationalism* (Wheaton: Victor, 1993), 21–56. In a previous publication I proposed a fourfold classification of American dispensationalism: Niagara Premillennialism, Scofieldism, Essentialist Dispensationalism, and Progressive Dispensationalism.

See Craig A. Blaising, "Dispensationalism: The Search for Definition," in Craig A. Blaising and Darrell L. Bock, eds., *Dispensationalism, Israel and the Church: The Search for Definition* (Grand Rapids: Zondervan, 1992), 13–24. Classical Dispensationalism in the threefold classification covers the first two of the fourfold classification, but it was intended to include Brethren dispensational thought as well. Obviously, these classifications are heuristic models. Individual writers have their own particular nuances. Further study on the history of the dispensational tradition, especially in the United States, is needed.

18. See Blaising, "Extent and Varieties of Dispensationalism," 23–24; Blaising, "Dispensationalism," 24–25.
19. Chafer, *Systematic Theology*, 4:47.
20. "In relation to the eternal destiny of the church saints, it is to be observed that their destiny primarily is related to a Person rather than a place. While the place looms with importance (John 14:3), the place is overshadowed by the Person into whose presence the believer is taken." These words by Pentecost (*Things to Come*, 562) capture succinctly the view of the earlier dispensationalists.
21. Darby's view of the heavenly destiny of the church is an intense experience of personal intimacy with Christ. This is explored by Gary L. Nebeker, "The Hope of Heavenly Glory in John Nelson Darby," (PhD diss., Dallas Theological Seminary, 1997), and also by Floyd S. Elmore, "A Critical Examination of the Doctrine of the Two Peoples of God in John Nelson Darby" (ThD diss., Dallas Theological Seminary, 1991). His view seems to be similar to the marriage mysticism that is found in Bernard of Clairvaux and subsequent writers. See Russell, *History of Heaven*, 116–17.
22. Chafer, *Systematic Theology*, 4:401.
23. Ibid., 4:327.
24. Chafer refers to his entire discussion of eschatology as "premillennialism," saying at the end of his introduction to his chapter on eschatology, "What premillennialism teaches will be the theme of following pages." Ibid., 4:284. He notes the modern revival of premillennialism within the sixty years prior to his writing, basically since the 1878 prophecy conference in New York City (see Sandeen, *Roots of Fundamentalism*, 147–61). American dispensationalists of the late nineteenth and early twentieth centuries primarily identified their view as premillennialism. It is only in the disputes of the 1930s with amillennialists (led by J. Gresham Machen and John Murray of the newly formed Westminster Seminary) that the term *dispensationalism* became more widely used to distinguish it from other forms of premillennialism. See Sandeen, *Roots of Fundamentalism*, 255–60; R. Todd Magnum, *The Dispensational-Covenantal Rift: The Fissuring of American Evangelical Theology from 1936–1944* (Milton Keynes: Paternoster, 2007).
25. Chafer, *Systematic Theology*, 4:327.
26. Ibid.
27. Ibid., 400.
28. Ibid. The pouring out of the Spirit on all flesh is developed in progressive dispensationalism to explain the revelatory nature of the church regarding the unity of all peoples in Christ and to each other as the key relational structure of the future multinational kingdom. See remarks below in this chapter.
29. Chafer, *Systematic Theology*, 4:400.
30. Ibid., 427.
31. Ibid.
32. Ryrie notes that the difference between dispensationalists and other premillennial views, such as the premillennialism of George E. Ladd, is the way in which the millennium is integrated into the entire system. "The doctrine of the millennial kingdom is for the dispensationalist an integral part of his entire scheme and interpretation of many Biblical passages." Charles Caldwell Ryrie, *Dispensationalism* (Chicago: Moody, 2007), 148. On the nondispensational premillennialism of George Ladd, see his chapter, "Historic Premillennialism," in R. G. Clouse, ed., *The Meaning of the Millennium: Four Views* (Downers Grove, IL: InterVarsity, 1977). See the discussion of historic premillennialism in

Craig A. Blaising, "Premillennialism," in *Three Views on the Millennium and Beyond*, ed. Darrell L. Bock (Grand Rapids: Zondervan, 1999). Ladd's critique of classical dispensationalism can be found in his books *Crucial Questions about the Kingdom of God* (Grand Rapids: Eerdmans, 1952) and *The Gospel of the Kingdom* (Grand Rapids: Eerdmans, 1959).

33. An example of a dispensational response to both of these challenges can be seen in John F. Walvoord, *The Millennial Kingdom* (Grand Rapids: Zondervan, 1959).

34. Ryrie, *Dispensationalism Today*, 146; cf. Ryrie, *Dispensationalism*, rev. ed. (Chicago: Moody, 2007), 159.

35. Hoyt, *End Times*, 232.

36. See the description of the millennial kingdom, including the sacrifices in the millennial temple, in Walvoord, "End Times," 1359–61. Also see the summary in Ryrie, *Basic Theology*, 510–11. A more extensive treatment of worship in the millennium is found in Pentecost, *Things to Come*, 512–31; and in Walvoord, *Millennial Kingdom*, 309–15.

37. "Though scholars have differed on this point, and some have attempted to support a restored earth and heaven, Scriptures are strong in their statement of the destruction of the old heaven and old earth. They are described as being 'destroyed by fire' and 'the elements will melt in the heat' (2 Peter 3:10, 12). In view of the tremendous energy locked into every material atom, the same God who locked in this energy can unlock it and destroy it, reducing it to nothing. . . . Out of this God could create a new heaven and a new earth as a basis for eternity. . . . The new earth will be totally different from the old earth, and one of those differences is that there will be no longer any seas. All the old landmarks will be gone, and the new earth will look different." John F. Walvoord, *Major Bible Prophecies* (Grand Rapids: Zondervan, 1991), 413–14. See also Walvoord, "End Times," 1363.

38. Walvoord, "End Times," 1365.

39. Ryrie, *Dispensational Today*, 147; also Ryrie, *Dispensationalism*, 160. He notes that Israel has both a "future" and a "heavenly hope."

40. "The glorious millennial reign will be the capstone of Israel's history. Though evidence seems to indicate that Israel will continue as a people into eternity, the millennium will be the final chapter of their history on the present earth." John F. Walvoord, *Israel in Prophecy* (Grand Rapids: Zondervan, 1962), 128. This does not mean the disappearance of Israel as a people, just the conclusion of their territorial reality. Elsewhere, he says that it is "an error to assume that national identity will be lost in eternity." Rather, "national identity seems a natural corollary to individual identity." Again, he writes, "Israelites will be Israelites throughout eternity." They continue as a distinct people group in the heavenly reality of eternity. John F. Walvoord, *The Nations in Prophecy* (Grand Rapids: Zondervan, 1967), 169–70.

41. Pentecost, *Things to Come*, 561.

42. "Some expositors feel that this [Rev. 20:11; 21:1] is to be explained on the basis of annihilation of the first heaven and the first earth and a completely new creation of heaven and earth . . . . If the 'first heaven and the first earth' is to be interpreted to mean the whole created order including space, then it leaves no place for the home of the redeemed and no place for the multitude of the lost. In fact, the wicked too are annihilated." Hoyt, *End Times*, 223–24.

43. Ibid., 224.

44. The dispensational debate between annihilation and renovation is particularly focused on the interpretation of the language of 2 Peter 3:10, 12. However, annihilationists seem to be misled by the majority text reading of 2 Peter 3:10. Rather than *katakaestai*, translated in the AV as "burned up," the critical text reading accepted by scholars today is *heurethesetai*, which Wolters has identified as a metallurgical term indicating refinement. This gives meaning to the other imagery of melting and burning. The idea is not obliteration but purification. See the discussion in Al Wolters, "Worldview and Textual Criticism in 2 Peter 3:10," *Westminster Theological Journal* 49 (1987): 405–13. See also the summary of the lexical and hermeneutical alternatives in Craig Blaising, "The Day of the Lord Will Come: An Exposition of 2 Peter 3:1–18," *Bibliotheca Sacra* 169 (2012): 395–99.

45. Hoyt, *End Times*, 223–26.

46. The term "new creation" is chosen in contrast to a traditional "heavenly" view of the eternal state. See Blaising, "Premillennialism," 160–64, for a summary contrast between what I describe as a "new creation model" of eternal life and what I term as a "spiritual vision model." The latter refers to a typical "heavenly" view. But see the various ways heaven has been conceptualized in Christian thought in Russell, *A History of Heaven*, and McGrath, *A Brief History of Heaven*. Here it is important to note that progressive dispensationalists affirm the present "heavenly" orientation of the church to Christ in heaven, to the "heavenly" city, and in fact all the "heavenly" orientation language of the New Testament. However, they do not interpret that language as indicating an eternal consummation in heaven. Rather, the heavenly orientation is to realities that *come to earth* in the future—Christ Himself, the City, etc. The reference in Hebrews 13:14, cited earlier in this chapter, is thus a key indicator of this future hope. The city in which we are enrolled and which is in heaven (Heb. 12:22–24) is "the city which is to come." This is the city that comes down to the new earth when it comes. We are accordingly looking forward to "the world to come" (Heb. 2:5).

47. Since there is a continuum, no explanation is required for the repeated stress in Scripture on eschatological blessings being everlasting. There is a direct connection between the original covenant promises of an everlasting blessing and the New Testament hope of everlasting life. "Biblical eschatology involves an ethical renewal, not an ontic renewal. The eschatological hope of the Bible is not for deliverance from the earth, but from sin. Creaturehood inevitably involves physical existence, and the redemption of creatures includes the redemption of creation." David L. Turner, "The New Jerusalem in Revelation 21:1–22:5: Consummation of a Biblical Continuum," *Dispensationalism, Israel and the Church*, ed. Blaising and Bock (Grand Rapids: Zondervan, 1992), 271.

48. For a progressive dispensational view of kingdom promise and fulfillment in Scripture, see Blaising, "The Kingdom of God in the Old Testament," and "The Kingdom of God in the New Testament," in Blaising and Bock, *Progressive Dispensationalism*, 212–83.

49. Note the reference to nations in the patriarchal promise (e.g., Gen. 12:3; 18:18; 22:18; 26:4; 27:29; 28:14), in the prophetic vision of the eschatological order (e.g., Isa. 2:2–4; Amos 9:12), in the commission of Christ (Matt. 28:19–20), and in the vision of the consummation given to John (Rev. 21:3, 23–22:4).

50. See Acts 11:1–18; 15:1–21; Eph. 2:11–21. Also see Blaising, "The Fulfillment of the Biblical Covenants," in Blaising and Bock, *Progressive Dispensationalism*, 190–91.

51. Ephesians 2:19–22. What unites the whole are the blessings of the new covenant promised to Israel, now granted to Gentile as well as Jewish believers. See Bruce A. Ware, "The New Covenant and the People(s) of God," in *Dispensationalism, Israel and the Church*, ed. Blaising and Bock (Grand Rapids: Zondervan, 1992), 68–97.

52. For progressive dispensational writings on the church, see Carl B. Hoch, Jr., "The New Man of Ephesians 2," and Robert L. Saucy, "The Church as the Mystery of God," in *Dispensationalism, Israel and the Church*, 98–126, and 127–55 respectively.

53. See Blaising, "The Kingdom of God in the New Testament," 251–62.

54. Ibid., 54, 262–70.

55. A key difference between progressive dispensationalism and earlier forms of dispensationalism is the fact that the church is not a separate group of the redeemed in the consummation but rather church saints have joined with the redeemed of other dispensations in a common salvific and pneumatological union with Christ and with one another.

56. See Blaising, "The Kingdom of God in the New Testament," 270–76. Also, see the argument for and description of the millennium in idem, "Premillennialism."

57. Blaising, "The Kingdom of God in the New Testament," 283.

9

Dispensationalism and Views of Redemption History

T. MAURICE PUGH

The one word that summarizes the story of the Bible is *redemption*. God works in human history to accomplish His redemptive plan, which is revealed in the Bible. That plan culminates in the rulership of His Son Jesus Christ (Eph. 1:11).

This process of God working out salvation is called redemptive history. It is the totality of God's plan to redeem: past, present, and future. God conceived His plan of redemption "before the foundation of the world" (Eph. 1:4), works it out in the present, and finalizes it in the future. Paul says that God is working "with a view to the redemption of [His] own possession, to the praise of His glory" (Eph. 1:14).

The activities of human history are not disconnected from the redemptive acts of God. Instead, God works in human history to accomplish His divine plan. He works "all things after the counsel of His will" (Eph. 1:11). Since the sinful fall of humanity, God has set in motion a redemptive plan of restoring lost sinners back into relationship with Himself.

God acts redemptively in history. Since history is forward moving, still en-compassing past events, a philosophy of understanding history emerges that "refers to the way one views the totality of world events of the past and present, and the futuristic direction, if any, toward which those events are moving."[1] God's redemptive program, then, provides a system for theologically interpreting the Bible and the movement of history. Richard writes,

> The Bible has many emphases, some of which are major and some of which are minor. Though its basic purpose is not to *construct* a philosophy of history, it does *contain* a philosophy of history, a theological grid through which one is to think about history. It provides a framework in which the historical process can be interpreted. Thus a Christian philosophy of history is *derived* from the Bible.[2]

So the Christian theologian has the advantage of relying on a system of interpretation to understand the redemptive story as it progressively unfolds in the Bible and therefore gains a theological perspective for seeing God's movement in history.

As a result, many theological traditions have attempted to develop a system of interpreting God's redemptive work in history. These approaches have attempted to compare the Bible's story line recorded from Genesis to Revelation with history's narrative being lived each and every day. Theologians have not discarded the interpretation of history as a secular responsibility. Instead, Christian theologians have almost unanimously agreed that they have the best resource for making sense of history—the Scriptures. God has revealed His will and work in the Bible.

However, "this interpretation of the meaning of historical events is the task of theology, and it is a task that is not without its problems."[3] There has been much debate, differences, and distinctions on a system of interpretation that has been properly constructed and contains the least amount of biblical inconsistencies. Therefore, it is important to examine the scope of redemptive history and consider the various systems of interpretation, to provide both a pastoral perspective and an ecclesiological application to the overall discussion.

THE STORY OF REDEMPTION

The Bible tells a story of redemption. It is not a book of random and unrelated stories, but stories knitted together to form a single theme of redemption.[4] In this redemptive narrative, God sovereignly works out His plan in history.[5]

Richard Lints further explains the biblical concept of redemptive history.

> A fundamental fact about the Scriptures is that they constitute a text with a developing story. It is a story that clearly progresses toward the accomplishment of specific goals. Redemption is an activity of God that unfolds over time. This unfolding movement in the biblical text is profoundly important to the accomplishment of its purposes. We must remember that Scripture not only witnesses to God's redemption but it is also an effective agent of that redemption. Biblical revelation progresses because it mirrors the progressive nature of redemption. The "story" of God's involvement with and redemption of his people is acted out on the stage of history with many distinct but related parts.[6]

A Developing Story

The biblical story of redemptive history, as Lints suggests, is "a developing story" that "progresses toward the accomplishment of specific goals." The metanarrative of creation, fall, redemption, and new creation, with the inclusion of covenantally particular episodes, constitutes the subjects of biblical revelation. Goldsworthy says, "The saving acts of God involve a new supernatural revelation from God given progressively throughout the whole history of redemption."[7]

Redemption may be considered the unifying principle of Scripture.[8] It links together the outworking of God's plans into a unified narrative. Although the biblical story includes divine promises, covenants, and dispensations, redemptive history connects them together into a unified story. Therefore, in a theological system, the unifying principle often governs the interpretation of all other issues, which provides an overall biblical structure and theological direction.

God is the divine author who sovereignly writes the redemptive story. He directs the actions according to His own purposes and brings them to His intended goal and conclusion.

> The Bible begins with the statement, "In the beginning," and ends with a book called "The Revealing," or "The Revelation." It is a fantastic look through time into eternity. The Bible describes a divine plan begun in the mind of God, and it ends with man before the face of God. It unfolds historically in time and space. Some events are purposed by God, and evil events are permitted by God. But all are a part of His divine will. In the wonderful pages of the Bible, God's plan gradually unfolds in time-space events, purposed and permitted, which ultimately results in the glory of God.[9]

The apostle Paul says God "causes all things to work together for good to those who love God, to those who are called according to His purpose" (Rom. 8:28); He "works all things after the counsel of His will" (Eph. 1:11); and God fulfills His promises in history. In redemptive history, "there is a detectable design to history, one imposed by God, the Lord of history and maker of the universe. As a result, history is directed toward the realization of a purpose or goal set by God."[10]

The Bible maintains the structure of a typical story: characters, plot, and drama, but woven within the biblical story is a redemptive theme orchestrated by God. In this redemptive story, the divine author is also the creator of men, superintendent of human affairs, and determiner of destiny. Kinman explains, "If we think of history as a canvas, and the Old Testament as a landscape depicting the work of God, we note that there are patterns in the way God works. He is the Creator and Lord of history. He promises something, and he does it. He works according to divine plan, not human expectation (for example, he chooses the humble but rejects the proud). He is Lord over history, and he works through history."[11]

God's Past and Future Revelations of Himself

In this unfolding of history, God reveals more and more of Himself. To see the totality of God's work, one must evaluate the past to see how God has revealed Himself, and the future, to anticipate God's future revelations of Himself to man. Ignoring the progress of revelation will lead to gross misinterpretations of the biblical data. Thus, the task of the biblical theologian is not to impose his own structure on the biblical narrative but to discover and display the inherent structure of the Bible's story. History is God's theater in which He promised to bring about His purposes for His people, and indeed the whole world.[12]

Redemptive history progresses towards a divinely determined destination. Kinman writes, "History is teleological: that is, it is goal-oriented; it is designed. This in turn presupposes a goal-setter, a planner, a designer."[13] God has predetermined the conclusion of the biblical story and predestined the grand finale of the redemptive drama. Each chapter of the story has been conceived in the mind of God, written out by His finger, and executed according to His sovereignty so that the end result corresponds with His providential plan; this, Paul repeatedly says, is "to the praise of His glory" (Eph. 1:6, 12, 14).

Redemptive history, then, is a progressively unfolding story. It is a narrative in motion, each scene increasingly and gradually revealing more of God's plans and purposes. The progressive nature of redemptive history means, "Christianity has as its *foundation* the acts of God in history and as its *goal* the further acts of God and his people in a redeemed and transformed earth."[14]

The Story's Central Figure: Jesus

As God's plan unfolds in history, Jesus becomes the central figure in the story, indeed the primary character of the redemptive narrative. He is the referent of the Old Testament narrative. On the road towards Emmaus, "Beginning with Moses and with all the prophets, Jesus explained to them the things concerning Himself in all the Scriptures" (Luke 24:27).

When Christ appeared on the worldwide stage, we know that in the "fullness of time . . . God sent forth His Son, born of a woman, born under the Law" (Gal. 4:4). Nelson summarizes, "Jesus Christ came at the fullness of time, long after the origin of the universe. But God planned the Savior's advent as the pinnacle which would fulfill all that came before and give purpose to all that came after."[15]

Jesus is the subject of the New Testament message. According to Paul, "We preach Christ crucified" (1 Cor. 1:23). The New Testament message proclaims that Jesus is God's redeemer in the redemptive story. Without Christ, there is no story of redemption. He "redeemed us from the curse of the Law, having become a curse for us—for it is written, 'Cursed is everyone who hangs on a tree' " (Gal. 3:13).

Ultimately, all of redemptive history climaxes and culminates in the glorious return of Jesus Christ. He concludes the divine story and finalizes the redemptive drama. Most importantly, Jesus is the summation and culmination of redemptive history. Paul summarizes the concept of redemptive history in Ephesians 1:10: God is working out in history His will and plan "with a view to an administration suitable to the fullness of the times, that is, the summing up of all things in Christ, things in the heavens and things on the earth." God works in history with a view and perspective of establishing an administration[16] in which He sums[17] up everything under the rule of Jesus Christ.

Everything and everyone will become subordinate to the King of kings; God is setting the stage so that when Jesus returns all things will be subject to His rulership. Every knee will bow and every tongue will confess that Jesus Christ is

Lord. "The revelation of God and in a very real sense the saving action of God reach their finality in Christ," writes Saucy. "All is finally summed up in him—all promises as well as all ministry for salvation. With the coming of Christ we have also reached the 'last days' of history. Not only that, but we have reached the realm of the heavenlies having come to the heavenly Jerusalem (Heb. 12:22)."[18]

There is consistency throughout the Bible that Jesus will be established as King of kings, the Messiah, and the anointed one in accordance with Old Testament prophecy. Jesus Christ culminates God's plan of redemption in history. Christ will return to earth to establish Himself as king in Jerusalem, sitting on the throne of David (Luke 1:32–33). Christ will be established as king executing the divine administration of God.

INTERPRETING REDEMPTIVE HISTORY

God executes His redemptive agenda in history and in accordance with His divine purpose. His plan of redemption is progressively revealed and unfolding in and throughout the pages of Scripture. As Richard has noted, "The Bible . . . provides a framework in which the historical process can be interpreted."[19]

Ephesians 1 on God's Plan

Paul describes the revealing of God's plan in Ephesians 1:

> He made known to us the mystery of His will, according to His kind intention which He purposed in Him with a view to an administration suitable to the fullness of the times, that is, the summing up of all things in the heavens and things on the earth. In Him also we have obtained an inheritance, having been predestined according to His purpose who works all things after the counsel of His will. (vv. 9–11)

The apostle continues by saying that "the Holy Spirit of promise . . . is given as a pledge of our inheritance, with a view to the redemption of God's own possession, to the praise of His glory" (vv. 13–14).

In these passages of the Scriptures, God has a redemptive plan that was established in eternity past, but works in history according to His will. God not only works His plan according to His will, but He does so with a "view"—a "perspective"—that is forward looking toward a perfect period of time (administration).

Approaches to Interpreting a Redemptive History

It is both clear and agreeable to most theologians and theological systems that God is unfolding a redemptive plan. However, the major point of disparity stems from the interpretive process for tracing the redemptive plan of God through history.[20] Simply stated, the question is, How does God fulfill His Old Testament promises in accordance with this redemptive continuum? What is the eschatological conclusion that culminates God's redemptive plan? Ryrie writes, "This interpretation of meaning of historical events is the task of theology, and it is a task that is not without its problems. The chief problem is that both covenant and dispensational theologies claim to represent the true philosophy of history as contained in the Scriptures."[21]

Within the last three to four hundred years, Bible-believing scholars have developed several distinct approaches to expositing the Bible's redemptive philosophy of history. Each approach has produced a system of theology—an approach to understanding redemptive history. Dispensationalism and covenant theology are two viable systems for interpreting God's redemptive history. Saucy adds: "Throughout the history of discussion between dispensationalists and non-dispensationalists numerous points of contention have been raised. These differences stemmed largely from the particular emphasis of each system in its understanding of biblical history."[22] He further writes, "One basic and fairly broad issue remains a point of contention between dispensationalists and non-dispensationalists—namely, God's purpose and plan in biblical history."[23] In other words, both systems have emerged as theological attempts to interpret and understand the progression of God's redemptive plan. Again, as Saucy explains,

> The fundamental issue between dispensationalists and non-dispensationalists is neither a basic hermeneutical principle nor the ultimate purpose of human history. The basic issue is the way we understand the historical plan and goal of that plan through which God will bring about eternal glory to himself. More specifically, it is the question of the purpose and plan of God within human history, i.e., from this creation until the inauguration of the eternal state. This inquiry involves not only the basic goal of history, but the meaning and integration of the various aspects of God's work during this period. We must understand not only what God intends to do, but how he accomplishes it. The call of Abraham, the election and formation of the nation of Israel, God's dealing with the church and the nations, and the various covenant arrangements—all these are facets of the historical plan that must be integrated and understood.[24]

On the one hand, as their name indicates, dispensationalists generally emphasize the differences in the various periods of human history brought about through the progressive revelation of God's salvation program. They recognize that there are differences in the way God deals with His creation. On the other hand, non-dispensationalists typically lean towards an emphasis on the unity of God's work in biblical history.[25] For the purpose of this discussion, covenant theology and dispensationalism will be the two primary theologies that will be examined in their approach to understanding God's redemptive history.[26]

COVENANT THEOLOGY

Covenant theology uses biblical covenants to provide a conceptual overview and an interpretive framework for understanding the overall flow of the Bible.[27] Covenant theologians insist this system emerges from a natural and ordinary reading of Scriptures. It is "a system of interpreting the Scriptures on the basis of two covenants: the covenant of works and the covenant of grace.[28] Some covenant theologians specify three covenants: works, redemption, and grace."[29] Horton says there is a "richness of this covenantal web and its centrality to the organization of the Bible's diverse teachings."[30] According to Showers, "Covenant theology can be defined very simply as a system of theology which attempts to develop the Bible's philosophy of history on the basis of two or three covenants. It represents the whole of Scripture and history as being covered by two or three covenants."[31]

Further, it is safe to say that covenant theology has been mostly associated with Reformed theology.[32] Phillips claims, "As Reformed theologians have long observed, the Bible does provide such a framework, which we call 'covenant theology.' It is through His covenants that God has acted in redemptive history. Covenant theology is not merely a Reformed approach to Scripture, but the Bible's own approach in presenting salvation."[33]

According to Horton, "Reformed theology is guided by a concern to relate various biblical teachings to the concrete covenants in Scripture as their proper context."[34] Horton suggests, "While some friends of and critics of Reformed theology have reduced Calvinism to 'five points,' or further still, to predestination, the actual confessions, catechisms, and standard doctrinal works of the Reformed tradition all testify to a far richer, deeper, and all-embracing faith in the God of the covenant. *Reformed* theology is synonymous with *covenant* theology."[35]

Spencer insightfully cautions readers to recognize that "Reformed theology is larger than covenant theology and that a person may align with Reformed theology without aligning with covenant theology."[36]

God's Covenantal Dealings as Context

In covenant theology, covenant is the matrix that holds together the structure of biblical faith and practice. God's covenantal dealings in history provide the context within which the unity of Scripture is recognized.[37] As Horton explains,

> So what brings all these themes together? What unites them is not itself a central dogma but an architectonic structure, a matrix of beams and pillars that hold together the structure of biblical faith and practice. That particular architectural structure that we believe the Scriptures themselves to yield is the covenant. It is not simply the concept of the covenant, but the concrete existence of God's covenantal dealings in our history that provides the context within which we recognize the unity of the Scripture amid its remarkable variety.[38]

Covenant theology uses the theological concept of covenant as the unifying principle for Christian theology. Systematic theology must make sense of the progress of revelation and the outworking of God's redemptive plan. It must have a system for interpreting God's salvific narrative. Theology must provide a unifying principle that connects these historical differences with the progress of revelation, thus providing answers for the past, present, and future. Covenant theologians see covenants as the means to accomplish these interpretive goals.

Essentially, all of the other covenants emanate from either the covenant of works or the covenant of grace. Covenant theology's basic premise is that, in eternity past, God determined to govern all of history on the basis of three covenants. The standard description of covenant theology views the history of God's dealings with mankind, from Creation to Fall to Redemption to Consummation, under the framework of the three overarching theological covenants of redemption, works, and grace.

Summary of the Covenants

The *covenant of redemption*, which precedes the other two, is one made among the three persons of the Trinity to elect, atone for, and save a select group of individuals unto salvation and eternal life. God the Father and the Son Jesus

Christ "covenanted together" for the redemption of lost sinners. In the covenant of redemption, the agreement is established first between God and humanity; it is solidified eternally within the Trinity. As Horton puts it, "The Father elects a people in the Son as their mediator to be brought to saving faith through the Spirit."[39] Enns explains, "In the eternal plan of God it was decreed that the Father would plan the redemption through election and predestination; the Son would provide redemption through His atoning death; the Holy Spirit would effect the plan through regenerating and sealing the believers (Eph. 1:3–14)."[40]

With a broader scope of covenant, the agreement was made within the Godhead with a desire to provide salvation for those chosen in Christ. The Son volunteered to take the place of those whom God gave to Him—the elect here on earth. According to covenant theologians, "The covenant of redemption, therefore, is as clearly revealed in Scripture as the Trinity and the eternal decree to elect redeem, call, justify, sanctify and glorify a people for the Son."[41]

The *covenant of creation/works* is the agreement that God made with Adam as the head of the whole human race, by which God required he be obedient to the law, resulting in eternal life; or, should Adam disobey, bringing eternal death. When God created man, He placed him in the garden of Eden and gave him one simple command: "From any tree in the garden you may eat freely; but from the tree of the knowledge of good and evil you shall not eat, for in the day that you eat from it you will surely die" (Gen. 2:16–17). We see the covenantal language (that is, an agreement between two parties, in this case, between God and Adam) implied in this command. Covenant theologians argue that Adam's obligation was perfect obedience to God. God's obligation was to provide eternal life in exchange for perfect obedience. Adam's penalty for failing to keep his part of the covenant was death to both Adam and his descendants.

The *covenant of grace* promises eternal life for those who receive forgiveness of sins through Christ. Some covenant theologians combine the covenants of redemption and grace. They are uncertain when the covenant of grace was established. Some argue it began with the promise of redemption in Gen. 3:15 when God told the serpent He would bruise his head and that the serpent would bruise the Man-Child's heel. Others argue it began with the covenant God made with Abraham in Gen. 12.

The covenant of grace links with the covenant of redemption to establish a salvific plan guaranteeing eternal salvation. Mankind fails to keep the covenant of works (creation), but God provides salvation in the covenant of redemption and the covenant of grace applies the works of Christ into the life of those chosen by God. According to Enns, "God provides His son as a guarantee for our salvation; through His grace God enables man to meet the demands of the covenant responsibilities by the gift of the Holy Spirit."[42] Jesus is the faithful Israelite who entered into an eternal covenant with the Father in the covenant of redemption, and fulfilled the requirements of God in the covenant of works so that we could inherit the promises according to a covenant of grace.[43]

Relationship of Promises with Israel and Church

Covenant theologians see God's promises to Israel fulfilled in the person and the work of the Messiah, Jesus of Nazareth, who established the church in organic continuity with Israel. Israel's relationship to the church incites significant discussions in both covenant and dispensational theologies.[44] However, covenant theologians insist on the *unity* and *continuity* of God's redemptive program throughout history. In covenant's understanding of the history of redemption no ultimate separation exists between Israel and the church.

The promise God made to Abraham in the formal ratification of the covenant of grace (Gen. 12; 15; 17), namely, that he would be the father of many nations and that in his "seed" all the families of the earth would be blessed, finds its fulfillment in Jesus Christ. The seed promised to Abraham in the covenant of grace is Jesus Christ, the true Israel, and all those who are united with Him by faith are also heirs of the covenant promises (Gal. 3:16, 29). In the Reformed-covenant view, the gospel of Jesus Christ directly fulfills the promises of the covenant of grace for all believers, whether Jews or Gentiles. Israel and the church are not two distinct peoples; rather, the church is the true Israel of God, "a chosen race, a royal priesthood, a holy nation, a people for God's own possession" (1 Peter 2:9). For covenant theology, God does not have a separate plan and purpose for Israel and another for the church. Instead, in the gospel of Jesus Christ, He is creating one redeemed humanity comprised of Jews and Gentiles from every tribe, tongue, and nation. According to Venema, "There is one way of salvation for all who believe in Jesus Christ. [Paul] simultaneously affirms that this salvation does not displace or supersede God's redemptive purpose for the Jews but, rather, fulfills it. The ongoing debate about Israel and the church needs to maintain the Apostle's balance, neither separating Israel and the church nor displacing Israel with the church."[45]

Covenant Theology and the End Times

Eschatology is the study of the end times. It seeks to interpret and understand the unfolding of future events. Any treatment of redemptive history seriously considers biblical eschatology as the end result of God's overall plan of salvation. Paul reminds us that God is redemptively working His sovereign program with the final consummation of history as His goal (Eph. 1:11).

Covenant theologians see the covenants as the organizing principles to unify the Old and New Testaments in a continuous theme in God's redemptive plan. However, there is flexibility and diversity in covenant theology's eschatology. Since God has a primary covenant of grace that provides one way of redemption to all humanity regardless of ethnic or national background, His eschatological plan applies to one redeemed humanity, not a separate and distinct plan for Israel and another for the church.[46] Eschatologically, this means that covenant theology understands the millennial kingdom as something other than a period of time when God fulfills promises made to the nation of Israel.[47] Generally, the millennial options acceptable to those who filter their biblical interpretations through the covenants are: amillennialism, postmillennialism, and what is sometimes referred to as historic premillennialism.

By amillennialism, covenant theologians generally do not mean no millennum as typically defined by the term. Instead, amillennialists do not believe in a *literal* thousand-year earthly reign that will follow the return of Christ. Hoekema says,

> The term amillennialism is not a happy one. It suggests that amillennialists do not believe in any millennium or that they simply ignore the first six verses of Revelation 20, which speak of a millennial reign. Neither of these two statements is true. Though it is true that amillennialists do not believe in a literal thousand-year earthly reign which will follow the return of Christ, the term amillennialism is not an accurate description of their view.[48]

Covenant's eschatology has developed a system of interpretation where God deals with the one redeemed humanity, and the millennial kingdom in Rev. 20 is in the process of being *realized* until the return of Christ. The kingdom of God is currently ruling through the Word and the Spirit moving toward the more glorious and perfect future kingdom when Christ will return to usher in the final state. Those reigning with Christ for the "thousand" years are Christians who have died and are already reigning with Him in heaven.[49] This view groups the significant events of redemptive history as occurring simultaneously after Christ's return.[50]

Postmillennialism is the second most common view among covenant theologians, which states that Christ returns *after* the millennium.[51] Gentry thoroughly defines postmillennialism:

> Postmillennialism expects the proclaiming of the Spirit-blessed gospel of Jesus Christ to win the vast majority of human beings to salvation in the present age. Increasing gospel success will gradually produce a time in history prior to Christ's return in which faith, righteousness, peace and prosperity will prevail in the affairs of people and of nations. After an extensive era of such conditions the Lord will return visibly, bodily, and in great glory ending history with the general resurrection and the great judgment of all mankind.[52]

In other words, God works through the church spreading the gospel and consequently "Christianizing" society to function more according to His standards. "The present age will gradually give way to the Millennium as a result of the progress of the gospel, but life will continue in its present form. Christ will return at the conclusion of the Millennium."[53] Unlike premillennialism and amillennialism where Christ returns to a world that is becoming progressively sinful, in postmillennialism, Christ returns to a society experiencing moral progress.[54] After Christ returns, He will establish the final eschatological series of events: the resurrection of the dead, final judgment, and the eternal state.

The "historic" premillennialism is the final eschatological option for those who interpret redemptive history through the continuity of covenants. Ladd explains this view: "Premillennialism is the viewpoint that states that after the Second Coming of Christ, He will reign for a thousand years over the earth before the final consummation of God's redemptive purpose in the new heavens and the new earth of the Age to Come."[55] However, there is no clear future distinction between national Israel and the church. The church will go through the tribulation, after which Christ will return to the earth to establish a millennial kingdom.[56] Incidentally, His reign does not begin in the future; Christ currently reigns from heaven. Thus, "The New Testament does not make the reign of Christ one that is limited to Israel in the millennium."[57] The kingdom of God was manifest through Jesus' public ministry. Upon His ascension into heaven and the "gift of the Spirit" at Pentecost, the kingdom is present through the Spirit, until the end of the age, which is marked by the return of Christ to the earth in judgment.

During the millennium, Christ will physically and visibly reign over the earth and His redeemed people will reign with Him. "The redeemed include both Jews and Gentiles. Though the Jews have for the most part been converted recently, after the ingathering of the Gentiles, they do not comprise a separate group, since there is only one people of God."[58] After the millennium, Satan will be defeated, then the final judgment, and the final state will be established.

DISPENSATIONALISM

Dispensationalism is another viable system for interpreting God's redemptive history. Dispensationalism is not first an articulation of theology, an outline of doctrinal belief, or a description of historical dogma, but first and foremost a system of biblical interpretation. Ryrie explains, "Dispensationalism, then, claims to be a help in supplying the answer to the need for biblical distinctions, in offering a satisfying philosophy of history, and in employing a consistently normal principle of interpretation. These are basic areas in proper understanding of the Bible. If Dispensationalism has the answers, then it is the most helpful tool in consistent biblical interpretation."[59]

Understanding Dispensationalism

Lightner defines dispensationalism as that "system of theology which interprets the Bible literally—according to normal usage—and places primary emphasis on the major biblical covenants—Abrahamic, Palestinian, Davidic, New—and sees the Bible as the unfolding of distinguishable economies in the outworking of God's major purpose to bring glory to Himself."[60] Several important characteristics of dispensationalism emerge from Lightner's definition: (1) it is a system for interpreting the Bible; (2) it places emphasis upon the biblical covenants; and (3) it focuses on the distinct periods in the outworking of God's plan and purpose. Bateman adds another significant characteristic highlighting Christ's eschatological role in fulfilling the biblical covenants in relation to the national Israel. He says,

> What marks a dispensationalist is the person's stress on the uniqueness of the church and confidence that a future millennial period exists in human history—when God will consummate His Abrahamic, Davidic, and new cove-

> nants with national Israel through the physical, earthly reign of Jesus Christ here on earth.[61]

Dispensationalism, then, is that system of biblical interpretation that interprets the Bible from the viewpoint of designated periods of time during which a particular revelation of God's will and mind is operative, and during which man is tested in relation to that particular revelation.[62]

Dispensation as a term and a concept, derived from the Bible, is a major argument of credibility for dispensationalists. A dispensation may be defined as a "distinguishable economy in the outworking of God's purpose."[63] The English word "dispensation" comes from the Greek word *oikonomia*, which corresponds to the concepts "household administration" and "stewardship" (Luke 16:2–4; Eph. 1:10; 3:2, 9).[64] Again, Bateman summarizes well,

> Theologically, the word is used to speak of (1) how God sovereignly and progressively reveals His salvation-history program in stages throughout human history (Hebrews 1:1–2), and (2) how human beings are to relate to God as He administers His program in various dispensations (John 1:17). For instance, the New Testament clearly speaks of a previous dispensation (Eph. 3:8–9, Col. 1:25–26), and a present dispensation (Eph. 3:2–3), and an anticipated or future dispensation (Eph. 1:9–10).[65]

Ryrie adds, "A dispensation is from God's viewpoint an economy; from man's, a responsibility; and in relation to progressive revelation, a stage in it."[66] Dispensationalists argue that this system of biblical hermeneutics provides a consistent and normative reading of the Bible. Theologically, it sees God working out His redemptive plan through the covenants and fulfilled eschatologically in Christ.

Characteristics of Dispensationalism

Unique Plans for Israel and for the Church

There are at least three central characteristics of dispensationalism that its adherents generally affirm.[67] First, there is a distinction between God's unique plan for Israel and His plan for the church. Blaising writes, "Among contemporary dispensationalists a general consensus exists that a distinction between Israel and the church is the essential distinguishing factor of dispensationalism."[68] Ryrie adds: "This is probably the most basic theological test of whether or not a person is a dispensationalist, and is undoubtedly the most practical and conclusive."[69] However, not all dispensationalists adhere to the same degree or sharpness of distinction.[70] Or as Blaising argues, "It is one thing to assert a distinction between Israel and the church; it is another to explain what the distinction is or what its implications are for dispensational theology."[71] However, almost all dispensationalists agree that a clear distinction must be maintained among God's promises, plans, and purposes for national Israel and the same for the church. The unconditional and unilateral promises that God made with Israel are certain to be fulfilled because they are based on His promises.[72] And even in Israel's failure, the church does not replace Israel in God's relationship with them. Israel has a future that is distinct from the church. "On this basis dispensationalists subscribe to a literal millennium for Israel, which Messiah will establish at His Second Advent (Rev. 19:11–19)."[73]

Emphases on Biblical Covenants and Divine Prophecy

Second, dispensationalism maintains significant emphases upon biblical covenants and divine prophecy in the structure of God's overall program. The biblical covenants reveals the promises and agreements that God makes, while divine prophecy reveals the predication, fulfillment, and the unfolding aspects of biblical covenants. Blaising and Bock assert,

> Dispensationalism finds the historical meaning of biblical prophecy relevant for understanding God's purpose for the earth and for its human inhabitants. There are other theological traditions which interpret Bible prophecy almost exclusively in relation to the present ministry of Christ in the church or to a believer's personal experience of salvation. Dispensationalism, however, interpreting these prophecies in a more "literal" manner, has always expected God's future blessings to include earthly, national and political aspects of life. Many of these blessings belong to a future dispensation which will be marked by the return of Christ to earth.[74]

Dispensationalism's system of biblical interpretation values the relationship between biblical covenants and divine prophecy. Variations within dispensationalism exist primarily around the nature of fulfillment,[75] but agreement is maintained that biblical covenants and divine prophecy are significantly united to properly understand God's philosophy of history. Dispensationalists trace the work of God in redemptive history in a large part by connecting the relationships of the covenants, and they see God's future work in fulfillment of His prophetic statements. The biblical covenants and the "Old Testament prophecies ultimately will be fulfilled exactly as God promised."[76]

A Premillennial View of Eschatology

Finally, a central feature of dispensational theology's interpretation of redemptive history is a premillennial eschatology. Consistent with the progress of revelation and the final stages of God's redemptive story, a premillennial eschatology allows for all of dispensationalism's systemic parts to work together toward a redemptive conclusion—the one-thousand-year reign of Christ on the earth. With its system of interpretation, its covenantal emphasis, and a distinction between Israel and the church, a premillennial eschatology provides the most viable conclusion for dispensationalists.[77] Blaising summarizes the key features of dispensationalism's premillennialism.

> Dispensationalism is a form of premillennialism. That is, it holds to the belief that Christ will return to this earth and rule over it for 1,000 years. Like most premillennialists, dispensationalists interpret biblical prophecy to teach that Christ will return during a time of trouble traditionally called "the Tribulation." However, unlike most premillennialists, most dispensationalists have advocated the doctrine of the pretribulational Rapture—the doctrine that Christ will come for the church prior to the Tribulation, resurrecting the dead in Christ, translating living believers into immortal life, and then taking the church with Him into heaven prior to His millennial return in which He will visibly rule the nations on earth.[78]

Most importantly, the millennium (and the eternal state that follows) completes the process of redemptive history. God will bring together His purposes and plans for Jesus, Israel, and mankind. Jesus will establish on earth a thousand-year reign of glory and peace. The millennial age will bring about the fulfillment of all that God has promised to the nation of Israel in the Old Testament. The Messiah will deliver Israel from their enemies, bring His righteous judgment to bear on the earth, restore Israel to glory, and establish a kingdom in which prosperity, righteousness, and peace will rule. Richard delineates the completeness of this kingdom on earth in fulfilling God's plans for history:

> The establishment of a kingdom on earth as the last phase in time and the climactic self-revelation of the glory of God was seen to be the purpose of his-

> tory. The premillennial system has a comprehensive unifying principle and a goal within time. It also meets the demands of a theodicy, a *heilsgeschichte*, and a Utopia, all resulting in God's glory. Only dispensational premillennialism has "an *eschaton* that delimits, a *telos* that affords meaning, and a finish that marks finality." It covers all of history, from the beginning of time (creation) to the end, when the kingdoms of the world will become the kingdom of the Lord (Rev. 11:15).[79]

Contra Richard, many dispensationalists believe that the reign of Christ in the millennium then transitions into the eternal state. And Christ's reign over a redeemed earth extends forever.

According to Daniel 2:44, "In the days of those kings the God of heaven will set up a kingdom which will never be destroyed, and that kingdom will not be left for another people; it will crush and put an end to all these kingdoms, but it will itself endure forever." Daniel forecasts that the Messiah will crush kings and their kingdoms and establish His own eternal rule.

SUMMARY: TWO THEOLOGICAL TRADITIONS

Two Viable Traditions

Covenantalism and dispensationalism are two viable theological traditions for providing a system that interprets God's redemptive history.[80] As its name indicates, the dispensational view tends to emphasize the differences in the various periods of human history brought about through the progressive revelation of God's salvation program. Covenants are crucial in dispensationalism, but dispensationalists view the covenants in terms of God's dealing specifically with Israel and promises He made to them, promises that ultimately will be granted to them. The national and earthly blessings that God promised to Israel will not be forfeited or nullified, neither will the church replace Israel as recipients for those earthly blessings. God maintains plans for Israel and the church; the promises He made to her in the Old Testament are not annulled. However, the promises to both Israel and the church are realized and experienced in the person of Jesus Christ.[81]

Covenant theology, on the other hand, leans toward an emphasis on the unity of God's work in biblical history.[82] Saucy adds, "Non-dispensationalists emphasize the unity of the historical working of God more than dispensationalists do. Although there may be some variations in how God administers the affairs of earth, there are basically stages in the development of a person from an infant to adulthood."[83] Important for covenant theology, then, "is a unity of the people of God that does not allow for a future place and purpose for the nation of Israel in the historical plan of God's redemption."[84]

Essentially, the continuity of covenant theology runs through three fundamental biblical covenants: works, redemption, and grace. These three covenants work together to define God's dealing with humanity and provide an overarching direction for God's redemptive story. For He made a Covenant of Works with Adam, promising eternal life for obedience and death for disobedience. Adam failed. Then God resolved man's problem through a Covenant of Grace in which He promised that sin would be overcome as a result of God's mediator—Jesus Christ who agreed, as a result of the Covenant of Redemption, to be God's provision for the sin problem. Saucy explains, "For traditional covenant theologians, the various economies of God are outworkings of the one covenant of grace."[85]

Dispensationalism and covenant theology can be understood to revolve around the issue of continuity versus discontinuity, that is, whether the development of God's redemptive story is solely and evenly continuous, or whether it is marked by some type of specific and designated periods in history. Spencer writes,

> The dispensational emphasis underscores the discontinuity of the advances and changes in God's administration of history. The covenant theology emphasis on the unity of the covenant of grace underscores the unity of God's program. Both views argue for *progressive* revelation, each at times accusing the other of neglecting that truth. Such accusations are mistaken on both sides and overlook the distinctive ways in which the phrase is used. "Progressive" for covenantal theologians means progress within an overall unity. "Progressive" for dispensationalists typically has meant progress with change and significant alteration. The different meanings highlight the distinctive perspectives of the two traditions.[86]

The degree to which the distinction between continuity and discontinuity is clarified will aid in the understanding of dispensational and covenant systems.

Amid the Differences, Many Similarities

Many similarities exist between these two systems: a high view of the authority of Scripture, a goal to interpret and understand accurately God's plan of redemption, the Old Testament prominence of Israel, and redemption through Christ. However, because their perspectives on continuity versus discontinuity differ, an equal disagreement occurs between Israel and the church in God's eschatological plan. Does the church replace Israel in God's redemptive plan so that Jews and Gentiles represent one redeemed people of God for all ages? Or does God maintain a unique plan for Israel and the church?

One cannot deny that there are some distinct and significant differences between dispensationalism and covenant theology. They differ on issues related to how, when, and why God fulfills His ultimate purpose in history, God's program for the nation Israel and the church, and the scope of the eschatological conclusion to God's redemptive story. However, both "figure prominently in contemporary theological discussions, particularly in evangelicalism where they often appear dominant."[87] Since both are dominant and significant systems of interpreting God's redemptive history, it behooves theologians to have a basic awareness and understanding of both traditions and their contribution to theological discussions.

PASTORAL AND MINISTERIAL IMPLICATIONS

One of the greatest privileges afforded to me is the opportunity to work and minister in two very important spiritual arenas—the church and the seminary—by merging my roles as professor and pastor, theologian and practitioner. I have had to take theoretical and theological concepts from the seminary and apply them in real-life scenarios in the local church. The most frequent question seminary students ask when discussing what seems like a theoretical and ethereal topic is: "What does this mean for ministry?" Conversely, the most common statement I hear from the church world is that while helpful in the seminary, this topic has nothing to do with what "we are experiencing in our daily lives."

So when it comes to redemption history, is this another topic that should be isolated and restricted to the seminary classroom, or is there meaning for the church? Theology is the study of God, our knowledge of His character, His work, and how we live in response to Him. As Lints concludes, "If God has in fact revealed himself, then this revelation should be normative for our thinking about God. If God has also given some indication about the purpose of history, then this revelation should be normative for our thinking about the world and our place in it."[88]

Therefore the story of redemption—how God sovereignly unfolds His redemptive plan—extends beyond the seminary classroom. God providentially works out His plan on earth to accomplish His divine purpose. The apostle Paul declared that God "works all things after the counsel of His will" (Eph. 1:11). Since God's plan operates on earth and in history, we live in the scope of His redemptive decisions. Then what is the implication and application of redemptive history for everyday life?

Trusting God

Trusting God is the first important implication of redemptive history. In the idea of redemption history, God is not idle or passive, but providentially working His plan. God promised redemption for the lost and blessings for the obedient. Ironically, He does not always specify exactly when those promises will be fulfilled. God told Abraham, "Go forth from your country . . . to the land which I will show you" (Gen. 12:1), hence the Promised Land. Therefore, trust and faith should become twin towers of a believer's life, the same for both Old and New Testament saints. The life of each prominent character of the Old Testament was lived according to God's covenantal promises. Abraham, Isaac, and David lived in anticipation of God fulfilling His promises. Covenant equals promise.

The same holds true for believers in every generation; we trust God on the basis of His covenantal promises, and our faith is rewarded appropriately. "And without faith it is impossible to please Him, for he who comes to God must believe that He is . . . a rewarder of those who seek Him" (Heb. 11:6). Faithful obedience to God and irrevocable trust in His promises enshrined heroic saints into the hall of faith (Heb. 11). Many struggle because they don't presently see God working. The principle "we walk by faith, not by sight" (2 Cor. 5:7) has always been the litmus test for a believer's spiritual maturity. God's work in redemptive history reminds us of the principle of faith, confidence, and belief in His sovereign work. It reminds us that God will complete His work and accomplish His plan. Paul says, "Faithful is He who calls you, and He also will bring it to pass" (1 Thess. 5:24).

Having Hope in God

What is "living hope"? The New Testament idea of hope is very different from our normal thinking about hope. We typically think about hope as a wishful desire for something in the future. That is not the way Peter or the rest of the New Testament writers describe hope. When Peter commands readers to "hope fully on the grace that will be brought to you at the revelation of Jesus Christ" (1 Pet. 1:13 ESV), he does not mean that it is an uncertain reality. The coming of Christ is a matter of complete confidence for all the writers in the New Testament. So the command "hope fully" means be intensely desirous and completely confident that Jesus Christ is coming again with grace for His people.

Another example outside 1 Peter would be Hebrews 6:11, which declares, "We desire each one of you to show the same earnestness in realizing the full assurance of hope to the end" (ESV). So we can define hope, in the New Testament sense, as full assurance or strong confidence that God's good work will be extended *to* us and *for* us in the future.

But there is something even more peculiar about Christian hope: Peter calls it "living hope." What does that mean? The opposite of a "living hope" would be a "dead hope," and that calls to mind a similar phrase in James 2, namely a *dead faith*: "Faith without works is dead" (2:26). James says that faith is "useless" (2:20); it is barren, fruitless, and unproductive. So "living faith" and, by analogy, "living hope" would be fertile, fruitful, productive hope. This is what "living" means in Hebrews 4:12 where it says, "The word of God is living and effective." So Christian hope is a strong confidence in God who has the power to produce change in how we live.

Jesus Christ represents the central figure in the redemptive work of God. The Father commissioned His Son to execute, inaugurate, and finalize His redemptive plan. This is possible because of the resurrection. Jesus is alive and therefore He is our hope. In keeping with redemptive history, God's promises made in the Old Testament are ultimately fulfilled in Jesus Christ. Our hope as believers is fulfilled in Jesus Christ as the resurrected Messiah. We have the full confidence that Jesus is fully capable and alive to mediate covenantal blessings, activate hope, and accomplish God's plan.

In *Theology of Hope*, Moltmann intends to recover the significance of the biblical eschatological perspective—especially that aspect of the early church that regarded the resurrection of Jesus Christ from the dead as the basis of their hope that all things would find their consummation through Him in the future. He writes, "The discovery of the central significance of eschatology for the message and existence of Jesus and for early Christianity, which had its beginnings at the end of the nineteenth century in Johannes Weiss and Albert Schweitzer, is undoubtedly one of the most important events in recent Protestant theology."[89]

According to Moltmann, Christian hope revolves around the Christian's expecting and awaiting the future of the crucified and resurrected Christ in the confidence of faith. Hope is nothing else than the expectation of those things which faith has believed to have been truly promised by God. Christian faith lives from the resurrection-fact of Jesus Christ. And Christian hope, which is rooted in the resurrection-faith, expects the promise of God to be fulfilled with regard to the universal future of Jesus Christ.

Depending on the Justice of God

Redemptive history reminds us of God's righteousness, justice, and peace. God will ultimately vindicate His promise to execute justice and righteousness on earth. God's righteousness means that He always acts in accordance with what is right and He is the final standard of what is right. "Righteousness and justice are the foundation of Your throne; lovingkindness and truth go before you" (Ps. 89:14). Consistent with God's character, righteousness and justice will be established on earth. God acts in conformity with His law and will administer His kingdom in accordance with the divine standard of righteousness.

The world is longing for evil, sin, unrighteousness, and wickedness to be addressed. Ultimately, all unrighteousness will be eliminated when the Prince of Peace, the Messiah, God's Son, sets up His kingdom and rules in justice, righteousness, and peace. In the eternal state, everything sin and Satan distorted will be restored, God's promises will be fulfilled, His righteousness will be fully vindicated and displayed, and every legitimate human longing for peace, justice, and righteousness will be met. God says of His Son: "Behold My Servant, whom I uphold; My chosen one in whom My soul delights. I have put my Spirit upon Him; He will bring forth justice to the nations" (Isa. 42:1); "He will faithfully bring forth justice. He will not be disheartened or crushed until He has established justice in the earth" (vv. 3–4).

Equally important, God expects those who are walking with Him in righteousness to represent and reflect His character of justice. In this regard, justice is the equitable application of God's moral law to all people without partiality. God expected Israel to reflect His character of justice. "To do righteousness and justice is desired by the Lord more than sacrifice" (Prov. 21:3). "Learn to do good; seek justice, reprove the ruthless, defend the orphan, and plead for the widow" (Isa. 1:17). God's character of justice will be reflected and administered in the future reign of Jesus. Justice and righteousness should also be reflected in the lives of Christians. Blaising and Bock remind us, "The church is a manifestation of the eschatological kingdom because it is an assembly of peoples whom the Messiah, acting with royal authority, has put into relationship with one another, bound by the inaugurated blessings of peace, righteousness, and justice through the Holy Spirit."[90] As our society struggles in the areas of fairness, discrimination, and exploitation, the church has the divine responsibility to reflect God's character of justice and fairness as an expression and in anticipation of the ultimate messianic realization.

Notes

1. Ramesh Richard, "Premillennialism as a Philosophy of History, Part 1: Non-Christian Interpretations of History," *Bibliotheca Sacra* 138 (1981): 14. Karl Lowith, *Meaning in History* (Chicago: University of Chicago Press, 1949), 1, defines a philosophy of history as "a systematic interpretation of universal history in accordance with a principle by which historical events and successions are unified and directed toward ultimate meaning."
2. Ramesh Richard, "Premillennialism as a Philosophy of History, Part 2: Elements of a Biblical Philosophy of History," *Bibliotheca Sacra* 138 (1981): 109.
3. Charles C. Ryrie, *Dispensationalism* (Chicago: Moody, 2007), 20.
4. It must be acknowledged that there have been numerous discussions attempting to develop a principle and primary theme that weaves together a single theme of Scripture and connect it to the work of God: kingdom, covenants, and the glory of God.
5. In *The Bible and the Future* (Grand Rapids: Eerdmans, 1979), 25–32, Anthony A. Hoekema summarizes the Christian view of history: "(1) *History is a working out of God's purposes.* God discloses his purposes in history. This is true primarily of what is commonly called 'sacred history' or 'holy history.' By 'sacred history' is meant redemptive history—God's redemption of his people through Jesus Christ. This redemption has its roots in Old Testament promises, types, and ceremonies; comes to its fulfillment in the life, death, and resurrection of Jesus Christ; and will reach its consummation in the new heavens and new earth which are still future. These histories are revelatory of God: they unveil or disclose his redeeming purpose with mankind." Hoekema further argues that "(2) *God is the Lord of history*" . . . who "rules over all (Ps. 103:19), even over the kingdoms of the nations (II Chron. 20:6)" . . . that (3) *Christ is the center of history* . . . ; that (4) *the new age has already been ushered in* . . . "and though not all men are by faith participating in the blessings of the new age [that] does not nullify the existence of the age;" [and that] "(5) *all of history is moving toward a goal: the new heavens and the new earth.* . . . The Bible therefore sees history as directed toward a divinely ordained goal. The idea that history has a goal is, as we have seen, the unique contribution of the Hebrew prophets."
6. Richard Lints, *The Fabric of Theology: A Prolegomenon To Evangelical Theology* (Grand Rapids: Eerdmans, 1993), 262–63.

7. Graeme Goldsworthy, *According to Plan: The Unfolding Revelation of God in the Bible* (Downers Grove, IL: InterVarsity, 1991), 59.
8. A unifying principle is a principle category from which all other issues are viewed. Many see the kingdom of God as the unifying theme of the Bible (Goldsworthy, *According to Plan*, 11). Others see the glory of God as the unifying theme of the Bible. Ryrie argues that the "unifying principle of the Bible is the glory of God and that this is worked out in several ways—the program of redemption, the program for Israel, the punishment of the wicked, the plan for angels, and the glory of God revealed through nature" (Ryrie, *Dispensationalism*, 247).
9. Tommy Nelson, *The Big Picture* (Dallas: Hudson Press, 1999), 17.
10. Brent Kinman, *History, Design and the End of Time: God's Plan for the World* (Nashville: Broadman & Holman, 2000), 2. There are two interpretations of history. According to Hoekema, "The first of these is found among the ancient Greeks. The Greeks had what may be called a 'cyclical' view of history: things occur in endlessly repeated cycles, so that what is happening today will [someday] be repeated. On the basis of such a view it is, of course, impossible to find any real meaning in history. . . . The Greek view of history is incompatible with the Christian view, which sees history as a fulfillment of God's purpose and as moving toward his goal. For the writers of the Bible history is not a meaningless series of recurring cycles but a vehicle whereby God realizes his purposes with man and cosmos. The idea that history is moving toward divinely established goals, and that the future is to be seen as the fulfillment of promises made in the past, is the unique contribution of the prophets of Israel. . . . A second interpretation of history which must be rejected is that of the atheistic existentialist. For existentialism of this type, history is without meaning. No significant pattern can be found in history, no movement toward a goal; only a meaningless succession of events. . . . The existentialist view of history is also incompatible with the Christian view" (Hoekema, *The Bible and the Future*, 24–25).
11. Kinman, *History, Design and the End*, 15.
12. Michael Horton, *Introducing Covenant Theology* (Grand Rapids: Baker, 2006), 30.
13. Kinman, *History, Design and the End*, 10.
14. Ibid., 26.
15. Nelson, *The Big Picture*, 19.
16. The Greek term *oikonomia* "has two nuances: first, the position or office an administrator, as used of [a] management of a household, or of a state; and, second, of the activity of administration and thus arrangement, order, plan, strategy" (Harold Hoehner, *Ephesians: An Exegetical Commentary* [Grand Rapids, Baker, 2002], 217). Hoehner recognizes that outside of Paul, Luke uses the term to refer both to office and activity. He argues that in this context, "it refers to the second translation, meaning activity, administration or dispensation." However, this context also indicates that one cannot overlook the reality that in the dispensation where God is summing up all things under the headship of Jesus Christ, the position of administrator must be considered as well. In other words, God is bringing all things under Jesus, the administrator, who will establish His rulership in accordance with the dispensation of God.
17. Hoehner says, "According to his good pleasure God purposed to unite, under one head, all things in Christ" (Hoehner, *Ephesians*, 216).
18. Robert L. Saucy, *The Case for Progressive Dispensationalism* (Grand Rapids: Zondervan, 1993), 32.
19. Richard, "Premillennialism as Philosophy of History: Part 2," *Bibliotheca Sacra*, 102.
20. Showers writes that "a philosophy of history has certain characteristics. First, it offers a systematic interpretation of history. In other words, it explains the *why* of historic events in an organized way. Second, it covers the whole scope of history from beginning to end. It explains why things happened in the past, why the world is where it is in the present, and the *what* and *why* of the future. Third, a philosophy of history has a unifying principle which ties together and makes sense of events, distinctions, and successions. Fourth, it assigns ultimate meaning to history. It demonstrates that the flow of history has an ultimate goal or purpose, that events are not disjointed or unrelated to each other, and that future events are the grand climax toward which all previous events have been moving"; in

Renald E. Showers, *There Really Is a Difference: A Comparison of Covenant and Dispensational Theology* (Bellmawr, NJ: The Friends of Israel Gospel Ministry, 1990), 2.

21. Ryrie, *Dispensationalism*, 20–21.

22. Saucy, *The Case for Progressive Dispensationalism*, 13.

23. Ibid., 19.

24. Ibid., 20–21.

25. Ibid., 13.

26. Spencer argues that it is error "to consider covenant theology and dispensationalism as the only available options, particularly for ecclesiological and eschatological matters. Consequently to refute dispensationalism is to establish covenant theology or vice versa. This error perhaps is more commonly found in dispensational writings, but it occurs in covenant works as well. This results in a narrowed focus and a misconstrual of the significance of the contrast between these two points of view" (Stephen R. Spencer, "Reformed Theology, Covenant Theology and Dispensationalism," in *Integrity of Heart and Skillfulness of Hands,* ed. Charles H. Dyer and Roy B. Zuck [Grand Rapids: Baker, 1994], 239).

27. Horton summarizes, "The covenant is the framework, but it is far from a central dogma. The various covenants are visible and significant, in some 'rooms' (i.e., topics) more than others. The covenant of redemption is prominent in discussion of the Trinity, Christ as mediator, and election, while the covenant of creation is more obvious when we talk about God's relationship to the world (especially humanity), and the covenant of grace is most visible when we take up the topics of salvation and the church. However, whenever Reformed theologians attempt to explore and explain the riches of Scripture, they are always thinking *covenantally* about every topic they take up" (Horton, *Introducing Covenant Theology*, 14).

28. Spencer writes, "Covenant theology may be understood in at least two senses. It can designate a theology in which the concept of covenant plays a significant or even central role, so that it is basic to the understanding of Scripture and the program of redemption. It also can designate a theology in which covenant is the explicit structural principle around which a theological work is written. Both of these uses are appropriate but they are not equivalent. A theology obviously may be covenantal in both senses, or it may be covenantal in the first meaning, but not the second" (Spencer, "Reformed Theology, Covenant Theology, and Dispensationalism," *Integrity of Heart*, 241).

29. Paul Enns, *The Moody Handbook of Theology* (Chicago: Moody, 1989), 203; Horton ascribes the "biblical-theological development of this theme to the traditional Reformed concept of three overarching covenants: the covenant of redemption (an eternal pact between the Father, Son, and Holy Spirit), the covenant of creation (made with humanity in Adam), and the covenant of grace (made with believers and their children in Christ)" (Horton, *Introducing Covenant Theology*, 77–78).

30. Horton, *Introducing Covenant Theology*, 11.

31. Showers, *There Really Is a Difference*, 7. Most will associate covenant theology with Reformed or Calvinistic theology. "*Reformed* theology is synonymous with *covenant* theology." Horton, *Introducing Covenant Theology*, 11.

32. Spencer affirms that "Covenant theology clearly has occupied the central place in the Reformed tradition, if by "covenant theology' one means a theology in which covenant is a significant concept for understanding the program of redemption and the relationship between the Old and New Testament" in "Reformed Theology, Covenant Theology and Dispensationalism," 243.

33. Richards Phillips, "Redemptive History," http://www.ligonier.org/earn/articles/redemptive-history.

34. Horton, *Introducing Covenant Theology,* 11.

35. Ibid.

36. Spencer, "Reformed Theology, Covenant Theology, and Dispensationalism," 239.

37. Horton, *Introducing Covenant Theology*, 13.

38. Ibid.

39. Ibid., 78.
40. Enns, *The Moody Handbook of Theology*, 508.
41. Horton, *Introducing Covenant Theology*, 82.
42. Enns, *The Moody Handbook of Theology*, 509.
43. Horton, *Introducing Covenant Theology*, 105.
44. Some covenantalists hold to replacement theology, or supersessionism, which is the view that "the NT church is the new and/or true Israel that has forever superseded the nation Israel as the people of God"; see Michael J. Vlach, "Various Forms of Replacement Theology," *Master's Seminary Journal* (2009): 57.
45. Cornelis Venema, "The Church and Israel: The Issue," http://www.ligonier.org/learn/articles/the-church-and-Israel-the-issue.
46. According to Hoekema, "Rev. 20:1–6 says nothing about an earthly reign of Christ over a primarily Jewish kingdom" (Anthony A. Hoekema, "Amillennialism," in *The Meaning of the Millennium: Four Views*, ed. Robert G. Clouse [Downers Grove, IL: InterVarsity, 1977], 155).
47. The term "millennium" derived from the Latin words *mille*, meaning a "thousand," and *annus*, meaning a "year." The term refers to a thousand-year period.
48. Hoekema, "Amillennialism," 155.
49. Hoekema, *The Bible and the Future*, 174.
50. Ibid. Strimple summarizes well: "The Old Testament does not teach a future millennial kingdom of Christ. Uniformly the Old Testament prophets speak of the Messiah's *everlasting* kingdom and its *everlasting* blessings. . . . Not only does the New Testament not teach a future millennial kingdom, in what it teaches us about Christ's second coming, the New Testament rules out an earthly millennial kingdom following Christ's return, because the New Testament reveals clearly that the following events are all concurrent; that is, all will occur together in one cluster of end-time events, one grand dramatic finale of redemptive history: the second coming of Christ, the resurrection of believers, the resurrection of the unjust, judgment for all, the end, the new heaven and new earth, and the inauguration of the final kingdom of God, the blessed eternal state of the redeemed" (Robert B. Strimple, "Amillennialism," in *Three Views on the Millennium and Beyond*, ed. Darrell L. Bock [Grand Rapids: Zondervan, 1999], 100).
51. In "Amillennialism," 175, Strimple notes, "Postmillennialists agree with amillennialists on three points: (1) postmillennialists do not understand the millennium as involving a visible reign of Christ from an earthly throne; (2) they do not think of the millennium as being exactly a thousand years in duration; (3) they place the return of Christ after the millennium."
52. Kenneth L. Gentry Jr., "Postmillennialism," in *Three Views on the Millennium and Beyond*, 13–14.
53. Enns, *The Moody Handbook of Theology*, 385.
54. Ibid., 386.
55. George Eldon Ladd, "Historic Premillennialism," in *The Meaning of the Millennium: Four Views*, 17. According to Enns (*The Moody Handbook of Theology*, 386), "The hermeneutical system of historic premillennialism distinguishes it from dispensational premillennialism. In historic premillennialism a distinction between Israel and the church is not maintained nor is a consistently literal interpretive method demanded." The Old Testament prophecies are now being applied and fulfilled in the New Testament church. Ladd ("Historic Premillennialism," 18–19) writes, "Dispensational theory insists that many of the Old Testament prophecies predict the millennium and must be drawn in to construct the picture of Messiah's millennial reign. This view is based upon the hermeneutic that the Old Testament prophecies must be interpreted literally. . . . The opposite to a literal hermeneutic of the Old Testament is a 'spiritualizing' hermeneutic, that is, a hermeneutic which finds the Old Testament prophecies fulfilled in the Christian church. Thus amillennialists usually find a 'spiritual' interpretation of the millennium. The millennium is not a literal reign of Christ on the earth; it is

either the reign of Christ in this age in his church; or it is the reign of the martyrs after death in the intermediate state."

56. "The Second Coming of Christ will not be a two-stage event, but a single occurrence. When Christ comes again, believers who have died will be raised, believers who are still living will be transformed and glorified, and then both groups will be caught up together to meet the Lord in the air. After this meeting in the air, believers will accompany the descending Christ to earth" (Hoekema, *The Bible and the Future*, 181).

57. Ibid., 29. According to Ladd, "A millennial doctrine cannot be based on Old Testament prophecies but should be based on the New Testament alone. . . . The only place in the Bible that speaks of an actual millennium is the passage in Revelation 20:1–6. Any millennial doctrine must be based upon the most natural exegesis of this passage" (*Historical Premillenialism*, 32).

58. Hoekema, *The Bible and the Future*,181.

59. Ryrie, *Dispensationalism*, 24.

60. Robert Lightner, "Theonomy and Dispensationalism," *Bibliotheca Sacra* 143 (1986): 33.

61. Herbert W. Bateman, "Dispensationalism Yesterday and Today," in *Three Central Issues in Contemporary Dispensationalism*, ed. Herbert Bateman IV (Grand Rapids: Kregel, 1999), 22. He adds, "Since its early beginnings, however, distinguishing characteristics of dispensationalism have undergone clarification, modification, and change."

62. Roy Aldrich, "An Outline Study of Dispensationalism," *Bibliotheca Sacra* 118 (1961): 134.

63. Ryrie, *Dispensationalism*, 28.

64. "Dispensationalism views the world as a household run by God. In His household God is dispensing or administering its affairs according to His own will and in various stages of revelation in the passage of time. These various stages mark off the distinguishably different economies in the outworking of His total purpose, and these different economies constitute the dispensations. The understanding of God's different economies is essential to a proper interpretation of His revelation within those various economies" (Ryrie, *Dispensationalism*, 34–35).

65. Bateman, *Three Central Issues in Contemporary Dispensationalism*, 47.

66. Ryrie, *Dispensationalism*, 36.

67. Ibid., 45ff. Ryrie refers to them as the *sine qua non of dispensationalism* (the absolute indispensable part). However, I am not necessarily summarizing from Ryrie's declaration. In fact Blaising suggests as well, the fact that the other two (supporting) elements of Ryrie's triad seem less than tenable, at least in the way he stated them. This characteristic, according to many, seems to be truly representative. See Craig A. Blaising, "Dispensationalism: The Search for Definition," in *Dispensationalism: Israel and the Church: The Search for Definition* (Grand Rapids: Zondervan, 1992), 23.

68. Craig A. Blaising, "Development of Dispensationalism," *Bibliotheca Sacra* 145 (1988): 273.

69. Ryrie, *Dispensationalism*, 46.

70. Stanley Toussaint, a traditional dispensationalist, agrees that "progressive dispensationalism still makes something of a difference between Israel and the church, but that distinction is not nearly as sharp" (Stanley D. Toussaint, "Israel and the Church of Traditional Dispensationalist," in *Three Central Issues in Contemporary Dispensationalism*, 230).

71. As cited in Toussaint, "Israel and the Church of Traditional Dispensationalist," 230.

72. Burns provides an excellent summary of additional questions raised when discussing the issues related to Israel and the church. "How was Israel distinctive as a people of God among the nations? Why has Israel rejected the incarnation of Torah while Gentiles have found favor with Yahweh seemingly apart from the Torah? Has the church 'replaced' Israel as a 'reconstituted' people of God? Is Israel distinct from the church as people of faith in God? To what extent or degree are the two biblical entities distinct? Does the olive tree metaphor describe a simultaneous or a successive salvation of Gentiles and Jews in the present age? Why does the New Testament discuss the relationship of 'Jews' and 'Gentiles' more explicitly than implied 'Israel' and 'church' contrasts? Is there a key text, or a limited num-

ber of crucial passages, for debating the differences between divergent theological approaches to the subject? Can 'integrative questions,' involving a number of texts and issues, result in a clarification, or even resolution, of polarizing differences between evangelicals about Israel and the church? What is the future of theological discussion, when many scholars in different traditions agree about most eschatological issues except for the Millennium? Answers to these and related questions must begin with the distinctiveness of Israel as evidenced in its divinely bestowed privileges and prerogatives" (J. Lanier Burns, "Israel and the Church of a Progressive Dispensationalist," in *Three Central Issues in Contemporary Dispensationalism*, 265).

73. Enns, *The Moody Handbook of Theology*, 523.

74. Craig A. Blaising and Darrell L. Bock, *Progressive Dispensationalism* (Wheaton: Victor Books, 1993), 18.

75. The nature of fulfillment centers on the relationship between Old Testament promises and prediction and the way in which they are fulfilled in the New Testament. The nature of fulfillment seeks to answer questions such as: Is it a total and complete fulfillment? A partial fulfillment? Or the inauguration of a fulfillment? What's the difference between a literal and a spiritual fulfillment?

76. Charles H. Dyer, "Biblical Meaning of 'Fulfillment,' " in *Issues in Dispensationalism*, ed. Wesley R. Willis and John R. Masters (Chicago: Moody, 1994), 71.

77. According to Ryrie, "There are those who are premillennial who definitely are not dispensational. The covenant premillennialist holds to the concept of the covenant of grace and the central soteriological purpose of God. He retains the idea of the millennial kingdom, though he finds little support for it in the Old Testament prophecies. The kingdom in his view is markedly different from that which is taught by dispensationalists, since it loses much of its Jewish character due to the slighting of the Old Testament promises concerning the kingdom. Many covenant premillennialists are also posttribulationalists, and that seems to be a logical accompaniment of the nondispensational approach. At any rate, being a premillennialist does not necessarily make one a dispensationalist. (However, the reverse is true—being a dispensationalist makes one a premillennialist)" (Ryrie, *Dispensationalism*, 45–46).

78. Craig A. Blaising, "The Extent and Varieties of Dispensationalism," in Craig A. Blaising and Darrell L. Bock, *Progressive Dispensationalism* (Grand Rapids: Baker, 1993), 19.

79. Ramesh Richard, "Premillennialism as Philosophy of History, Part 3" *Bibliotheca Sacra* 138 (1981): 211.

80. Spencer writes, "Continuity theologies, emphasizing the unity of the Testaments and of Israel and the church, have predominated since the second century, but covenant theology originated in the Reformed wing of the Protestant Reformation. Alternative continuity theologies would include, among others, the Lutheran law/grace dialectic, Roman Catholic theology, and the Eastern Orthodox Church. Anabaptist theologies are discontinuity in character as is much of Baptist theology (at least insofar as it advocates a 'believer's church' view). Some theological traditions are not necessarily committed to either 'continuity' or 'discontinuity.' Anglicans hold to 'covenantal continuity' (especially 'Anglo-Catholics'), or to 'covenantal continuity' (e.g., J. I. Packer and a significant portion of the Puritan movement, namely, the non-Dissenter, non-Presbyterian, non-Congregational wing), or to 'discontinuity' (e.g., W. H. Griffith Thomas). The Methodist Episcopal tradition, derived from the Anglican, is similarly variable" (Spencer, "Reformed Theology, Covenant Theology, and Dispensationalism," 253–54).

81. Progressive dispensationalism has presented itself as an additional option for interpreting God's redemptive history and it offers somewhat of a mediating position relying on an idea of both continuous and discontinuous approaches in its system of interpretation. As Saucy writes, "There is a mediating position between non-dispensationalism and traditional dispensationalism that provides a better understanding of Scripture. This view seeks to retain a natural understanding of the prophetic Scriptures that appear to assign a significant role to the nation of Israel in the future, in accordance with a dispensational system. But it also sees the program of God as unified within history, in agreement with non-dispensationalists, and it denies a radical discontinuity between the present church

age and the messianic kingdom promises" (Saucy, *The Case for Progressive Dispensationalism*, 27). Progressive dispensationalists do not believe that the church has replaced Israel or that the Old Testament covenants are now being completely fulfilled in the church. Progressive dispensationalism (PD) maintains a distinct separation between Israel and the church, a prerapture tribulation, and the return of Christ to establish His earthly kingdom during a literal 1,000-year millennial kingdom. However, some of the distinctions of progressive dispensationalism are as follows: (1) hermeneutically, PD advocates what they call a "complementary" hermeneutic that suggests that in a normal reading of the Old Testament, concepts and themes work together with the New Testament in a way that completes, expounds, or expands what has already been discussed so that they are able to be applied to a wider audience than just Israel while maintaining their initial commitment to Israel; (2) with regards to the covenants, PD argues that the covenants, as an *initial* aspect, are being realized in the church. "To say that such a realization occurs in the church is not to deny that these covenants were originally or ultimately for national, ethnic Israel. It is rather to note that because of the work of Christ, who is the key to fulfillment, initial fulfillment becomes possible in the context of the church. . . . Progressive dispensationalism's emphasis of this point of continuity in Christ makes it different from previous expressions of dispensationalism" (Bock, "Covenants in Progressive Dispensationalism," in *Three Central Issues in Contemporary Dispensationalism*, 171–72).

82. Saucy, *The Case for Progressive Dispensationalism*, 13.

83. Ibid., 22.

84. Ibid., 23. In addition, Saucy writes, "Perhaps the view most commonly held among evangelical non-dispensationalists is that Israel's future is simply an incorporation of that people into the church" (ibid.).

85. Ibid., 22.

86. Spencer, "Reformed Theology, Covenant Theology, and Dispensationalism," 252. Spencer adds, "The distinctive of covenant theology is that it uses the concept of divine covenants as the central rubric for interpreting Scripture. Its distinctive is not its emphasis on continuity, but rather its use of covenant as the means of emphasizing continuity. It belongs, as it were, to the genus of continuity theologies, but is a distinct species within that genus.

87. Ibid., 238.

88. Lints, *The Fabric of Theology*, 8.

89. Jürgen Moltmann, *Theology of Hope* (Minneapolis: Augsburg Fortress, 1993), 37. Jürgen Moltmann was born in Hamburg, Germany, in 1926. He fought in World War II, but was eventually captured by the British in Belgium in 1945 and held as a prisoner of war until 1948. He saw the collapse of his native Germany and all of its institutions. While in the camp in Belgium, an American chaplain gave him a Bible and the Scriptures changed his life.

90. Blaising and Bock, *Progressive Dispensationalism*, 287.

10

Dispensationalism and Its Worldwide Impact

OSCAR A. CAMPOS

Dispensationalism has been a growing, influential, and diverse tradition that emerged alongside and within the larger movement known as "evangelicalism." As a theological system grounded in a particular interpretive approach, emphasizing the spiritual life as well as evangelism and missions, dispensationalism has also been a populist movement, a "people's movement."

Having originated in late nineteenth century with the former Anglican minister John Nelson Darby and the Plymouth Brethren in Great Britain, dispensationalism has had a worldwide impact. Darby and other Brethren teachers of the time characteristically preached on spiritual and personal conversion and an ecclesiology of the body of Christ (instead of a national institutional church), and they emphasized biblical prophecy. These Brethren teachers traveled to countries in Europe (like Spain, France, Holland, Italy, Germany, and Switzerland), the United States, Canada, and New Zealand, preaching and teaching in churches and Bible conferences. By and large, this was a revivalist movement, influencing conservative Christianity. Brethren congregations were also born in different places. Adding to Darby's prolific writing work, his teachings became widely spread in the West, especially in the English-speaking world.[1] Darby's and Brethren teaching were clearly identified as dispensational, futuristic premillennial, and conservative (fundamentalist).

At the same time, as the twentieth century approached, Christianity in general was in decay as the West was entering a "post-Christian era" as the aftermath of modernity. Thus North American conservative Protestantism, in good measure, was very receptive to fundamentalist and dispensational premillennialist teaching. As a result, the identity of Christianity and the nature of missions were redefined as conservative Protestantism was renewed as a movement later known as evangelicalism. Certainly, evangelicalism represented a new era of spiritual, social, and ecclesiastical understanding. Dispensational premillennialism was part of this historical transition.

DISPENSATIONALISM AND THE FAITH MISSIONS MOVEMENT

American (and British) evangelicalism rapidly experienced considerable growth and transformation at home and abroad, becoming a global movement. Among several historical factors that likely contributed to the rise of evangelicalism and its worldwide impact are premillennialism, fundamentalism, and the "faith mission movement."

The faith mission movement has been the main vehicle for evangelicalism into the world throughout the twentieth century. Basically a North American phenomenon, evangelicalism's missions movement emerged at the end of the nineteenth and early twentieth centuries, and still functions today,[2] and it is reproduced in other parts of the world, especially in contemporary majority world missionary movement.[3]

As already suggested, it has been recognized that the two main features that influenced the expansion of the faith missions movement were: premillennial theology (especially dispensational premillennialism) and fundamentalism. These two elements that helped shape the identity and missiological approach of dispensational evangelicalism in North America have been also taken to the world through missions for more than a century now.

Although there has been controversy over the key originating factor of the faith missions, it seems that premillenialism was the spark that ignited the fire of the new wave of missions.[4] It was a rediscovered theological conviction. A new generation of missionaries and donors were convinced of the urgency to preach the gospel message of salvation before the second coming of the Lord. As a result, they "overflowed the insufficient denominational missionary structures."[5] Dana L. Robert describes that theological element as a "mission revival." She explains, "Little did the average Christian of 1880 realize that the age of foreign missions would irrevocably change the religious landscape at home. By the early twentieth century, American missions had not only influenced the developing world, but a constellation of separatist evangelical missions, often called 'faith missions,' had emerged from the heady enthusiasm of the mission revival."[6]

To argue in favor of that chronological sequence within the faith mission movement, Robert emphasized that "it would be easy to read twentieth-century theological controversy between so-called liberals and evangelicals back into the origins of the faith missions of the 1890s. But evangelicals of late nineteenth century did not join faith missions as a protest against liberalism in the established denominations."[7] She also argued that "premillennialist mission theory" was adopted first by such denominational leaders as A. T. Pierson, A. J. Gordon, A. B. Simpson, and others, who later became the fathers of the faith missions.[8] Denominational missionary structures were unable to channel the massive response from the new missionary force that emerged motivated by premillennialism. Robert even goes further by stating that the so-called crisis of missions was related to the premillennialism taught in the Niagara Bible Conferences by people like the "British missionaries" George Mueller and John Nelson Darby,[9] thus disclosing an even stronger connection between the faith missions movement and dispensational premillennialism.

DISPENSATIONALISM AND PREMILLENNIALISM

Taking a step backward, the history of modern premillennialism began during the early nineteenth-century millennialist revival, both in England and America.[10] Millennialism, the teaching of a literal millennial kingdom of Christ on earth, reappeared after centuries of amillennial theological dominance (the interpretation that there was a present nonliteral millennial kingdom of Christ on earth) and was popular among Catholics and early Protestant traditions. The emphasis of this initial movement was on a "historicist pre-millennialism" also called "year-day theory," which focused on predicting dates for the second coming of Christ by correlating contemporary historical events and world or religious leaders with Bible prophecy.[11] As it is known, the failure of those predictions was a discredit and a setback of millennialism, since these predictions were highly publicized and resulted in embarrassment for the premillennialist position.[12]

Years later, a "futuristic" type of premillennialism reappeared by the second half of the nineteenth century. It differed from "historicists" in the fact that this premillennialism expects the second coming of Christ at any given moment and does not believe in the human ability to determine specific dates according to interpretation of contemporary historical events and current world personalities.[13]

It was within futuristic premillennialism that the concepts of "rapture" and "dispensations," among other dispensationalist doctrines, were introduced and rapidly spread. This "dispensational futuristic premillennialism" was an outgrowth of the teachings of John Nelson Darby[14] and the following Niagara Bible Conference movement.[15] Those teachings were later collected by Cyrus I. Scofield in the well-known *Scofield Reference Bible,* which popularized and identified these teachings with the name "dispensationalism."[16]

DISPENSATIONALISM AND ITS WORLDWIDE IMPACT

The relevance of the history of dispensationalism has to do with its wide influence on evangelicalism in Great Britain and North America and on the faith mission movement, especially as it was taken to the rest of the world. Its influence expanded beyond particular local churches, denominations, Christian educational institutions, and mission agencies due to the urgency for preaching the gospel to the lost before the second coming of Christ (premillennialism), and to the popularity of the *Scofield Reference Bible* taken to the mission fields by a new wave of missionaries mostly within the faith missions movement. The new generation of missionaries was provided with a resource for biblical study and teaching for them and their ministries—a "handbook" to be taken to the missions fields of the world, where there was no access to theological libraries.[17]

Dispensational Premillennialism and Fundamentalism

No doubt dispensational premillennialism was also related to fundamentalism. At that time (the late nineteenth and early twentieth centuries), fundamentalism was a general and simple designation for conservative Protestantism in contrast to the liberal theology and modern culture being embraced by humanistic education and society. The Bible conference movement became the common ground for both (premillennialism and fundamentalism), because premillennialism and the Bible conference movement appealed mostly to conservative Protestants.[18] Robert described this process while identifying some of the fundamentalist denominational leaders who became first influenced by the premillennialist missiological approach. She explains,

> Muller then convinced Pierson of a premillennial interpretation of Scripture: that the condition of the world would in fact worsen until Jesus returned to usher in the millennium. Late-nineteenth-century premillennialism's view that human effort could not in fact bring in God's kingdom seemed to Pierson to be both more scriptural and more consonant with reality as he experienced it in his own ministry in urban Detroit.
>
> After he became a premillennialist, Pierson began to participate in Niagara Bible conferences, a regular fellowship of church leaders, mostly Presbyterian and Baptists, who had become convinced of a premillennial interpretation of Scripture. Many Niagara participants had been converted to premillennial exegesis by British "missionaries" such as George Muller and John Nelson Darby, who traveled through the United States in the 1870s and 1880s. Niagara participants tended to be prominent urban pastors or evangelists—like Dwight L. Moody of Chicago, A. J. Gordon of Boston, James H. Brookes of St. Louis and others—who felt a strong commitment to evangelism as a solution to urban social problems. Today scholars consider the Niagara conferences to have been a primary breeding ground for what became fundamentalist biblical exegesis.[19]

Although American fundamentalism is a larger cultural phenomenon in itself, it also had a missiological impact alongside dispensational premillennialism in the world.[20] The faith mission movement reflected both the premillennialist fervor and, surely, the theological zeal and culture of fundamentalists against modernism within and outside of different denominational settings.[21] This combination of elements led to a different way of financing and organizing missionary efforts. Denominations lacked funds for the increasing missionary forces motivated by premillennialism while being "affected" by modernism. Edwin L. Frizen, Jr. explains:

> As the leadership of the denominational boards was increasingly assumed by those holding a liberal theological or social-gospel position, more workers and support came to the nondenominational missions. This was based upon the convictions and decisions of individual Christians and individual churches that wanted the missionaries they sent out and supported to go with agencies that held firmly to the authority of the Scriptures and demonstrated evangelistic fervor.[22]

The Interdenominational Foreign Mission Association (IFMA)

Faith missions were named in ways that reflected their organizational character: Nondenominational, interdenominational, or independent missions.[23] More specifically, the name "faith missions" was given because of their independence from denominational funds and denominational missionary boards. As Frizen said, "Nondenominational agencies were formed to operate on the basis that the Lord would provide by faith the support needed for ministries that He directed His servants to enter."[24]

In 1917 representatives of several faith missions, including the Central American Mission, founded the Interdenominational Foreign Mission Association of North America "for the purpose of strengthening the cause of the so-called 'faith missions.' "[25] All its members had to adhere to the "conservative positions in matters pertaining to the fundamental doctrines of the historic Christian faith."[26] However, it should not be ignored that fundamentalism was not limited to premillennialism, which in turn was not restricted to dispensationalism, as the faith missions are not exclusive to dispensational premillennialism either. It is also necessary to recognize that dispensational premillennialism and fundamentalism have been historically bound within the faith mission movement.

DISPENSATIONALISM AND CURRENT GLOBAL EVANGELICALISM

As the faith mission movement carried to the world the gospel news of salvation, dispensational evangelicalism became a growing phenomenon. It "now exercises a global influence."[27] Its impact and growth now reaches Africa, Asia, the South Pacific, Europe, and Latin America, even though missions literature typically does not elaborate on evangelical theological differences and backgrounds like the ones treated in this chapter; they are just implied or included in the missionary movement.[28] It is important to remember that dispensational premillennialism is a popular, revivalist grassroots movement worldwide.[29]

Another sign of the times is that in the last decades, the so-called mission fields overseas, especially in the majority world, have become a global missionary force to the rest of the world. Again, evangelicalism is the branch of Christianity growing the most.[30]

A CASE STUDY: GROWTH IN LATIN AMERICA

The considerable growth of evangelicalism in Latin America illustrates very well the global growth of evangelicalism, and especially it reveals the influence of dispensational evangelicalism.[31] Dispensationalism and fundamentalism are foundational aspects in the missiological practices of most evangelical groups in Latin America, which are related to the North American faith missions. Furthermore, the influence of dispensational premillennialism in Latin America, and the world for that matter, is so overwhelming once it is accepted that the popular and fast-growing Pentecostal and charismatic movements are also identified with dispensationalism.[32]

The Pentecostal Influence

Studies demonstrate that about 70 percent of all evangelicals in Latin America are Pentecostals or Charismatics. Therefore, since Pentecostalism represents the majority of evangelicals, the popularity and influence of traditional dispensational evangelicalism in Latin America, as in many parts of the world, cannot be denied. These topics were documented and brought to international attention through the well-publicized studies of David Stoll and David Martin in the 1990s.[33]

Stoll, an anthropologist, concluded: "Dispensationalists did not approve of the new manifestation. . . . But many Pentecostals took up dispensationalism anyway, reshaped it, and organized their own, more enthusiastic variant of fundamentalism."[34] Martin, a sociologist, also describing the growth of Pentecostalism in Latin America, wrote: "The balance of numerical power has now passed unequivocally from the older denominations to the conservative evangelicals and, above all, to the Pentecostals. The older denominations were themselves quite conservative theologically, but they were fairly staid in style. The newer denominations are, if anything, more conservative and for the most part they are charismatic."[35]

Since its very roots are in North American soil, Pentecostalism embraced dispensational theology, like in the case of Albert Benjamin (A. B.) Simpson, a Presbyterian premillennialist who founded the Christian and Missionary Alliance as a faith mission, and who became related to the Pentecostal movement, especially the Assemblies of God—a major evangelical force in Latin America and the world.[36] As Douglas A. Oss affirmed: "Historically Pentecostals have considered themselves to be dispensationalists. Early Pentecostals were influenced significantly by dispensationalism and American Fundamentalism. The *Scofield Reference Bible* was endorsed by official Assemblies of God publications, and the denomination's chief organ, *The Pentecostal Evangel*, commonly affirmed the dispensational stance of the movement."[37] As a matter of fact, the Assemblies of God Statement of Faith is completely dispensational even today.[38]

Mike Berg and Paul Pretiz identified some of the faith missions represented in Latin America. They relate those mission agencies and their theology with the growth of evangelicalism:

> With a loss of confidence by many in the theology of the mainline denominations and their respective missions, thousands of more conservative Christians found a vehicle for their missionary outreach in such societies as CAM International (originally the Central American Mission, founded by C. I. Scofield of the dispensational Scofield Bible) or TEAM (The Evangelical Alliance Mission). The first CAM couple went to Central America in 1891. . . .
>
> Despite failures and set-backs, however, the faith mission wave touched the length and breadth of Latin America. One mission specialized in radio. The World Radio Missionary Fellowship established the first missionary radio station, HCJB, in Quito, Ecuador, when the country had only a handful of people with receivers. Another, the Latin American Evangelization Campaign (later, the Latin America Mission), began in 1921 by conducting citywide united evangelistic campaigns. Wycliffe Bible Translators and New Tribes Mission reached Indian populations in the jungles and in the mountains.[39]

All the features mentioned as forces behind faith missions translate into some characteristics that establish evangelical identity in general and that of dispensational evangelicalism in particular. This is supported by the fact that most of the well-known dispensationalist writers (Scofield, Chafer, Pentecost, Walvoord, and Ryrie) have been translated into Spanish as in other languages. Their books are popular readings and textbooks among the churches and educational institutions related to the dispensational faith missions in Latin America.[40]

Marks of Latin American Evangelicalism

Latin American missiologist Orlando Costas described three marks of evangelicalism in Latin America. He attached them to what he called "its pre-dominantly Anglo-Saxon progenitor and counterpart" (meaning North American conservative evangelicalism).[41] They are: "Insistence on (1) the authority of the Bible in all matters of faith and practice; (2) conversion as a distinct experience of faith in Christ as Lord and Saviour, which distinguishes the Christian from the non-Christian; and (3) the practice of evangelization as the fundamental dimension of the mission of the Christian faith."[42]

Those characteristics help to define what evangelicalism is and to show the evangelistic impulse of its missiology. Christian *praxis* and belief are joined together.

Costas also agreed that the same evangelical marks characterize Pentecostals and the majority of mainline denominational churches in Latin America, noting, "This explains why the term 'evangelical' is used in Latin America in reference to all Protestants irrespective of their denominational affiliation."[43] Read, Monterroso, and Johnson also agreed with this assessment (although from a different perspective than Costas), stressing evangelical commitment to its evangelistic mission. They wrote:

> The particular affiliation of a mission and its consequent commitment to a particular theological position are almost meaningless issues in Latin America so far as the related churches are concerned. Instead there is an overwhelming general agreement among Evangelicals on theological issues. For missionaries, though, North American and European affiliations are very important, and to the extent that the Churches of Latin America are still dependent on the missions, they are inevitably influenced by such affiliations.[44]

Although evangelicals have common characteristics in Latin America, there are still normal differences according to particular theological emphasis. Some of the differences include the Pentecostal stress on the "charismatic experiences," while mainline churches stress their theological and historical ties, and ecumenism.[45] However, as Berg and Pretiz explain, Latin American evangelicalism includes those historical churches or mainline denominations that remained "evangelical" in Latin America while their mother denominations in North America were becoming "liberals."[46] It also includes some newer non-Pentecostal denominations, and a large number of Pentecostal-charismatic groups or "denominations" as well, which contain the largest segments of the evangelical population in Latin America.[47]

Evangelical history in Latin America is now over one hundred years old. But as we have seen, it was not until the second half of the twentieth century that its growth became generally recognized. It has attracted the attention of the dominant Catholic Church and of the general public as well.

DISPENSATIONALISM AND THE GREAT COMMISSION

The mission of the church within dispensational evangelicalism in Latin America and the rest of the world has been understood as the fulfillment of the Great Commission as described in Matthew 28:19–20.[48] That by itself leads to the obedience to our Lord's commandment of spreading the gospel to all corners of the earth in some strategic way in time. However, relating the Great Commission to a "futuristic" (imminent) premillennial second coming of Christ ignites evangelism in particular ways. This approach emphasized urgency and "rapid evangelization" because, "like the early church, they believed that Jesus' Second Coming was just around the corner."[49] In this way, dispensational premillennialism influenced the advancement of missions into the world, as it is seen in the growth of dispensational evangelicalism around the world today.

Dispensational evangelicalism took its evangelistic zeal to the world. Their evangelism focused on the personal experience of spiritual transformation called "the new birth" in reference to John 3:3–8, which stresses the primary spiritual nature of the gospel transformation.[50] This focus rested on a personal relationship to Jesus the Messiah, the Redeemer, God's Son, and consequently to the only and true God of the Bible for transformation, instead of a professing religious affiliation and Christian cultural ethics.

Norman Kraus, commenting on the historical British and American Plymouth Brethren movement and its influence on the teaching of mission as evangelization, said: "They held that the primary task of the church is evangelism, that is, the verbal proclamation of the Word."[51]

While evangelical missiology in general has widened its missions focus, dispensational premillennialism has also grown in its theology of redemption history and its ecclesiological outreach in missions in a variety of services to our needy world. The gospel is being preached and lived out in service so the lost and needy can meet Jesus the Savior for everlasting transformed life for the glory of God.

Notes

1. Larry V. Crutchfield, *The Origins of Dispensationalism: The Darby Factor* (Lanham, MD: University Press of America, 1992), 6–13.
2. J. Herbert Kane, *Understanding Christian Missions*, 3rd ed. (Grand Rapids: Baker, 1982), 160.
3. Steve (Heung Chan) Kim, "A Newer Missions Paradigm and the Growth of Missions from the Majority World," in *Missions from the Majority World*, ed. Enoch Wan and Michael Pocock, Evangelical Missionary Society Series No. 17 (Pasadena, CA: William Carey Library, 2009): 1–34.
4. Ernest R. Sandeen proposed a well-documented thesis that by the second half of the nineteenth century it was millenarianism that gave life to fundamentalism and not the opposite. See Ernest R. Sandeen, *The Roots of Fundamentalism: British and American Millenarianism 1800–1930* (Chicago: University of Chicago Press, 1970).
5. Edwin L. Frizen, Jr., *75 Years of IFMA, 1917–1992: The Nondenominational Missions Movement* (Pasadena, CA: William Carey Library, 1992), 69.
6. Dana L. Robert, "'The Crisis of Missions': Premillennial Mission Theory and the Origins of Independent Evangelical Missions," in *Earthen Vessels: American Evangelicals and Foreign Missions, 1880–1980*, ed. Joel A. Carpenter and Wilbert R. Shenk (Grand Rapids: Eerdmans, 1990), 29. The phrase "separatist evangelical missions" refers to the independent nature of these mission organizations, which were "separated" or "apart" from the common denominational mission organizations.
7. Robert, in line with Sandeen's thesis, argues that the faith missions did not originate with the controversies between liberals and "evangelicals" but with premillennialism. Robert, "The Crisis of Missions," 30. See also the concept of "applied eschatology" in Klaus Fiedler, *The Story of Faith Missions* (Oxford: Regnum Books International, 1994), 272–81.
8. Fiedler also identifies the influence of premillennialism in A. B. Simpson and the Christian and Missionary Alliance, James Hall Brooks and the Gospel Missionary Union, C. I. Scofield and the Central American Mission, Paul Fleming and the New Tribes Mission, among others. Ibid.
9. Robert, "The Crisis of Missions," 31–34. Joel A. Carpenter, in the same book, prefers to call Robert's view a "premillennialist proto-fundamentalism." While Carpenter is giving continuity to Robert's theory, at the same time he explains that there was a mission debate later on within fundamentalism, and that it was one of the "most explosive issues in the fundamentalist-modernist controversies." Joel A. Carpenter, "Propagating the Faith Once Delivered: The Fundamentalist Missionary Enterprise, 1920–1945," in *Earthen Vessels*, 92–93.

10. Another increasingly popular position in American Protestantism in the eighteenth and nineteenth centuries was postmillennialism, the teaching that the kingdom was being established as the world was increasingly Christianized. For a comprehensive study on these different positions, see *The Meaning of the Millennium: Four Views,* ed. Robert G. Clouse (Downers Grove, IL: InterVarsity, 1977); Millard J. Erickson, *Contemporary Options in Eschatology: A Study of the Millennium* (Grand Rapids: Baker, 1987); Stanley J. Grenz, *The Millennial Maze* (Downers Grove, IL: InterVarsity, 1992).
11. Sandeen, *The Roots of Fundamentalism*, 8–18; Fiedler, *The Story of Faith Missions*, 272–81.
12. Sandeen, *The Roots of Fundamentalism*, 42–58.
13. Ibid. See also Fiedler, *The Story of Faith Missions*, 276.
14. Mark A. Noll, *A History of Christianity in the United States and Canada* (Grand Rapids: Eerdmans, 1992), 376. For a comprehensive study on Darby, see Crutchfield, *The Origins of Dispensationalism: The Darby Factor*.
15. Later, some futuristic premillennialists disagreed with some of the dispensational teachings, especially with the pretribulational rapture of the church, and therefore they distanced themselves from it, conforming to the position called "historic" premillennialism. George Eldon Ladd is probably the most well-known representative of this position. For a good account, see Timothy P. Weber, "Dispensational and Historic Premillennialism as Popular Millennialist Movements," in *A Case for Historic Premillennialism*, ed. Craig L. Blomberg and Sung Wook Chung (Grand Rapids: Baker, 2009), 13–14.
16. *Scofield Reference Bible* (Oxford: Oxford University Press, 1909). In the introduction to the 1909 edition, Scofield mentions that his work is the result of the last thirty years of biblical studies, which he relates to the Bible studies and conference movement. This introduction is printed also in the following editions of that Bible. Craig A. Blaising, "Dispensationalism: The Search for Definition," in *Dispensationalism, Israel and the Church: The Search for Definition*, ed. Craig A. Blaising and Darrell L. Bock (Grand Rapids: Zondervan, 1992), 19–21.
17. In "The Crisis of Missions," 44, Robert described the *Scofield Reference Bible* as "a one-volume reference work for missionaries who had no access to theological libraries." Mark A. Noll agrees with Robert about the missionary intention of the *Scofield Reference Bible*, "which [Scofield] intended as a portable guide for missionaries more than a polished theological system." Noll, *A History of Christianity in the United States and Canada*, 378. See also Andrew F. Walls, "The American Dimension in the History of the Missionary Movement," in *Earthen Vessels*, 17.
18. Sandeen, *The Roots of Fundamentalism*, 132–61. See also Timothy P. Weber, *Living in the Shadow of the Second Coming: American Premillennialism, 1875–1982* (Chicago: University of Chicago Press, 1983).
19. Robert, "The Crisis of Missions," 34–35.
20. Fundamentalism in American evangelicalism is closely related to British evangelicalism. See Ian S. Rennie, "Fundamentalism and the Varieties of North Atlantic Evangelicalism," in *Evangelicalism: Comparative Studies of Popular Protestantism in North America, the British Isles, and Beyond, 1700–1990*, ed. Mark A. Noll, David W. Bebbington, and George A. Rawlyk (Oxford: Oxford University Press, 1994), 333–50. This work also proposes that the relationship between British and American evangelicalism expressed in fundamentalism is also evident in pentecostalism.
21. E.g., Chester Earl Tulga, *The Foreign Missions Controversy in the Northern Baptist Convention, 1919–1949* (Chicago: Conservative Baptist Fellowship, 1950), 9. Tulga mentions the controversy within the Northern Baptist Convention that was manifested in their 1919 convention in Denver, which led to the formation of The Fundamentalist Fellowship of the Northern Baptist Convention in 1920, later named Conservative Baptist Fellowship of Northern Baptists. He explained:

    "The modernists had captured most of the colleges and seminaries and attained to a large influence in others. The new interest in social reform and world reconstruction had taken on the terminology of the Gospel. Modernists, who had been hostile to missions as carried on by the orthodox, now became enthusiastic about the foreign missionary enterprise. The Great Commission was being interpreted in social terms, the old evangelical words were being invested with liberal meanings, the new missionary candidates were coming from liberal schools, the evolutionary philosophy of history guaranteed a better return from human effort than the individual Gospel message, so hostile modernism had become a missionary modernism."

22. Frizen, *75 Years of IFMA*, 69–70.
23. Ibid., 15. Frizen argues that the faith missions were part of a wide network of nondenominational evangelical organizations that were already common before the end of the nineteenth century. He also relates the origin of faith missions to the Bible conference movement. See pp. 51–82.
24. Ibid., 70.
25. J. Herbert Kane, *Faith Mighty Faith: A Handbook of the Interdenominational Foreign Mission Association* (New York: Interdenominational Foreign Mission Association, 1956), 8. Thirty-six missionary agencies were members of IFMA by 1956, of which at least twelve had ministries in Latin America; ibid., 169–71. By 1992 there were seventy-two agency members, and about twenty of those had some ministry in Latin America; Frizen, *75 Years of IFMA*, 444–46. See also *Mission Handbook: North American Protestant Ministries Overseas*, ed. Samuel Wilson and John Siewert, 13th ed. (Monrovia, CA: Missions Advanced Research and Communication Center, 1986), 37.
26. Kane, *Faith Mighty Faith*, 10. Cf. Frizen, *75 Years of IFMA*, 19, in which Frizen wrote of the theological position held by IFMA members: "Nondenominational missions hold to the basic historical fundamentals of conservative evangelical Christianity, usually stated in detailed doctrinal positions. In their firm adherence to the inerrancy of the Word of God, nondenominational missions have avoided the grave dangers of syncretism and neo-universalism prevalent today.
27. Catherine Wessinger, "Millennialism in Cross-Cultural Perspective," in *The Oxford Handbook of Millennialism*, ed. Catherine Wessinger (Oxford: Oxford University Press, 2011), 16.
28. See Sang-Bok David Kim, "Changes and Trends in World Christianity," in *Transformation: An International Journal of Holistic Mission Studies* 30, no. 4 (2013): 257–66.
29. Mal Couch, "Foreword," in *Dictionary of Premillennial Theology*, ed. Mal Couch (Grand Rapids: Kregel Publications, 1996).
30. Cf. Ralph Winter and David A. Fraser, "World Mission Survey," in *Perspectives on the World Christian Movement, A Reader*, ed. Ralph Winter and Steven C. Hawthorne, rev. ed. (Pasadena, CA: William Carey Library, 1992): 193–212. See also, William A. Dyrness, *Emerging Voices in Global Christian Theology* (Eugene, OR: Wipf & Stock, 1994); Peter Falk, *The Growth of the Church in Africa* (Bukuru, Nigeria: ALTS, 1997); and *Missions from the Majority World*, ed. Enoch Wan and Michael Pocock, (2009). There is abundant literature on evangelical world missions. However, as mentioned above, most of the time it does not elaborate on evangelical theological differences and backgrounds.
31. Emilio Antonio Núñez and William David Taylor, *Crisis and Hope in Latin America: An Evangelical Perspective*, rev. ed. (Pasadena, CA: William Carey Library, 1996), 160–63, 459–61. For statistics and percentages about the growth of the church in Latin America, see also Patrick Johnstone, *Operation World: The Day-by-Day Guide to Praying for the World*, 5th ed. (Grand Rapids: Zondervan, 1993), 62–67. Cf. Guillermo Cook, "Introduction: The Changing Face of the Church in Latin America," in *New Face of the Church in Latin America*, ed. Guillermo Cook, American Society of Missiology Series, ed. James A. Scherer and others, vol. 18 (Maryknoll, NY: Orbis Books, 1994).
32. Allan Anderson, *An Introduction to Pentecostalism: Global Charismatic Christianity* (Cambridge: Cambridge University Press, 2004).
33. David Stoll, *Is Latin America Turning Protestant? The Politics of Evangelical Growth* (Berkeley: University of California Press, 1990); and David Martin, *Tongues of Fire: The Explosion of Protestantism in Latin America* (Cambridge, MA: Basil Blackwell, 1990). See also Anne Motley Hallum, *Beyond Missionaries: Toward an Understanding of the Protestant Movement in Central America* (Lanham, MD: Rowman & Littlefield Publishers, 1996).
34. Stoll, *Is Latin America Turning Protestant*, 48–49.
35. Martin, *Tongues of Fire*, 52.
36. Robert, "The Crisis of Missions," 44. See Gary B. McGee, *"This Gospel . . . Shall Be Preached": A His-*

tory and Theology of Assemblies of God Foreign Missions to 1959 (Springfield, MO: Gospel Publishing House, 1986), 57–67. Cf. J. Kwabena Asamoah-Gyady, *African Charismatics: Current Developments within Independent Indigenous Pentecostalism in Ghana* (Leiden, The Netherlands: Brill, 2005).

37. Douglas A. Oss, "The Hermeneutics of Dispensationalism within the Pentecostal Tradition" (paper presented at the Dispensational Study Group of the Evangelical Theological Society, November 21, 1991), 2. Oss speaks from within the tradition. Now he is a professor at Assemblies of God Theological Seminary in Springfield, Missouri.

38. Cf. Anderson, *An Introduction to Pentecostalism*, 231–33; and The General Council of The Assemblies of God, "Statement of Fundamental Truths"; available at http://agchurches.org/Sitefiles/Default/RSS/AG.org%20TOP/Beliefs/SFT_2011.pdf.

39. Clayton L. ("Mike") Berg, Jr. and Paul E. Pretiz, *The Gospel People of Latin America* (Monrovia, CA: MARC, World Vision International and Latin America Mission, 1992), 47. A. B. Simpson and the Christian and Missionary Alliance and James Hall Brooks and the Gospel Missionary Union, as already mentioned, also worked in Latin America.

40. A curious note in the second page of Cyrus I. Scofield, *Hojas de Estudio Bíblico de Scofield* (Los Angeles: Casa Bíblica de Los Angeles, 1915) says that this work has been published (in Spanish) because of "a petition from the missionaries and pastors in the Spanish countries." This fact illustrates the singular role played by translations of the key dispensational writers.

41. Orlando E. Costas, *Theology of the Crossroads in Contemporary Latin America: Missiology in Mainline Protestantism, 1969–1974* (Amsterdam: Editions Rodopi N.V., 1976), 40.

42. Ibid., 40–41.

43. Ibid., 48.

44. William R. Read, Victor M. Monterroso, and Harmon A. Johnson, *Latin American Church Growth* (Grand Rapids: Eerdmans, 1969), 349. They expanded their assessment (on p. 351) by anticipating that:

    "A Latin American theological consensus will doubtless emerge which will reflect the realities of Latin culture and will by-pass foreign theological squabbles. Even Latin American use of the term *Evangelical* rather than *Protestant* indicates that the Church wishes to make its own way on its own terms regardless of what outsiders might feel about the Church. European and North American theological emphases concerning secularized Christianity find little echo in Latin America, where the Evangelical Church is too busy fulfilling its mission to be troubled by these theological issues."

45. Costas, *Theology of the Crossroads*, 47.

46. Berg and Pretiz, *The Gospel People*, 46.

47. Ibid., 71, 117. In reference to the particular growth of pentecostalism, see also Gary B. McGee, *"This Gospel . . . Shall Be Preached"*; Charles Troutman, *Everything You Want to Know about the Mission Field, but Are Afraid You Won't Learn until You Get There* (Downers Grove, IL: InterVarsity, 1976), 84; Christian Lalive d'Epinay, "The Pentecostal 'Conquest' of Chile," in *The Religious Situation: 1969*, ed. Donald R. Cutler (Boston: Beacon Press, 1969), 179–94.

48. Cf. Lewis Sperry Chafer, *Major Bible Themes* (Chicago: Moody, 1944), and Charles C. Ryrie, *A Survey of Bible Doctrine* (Chicago: Moody, 1972).

49. Robert, "The Crisis of Missions," 45.

50. Orlando Costas, "Conversion As a Complex Experience: A Hispanic Case Study," in *Latin American Pastoral Issues* 16 (January 1989): 8–32. Cf. Lewis Sperry Chafer, *He That Is Spiritual* (n.p.: Our Hope Publisher, 1918), 20.

51. C. Norman Kraus, "Introduction: Evangelism, Missions, and Church Growth," in *Missions, Evangelism, and Church Growth*, ed. C. Norman Kraus (Scottdale, PA: Herald Press, 1980), 20.